6.92 Russell & Russell 1-67 (Sweeringen)

THE BEGINNINGS
OF
MARXIAN SOCIALISM
IN FRANCE

THE BEGINNINGS
OF
MARXIAN SOCIALISM
IN FRANCE

Samuel Bernstein, Ph.D.

NEW YORK
RUSSELL & RUSSELL · INC
1965

PREFACE TO THE SECOND EDITION

Over thirty years ago, when this book first appeared, it was at once praised and assailed. Well disposed critics said it was a lucid and a hitherto unchronicled story, and a definitive contribution to the subject. Critics with a severe bent of mind, while acknowledging that the book had merits, found it inadequate under two general heads: a narrowness of scope; and an underestimation of French economic history in the decade after the Paris Commune. Looking back at these observations with a detachment acquired with the passage of time, I can own to their validity. Full account would be taken of them were I to revise the book. Not so, however, of the strictures of the captious dogmatists who lectured me for not having brought into focus the ideological bonds between Marx and Blanqui. It can be said that this was not criticism but an animadversion inspired by presumption. Since these reviewers showed that their knowledge of Blanquism, not to mention Marxism, was deplorable, I feel obligated to mark out, from the vantage ground of a long acquaintance with the Blanquist manuscripts, the big differences between the two schools of thought. This will find a place in a later part of the preface.

Pertinent to the present purpose is the notice to be taken of the useful literature and documentary material that have appeared in the thirty odd years that have elapsed since the first edition, and what is equally to the point, of my own reevaluation of the text. In view of the mounting interest in nineteenth century French social history the first chapter

v

assumes more importance today than it had three decades ago. It spans a period between two revolutions, each of which was seen as a threat to the social order not only of France but of Europe as a whole. The restoration of Bonapartism was calculated to maintain a relative equilibrium which the Holy Alliance had failed to achieve. Yet, Louis Napoleon's terror could not secure the social peace his backers had hoped for. The reports of his Procureurs généraux, at the National Archives in Paris, testify that even his despotic rule could not in its first eight or nine years prevent economic breakdowns, rising food costs, plots, strikes and sporadic outbreaks. Though they were quickly put down, they signalized seething discontent.

There were unsettling events that were not his doing. For example, the economic crisis of 1857, which affected the whole Atlantic community, stirred considerable unrest in France not merely among workers, but also among the bourgeoisie and the peasants, reputed to be devoted to the regime. A source of French opposition, still more disconcerting, was the depression of 1866. In her erudite work, *La chute du second empire et la naissance de la troisième république en France*, 1959, E. Jéloubovskaïa provides the evidence on the impact of this depression and the resulting damage to the imperial system. People were troubled with perplexing doubts about its worth to France.

For almost simultaneously Napoleon suffered diplomatic and military defeats in the Austro-Prussian War and in the Mexican adventure. He had dreamed of being the loud speaker of the European Continent and a voice in the Western Hemisphere. Frustrated in both aims, he had to face at home issues on which pivoted the fate of his rule.

His prestige was fading. Bound up with the Mexican adventure was his ill conceived pro-Confederate policy during the American Civil War. I have shown in my *Essays in Political and Intellectual History,* 1955, that the wretchedness it caused among textile workers in France was relatively as great as that of textile workers in England. The outcome was the further discrediting of Bonapartism among French workers. It was not generosity that motivated Louis Napoleon to relax restrictions on labor combinations in 1864, just when currents of anti-slavery sentiment were reported by his faithful Procureurs généraux. The currents also coincided with the call of sixty leaders of labor for independent political action.

This is not to imply that French organized labor of the 1860's stood far to the left. The fact was that it was conservatively oriented. It was by and large inspired by Proudhon. Specifically this meant that it was reticent on politics, defended the craft industries against technological innovation, demanded freedom to organize and assemble, on a par with the capitalists, and extolled cooperation as the means of its earthly salvation. An expanded version of the same program was advocated by Proudhonists at the congresses of the First International which will be considered below. Since Proudhon's name has been introduced it may be appropriate to review his teachings both from the angle of his post World War II disciples and from the viewpoint of his own posthumously published writings.

Rereading the section on Proudhon in the text, I was disturbed by the general picture. Traits were missing which had been revealed during the Second World War. The establishment of the Vichy régime created a Proudhon cult which

Georges Sorel and his few disciples on the Right had attempted unsuccessfully. Under the Vichy government Proudhon's writings were drawn on by all shades of politicos, from neo-socialists to royalists, to justify the "new order" and to sully everything incompatible with it.

Proudhon was the vogue. But his name had to be cleared of the calumny it had been encrusted with, thanks to his audacity. For back in the 1840's he had flung at the public the startling paradoxes, "God is evil!" and "Property is theft!" He did not really mean what he had said, wrote the Jesuit Father, Henri de Lubac in his learned work *Proudhon et le christianisme*. And the reverend father was right. Going further into the subject, he proved beyond any doubt that with all his anti-theistic invective Proudhon was deeply religious, far more religious than socialist. Withal he was a tireless reconciler of atheism and Christianity in divine justice. Father Lubac also manifested sympathy with Proudhon's views on women and the family. These, after all, have been more or less in keeping with Catholic pronouncements. So has antiracism. But on this absorbing question Proudhon was an unregenerate transgressor.

For Proudhon is a liability to any organization or faith that reveres him as a fountainhead of wisdom and yet preaches the brotherhood of man. Nowhere are more anti-Semitic sentiments to be found than in the recently published first two volumes of his *Diary (Carnets)*, 1961. In *The General Idea of the Revolution in the Nineteenth Century* he had set himself the goal of achieving "the universal communication of races." A decade later, in *War and Peace,* he approved of a racial hierarchy. As a logical sequence he approved Negro slavery in the United States. In his *Lettres au citoyen Rolland,* 1946, he confessed "that I would be very sorry if the slave states of North America were beaten by the so-called liberal and democratic states. I am a partisan of divine right, and I have a horror of liberty."

His vulgar estimate of women does not merit space here. More relevant to the present analysis is Jacques Bourgeat's *P. J. Proudhon, père du socialisme français,* 1943, published in Paris in the Vichy period. Its object was in line with Father Lubac's book, for it argued that, despite Proudhon's stigmatic formula on property, his stand on the social problem was very similar to that of Catholic sociologists. The question arises, what did he do to earn the title, "Father of French Socialism?" Bourgeat answered that he promised to eliminate the class struggle by melting into one class the proletariat and the petty bourgeoisie. The fusion would effectively resist the concentration of wealth on the one hand and the socialist argument on the other. It was but another way of saying that the "Father of French Socialism" was antisocialist. His utopia was a social balance on a mediocre level, an equilibrium which subdued antagonisms, class antagonisms in particular. This ideal way of life was the best conceived and the best calculated to prevent fundamental change. Proudhon's so-called socialism ended in stagnation.

He considered himself the champion of the workers. Under this head, however, he placed the shopkeeper, the artisan and the peasant. For the common people, the wage earners, he had but contempt. They were the "vile multitude," especially when they agitated vigorously for their demands and struck. His labor program resembled in key respects what has since been known as corporatism. He made many references to history, but he had little respect for historical science or for that matter for science in general. Who spoke more of justice than he? In his sense, however, it was the eternal absolute, in words his own, "the mystery of mysteries," upon which he relied to hold society in equipoise. Obviously he reckoned without the compelling forces of history.

I must now turn to the critics who chided me for having avoided areas of agreement between Marx and Blanqui. Actually attempts to approximate them have for some time made by two separate schools of thought. On the one hand, adherents to the principles of Edward Bernstein have maintained that the two revolutionaries were alike partial to conspiracy and violence; on the other, communists, especially among the French, have held firmly that both had communism as their goal and revolutionary dictatorship as their means. Now, it is a matter of record that Marx did not altogether rule out conspiracy. It was the only possible method under systems like Tsarism and Bonapartism. But he considered it useless, in fact baneful, as a general practice. Thus he termed conspirators alchemists of revolution. By the same token he viewed the *coup de main* as an adventurer's way to power.

Indeed, Blanqui believed that the future belonged to communism. But in his own mind the road to it was very tenuous. He was essentially an activist. The capital-labor dispute crops up repeatedly in his writings; and he never wavered in his optimism on labor's ultimate triumph. Among his French contemporaries, no one, with the exception of Alexis de Tocqueville, was his equal as a political analyst. Not one of them struck more bruising blows at capitalism than he did. For all that, he did not look upon the working class, as did Marx, as the principal motor of history. From Blanqui's standpoint, the workers' striving to obtain their immediate needs was secondary to the struggle against spiritualism, his reason being that their liberation from supernaturalism was preliminary to their emancipation from capitalism.

The separate outlooks derived from different philosophies of history. Marx had concluded that a cause and effect relationship existed between man's means of earning a living and the forms of his thought and action. Blanqui put his faith in the propelling force of ideas, in their power to set off a hurricane of revolution, irrespective of circumstances or of such pivotal factors as time and place. Accordingly he gave high priority to the propagation of atheism. In other words, he was a militant materialist who waged war on all types of spiritualism, Comtism included. His was a materialism that was closer to Holbach's than to Marx's. Like Holbach he judged the struggle against religion foremost because he thought it was the strongest rampart of the established order.

The presumed likeness between Blanquism and Marxism turns out, upon inquiry, to be superficial. The first cannot even be ranked as a socialist system because its ideas were never pulled together and rounded out. Eclectic is the term that best characterizes Blanqui's socialism. Embedded in his massive writings are gems of thought at once penetrating and prophetic. But they do not make a firm pedestal on which to raise him among the seminal minds of socialist thought.

He seems to have had more in common with Michael Bakunin, the Russian anarchist, than with other contemporary professional revolutionaries. Blanqui, like Bakunin, depended on conspiracy and made atheism a central programmatic tenet. They were both romantics, counting on bands of determined men to blast open the roads to their respective goals. Akin to their romanticism was their messianic nationalism. For each one was persuaded that his country had the historic mission to start Europe on the revolutionary course which would end in the overturn of the whole social order. And finally, the one hated Germans and Jews as heartily as did the other.

Such were Blanqui's principal prepossessions. Though they cannot be accounted for in a preface, this much can be said. His reading roamed over many fields, but thirty-three years behind prison walls were more than enough to stunt the development of the most fertile ideas. Thus his economic thinking did not rise above the level of the handicrafts; and his philosophy of history consisted of concepts garnered from French eighteenth century *philosophes* and nineteenth century utopian socialists. He urged his disciples to spare no effort in order to win the workers to his ideas. But the gains were small. For how could they be expected to take to a program which gave second place to the bread-and-butter question?

Nevertheless, Blanqui's was a politically acute mind. It was unfortunate that he saw things from narrow, Gallic perspectives; but he saw them *en bloc*, immensely integrated to attain a society for the general good. In the pursuit of that object he took the most unpopular and the most hazardous road. "And that has made all the difference," as Robert Frost would say. He came to personify the nineteenth century spirit of revolution in France, and this excited Marx's interest in him.

The interest, dating from 1848, was apparently enduring, according to the published and unpublished sources. Of all the episodes and movements in which it manifested itself, only one needs some attention here, namely, the First International, in which Marx endeavored to enroll Blanqui and his party. Nearly all of its members were young men and disciplined. Apart from being energetic and, for that reason, serviceable to the sprawling Association, they could be useful in still another way, it occurred to Marx. They would neutralize the increasing power of the French Proudhonists. Consequently, acting through intermediaries, he persuaded Blanqui to send delegates to the first congress at Geneva in 1866. Suffice it to say, without entering into sordid and wearisome details, that they were ejected from the meeting hall by the Proudhonists and their allies. Another attempt to bring over the Blanquists was made in 1867. But it was all in vain.

The fact was that Blanqui had a low opinion of the International almost from the start. He conceded in 1868 that it was making progress, but not the palpitating progress he was looking for. The Association, he wrote, was a victim of ambitions, and an inconsequential factor in the march of events. Actually they towed it like a barge. It could not impose its program, for it had no power over the masses. Such a body could not win his confidence.

The indictment was severe. The charges can be discounted, or at least minimized, if it is borne in mind that they stemmed from one who had never understood the purpose of a mass organization. The societies he had known were secret, small, well-knit, disciplined, trained for insurrection. The First International had none of these characteristics. Its object, at least as far as the near future was concerned, was not to revolutionize Europe, the claims of Continental police chiefs and foreign ministers notwithstanding. It had arisen, partly at any rate, to meet the challenge of employers who were importing cheap labor in order to beat down wages, defeat strikers and ruin rising trade unions. In other words, its object was to defend the immediate interests of labor internationally. The assistance it was instrumental in bringing to distressed workers' families, its forthright support of President Lincoln, its advocacy of Poland's liberation and its denunciation of saber-rattling dynasts made it the cynosure of people in Europe and in the United States who counted on democratic institutions to secure the good life.

There was no firm meeting ground between the First International and Blanqui's party. The first could not tolerate a program which made atheism a cardinal tenet; and it put in the foreground the working class which had no place in the insurrectionary strategy of the second. The incompatibility of the two organizations might have caused Blanqui to show a temporary interest in Bakunin's International Alliance of Socialist Democracy. Thus a Blanquist was present at its founding in September 1868. It was a public society, grafted on a secret one, dating from 1864 and reorganized in 1868 under its new name.

Blanqui's brief flirtation with Bakunin's Alliance might have escaped Marx's notice. At any rate, it drew heavier the line of separation between Marxism and Blanquism. But it does not gainsay the earlier remark that, by his tireless struggle against the bourgeois order, paid with more than three decades of confinement in closely guarded prisons, Blanqui became the embodiment of the nineteenth century revolutionary spirit in France. That, and not his dogmas, mattered to Marx and induced him to speak of Blanqui as the head and heart of the French workers' party. It does not mean, however, that Marx shared either his conception of the road to power or his understanding of the end to be attained.

The section on the First International requires amending in two respects. More emphasis should be placed on its militancy in the final years of the Second Empire; and the range of the narrative needs broadening. As for the first, two major points can be made here. First, an impending war between France and Prussia was forcing French Internationalists to take a hand in politics contrary to Proudhonist teachings. Second, and equally out of keeping with them, were the waves of strikes, evidenced by the police dossiers of those years. Many of the more important strikes were led by Internationalists. Struggles over hours and wages turned into political struggles in which the imperial government took the side of the employers. Willy-nilly the Proudhonist-directed International in France had to take a political course. Louis Napoleon had tried at considerable cost to gain the support of labor. But economic breakdowns and Internationalists' agitation rendered his methods vain. The International in France, with its nuclei of trade union federations in the principal cities of France, alone loomed as the challenge to his power at home. Consequently, before going to war with Prussia he ordered the arrest of its leaders throughout the country.

The second, that is, widening the range of the narrative, may be better achieved by referring here to a number of publications that appeared to mark the centenary of the Association's founding. First, from the point of over-all value, are the Minutes of the General Council of the First International of which the first two volumes, covering the years 1864 to 1868, have been published by the Institute of Marxism-Leninism in Moscow. The first volume, it should be noted, includes the proceedings of the London Conference of 1865. Three other volumes have been promised. When the Minutes have all been published, they will constitute a unique original source on the First International and on the labor movement of the Western world from 1864 to 1872. Less important, yet noteworthy are the two sets of documents and essays, edited by Jacques Freymond. The first, *La première internationale, recueil de documents,* 1962, consists, as the title suggests, of documents which, with few exceptions, have been scarce items. The second, *Etudes et documents sur la première internationale en Suisse,* 1964, contains a number of original pieces bearing on the International in the Jura and on the Bâle Congress in 1869. Of special worth are the hitherto unpublished minutes of the Geneva Section of the Alliance of Socialist Democracy, during 1869 and 1870, edited by Bert Andréas and Miklós Molnár. Along with these volumes may be cited the special centenary issue of the monthly *Cahiers de l'Institut de science économique appliquée* which reprinted several rare documents and ran a lengthy bibliography of the literature on the First International. A similar bibliographical survey was prepared by Chimen Abramsky for the August 1964 *Bulletin of the Society for the Study of Labour History.* Also, thanks to the long held plan of the International Committee of the Historical Sciences, we now have a three volume catalogue of the International's official publications, including its far-flung press.

It is not beside the point to mention in this context the reprint in 1963 of Johann Philipp Becker's *Der Vorbote* which appeared monthly without interruption from 1866 to 1871. During these six years it served as the organ of the International, published reports of its congresses, releases of the General Council and of sections in Europe and in the United States as well as news-items on the labor movement as a whole.

Literature of recent date with a direct bearing on the International in France has been either meager or inadequate. The exception has been the high-level work of Jacques Rougerie who edited and evaluated for *Annali*, 1961, the documents of the International in Lyons. By contrast, the book by Jacques Duclos, *La première internationale*, 1964, is superficial and inaccurate. Little account has been taken of the latest scholarship, especially in languages other than French. Even the Marx-Engels *Correspondence*, cited in the bibliography, is the French version of the expurgated Bernstein-Bebel edition, instead of the full text in the *Gasamtausgabe*.

Little, if any, substantial change is called for in the section on the Paris Commune. The charge of publicists and politicos that it had been plotted by the First International belonged to the crowded realm of deceit, as I first pointed out. And what I have since read has confirmed my original conclusion. The charge was a wily device for misleading public opinion in the tight-drawn situation caused by the Long Depression of the 1870's. Labor strikes were equated with Paris Communes in the making, behind which lurked the First International, even after it had been quietly laid to rest in Philadelphia.

All the above comments relate to the first chapter. For the other three no significant data has turned up which requires their fundamental revision. The fat police dossiers on the labor congresses from 1876 to 1880, handed over by the Ministry of the Interior to the National Archives a number of years ago, add only brief biographic notes, interspersed with thumbnail sketches where the police agent had a flair for characterization. However, police data on industrialized areas, during the years of the first three congresses, contain vital information. They refer to business failures, to layoffs, wage cuts and many strikes. This amounted to saying that the effects of the Long Depression were felt in France during the first three labor congresses, a fact which had some bearing on the triumph of the socialists at the Congress of Marseilles.

The book leaves no doubt about Marx's concern for the emerging French Labor Party. This accounts for the direct hand he had in drafting its program. Still another question appears to have been the object of his solicitous thought. Who among the French socialists had the national standing to endow the nascent Party with prestige? Looking at the French scene from across the Channel, only Blanqui, it seemed to him, had the essential qualifications. He had been made nationally prominent by the sustained campaign for amnesty with his name as the emblem. His socialist ideas were misty, to be sure, but neither had those of other French socialist spokesmen been cleared of confusion. As Marx saw it, Blanqui's ideas were, for the time being at least, less consequential than his name which had become a standard for all those who aimed at a socialist alternative to the bourgeois order.

These remarks are preliminary to the following letter I came upon in the Blanqui manuscripts. It was addressed by Lafargue to Blanqui on June 22, 1879. But it is obvious from the contents that Marx inspired it. After a few statements about Blanqui's long martyrdom and his recent liberation from prison, Lafargue went directly to the point. "You are coming into view at the time when we are most in need of a man to form the party of the proletariat and to launch it for the conquests of power." The bourgeoisie, continued Lafargue, had ended its revolutionary role, whereas the Paris Commune had shown that the proletariat still had its part to play. All it needed was organization and leadership, and Blanqui's past made him its logical standard-bearer. Lafargue invited Blanqui to take a few weeks of rest at his home in London. And he ended: "Marx who has watched your political career with so much interest would be very happy to make your acquaintance."

There is no evidence that Blanqui answered Lafargue's letter. In any event, it casts a beam of light on the background of the French Labor Party at its foundation. In this setting it can also serve as the terminal point of the preface. For it advances the purpose I set myself, that of reexamining the text with the advantage of recent publications and with the benefit of my further research and changing outlook.

April 1965.

S.B.

PREFACE

The story of the beginnings of modern socialism in France has been a neglected field. Nothing has been written in English on this subject, and in French it has been treated only very briefly. It is for this reason that the present attempt has been made to write the history of the slow entrance of Marxian socialism into France. The first chapter is intended as an introduction to the essay. It aims to give a brief survey of the labor and cooperative movements in the time of the Second Empire, of the socialist theories which captivated the minds of a number of labor leaders and intellectuals after 1860, and of the founding of the First International in France and of its growing influence among the workers during the few years preceding the Commune. The purpose of the section on the Commune is to show: that the revolt of March 18th was a republican, patriotic and proletarian movement; that, despite the presence of socialists in its government, the Commune was not socialistic; that the International cannot be held responsible for the revolt; and that the defeat of the Commune, resulting in the decapitation of the labor and socialist movements in France, was a turning point in the history of these movements.

In the second chapter an effort has been made, first, to describe the state of fear which the Commune engendered among the governing authorities and among the various schools of social thought, and to indicate how they planned to placate the workers in order to prevent any possible recurrence of an outbreak; secondly, to portray the weak beginnings of the labor movement after the Commune, the timidity of the leaders, the moderation of their demands, and the reasons why producers' cooperation became labor's open sesame of social emancipation. It is because cooperation appeared to most labor leaders and workers as the cure-all of the prevailing social and economic maladies that many pages have been devoted here to an exposition of its doctrine and to the arguments of its opponents.

The third chapter treats of the beginnings of Marxian socialism in France, and of its slow spread during the eight years following the Commune. At no time during this period, not even at the Marseilles Congress in 1879, did the socialists represent a majority in the organized labor movement. If collectivism won a victory over cooperation at the Congress of Marseilles, it was because the socialist leaders were more active than the exponents of cooperation, and because the socialists had succeeded in having themselves represented in large numbers.

The fourth and last chapter aims to tell how the program of the French socialist party, written by Marx, was officially adopted in July, 1880, by the local congress of the Federation of the Center against the opposition of the anarchists. In order that the reader may appreciate the attitude of these anarchists toward the program, it was deemed advisable to summarize the chief tenets of their system of thought. An analysis of the doctrines of all the anarchist schools would have led us too far away from the particular subject of our inquiry. It was therefore decided to limit the discussion to the "anarchist communists" who, of all the schools of anarchism, had developed by 1880 the clearest formulation of anarchist doctrine.

PREFACE

For the purpose of this essay the fourth National Socialist Labor Congress, meeting at Havre in 1880, may be considered a good stopping place. Here the socialists, having separated themselves from the pure trade-union leaders, proceeded to hold in Havre a congress of the French socialist party. This congress adopted the Marxian program as the platform of the party. Thus modern socialism was definitely launched as a movement in France.

It is extremely difficult to determine the reactions of the French workers toward political and economic questions during the few decades after the Commune, and particularly during the first of these decades. The available records do not contain expressions of their views. The author, therefore, has accepted the opinions of the leaders as the reflection of the ideas of the workers in the respective organizations. Furthermore, it is equally difficult to estimate the numerical strength of organized labor during the period covered in this essay (1871-1880), because labor organizations, regarded with suspicion by the government, were eager to conceal the number of their adherents.

I wish to take this opportunity to acknowledge my appreciation to the following: to Professors Carlton J. H. Hayes and Geroid T. Robinson for their careful reading of the manuscript, and for their many valuable suggestions; to my friend, Mr. E. M. Cohen, for the stimulating questions he so frequently brought forward, and for evoking numerous discussions which helped to clarify some of my ideas; to Dr. H. Davidson, for his suggestions on style; to Miss C. Winchell and Mr. F. W. Erb of the Columbia University Library, and to M. Etienne Martin Saint-Léon, director of the library of the Musée Social in Paris, for their assistance in locating sources; and to my wife, who made it possible for me to prepare this essay.

Samuel Bernstein

CONTENTS

CONTENTS

CONTENTS

CONTENTS

CHAPTER I

THE LABOR AND SOCIALIST MOVEMENTS IN THE TIME OF

THE SECOND EMPIRE; THE COMMUNE

1. The labor and cooperative movements

The French socialist and labor movements of the nineteenth century have two significant historical landmarks: 1848 and 1871. During each of these years, labor and socialism experienced a bloody defeat, resulting in the disintegration of their organizations and in the discrediting of their then prevailing doctrines. Each catastrophe was followed by a lull in labor agitation and in socialist propaganda, only to be succeeded, however, by a reawakening under the stimulus of new doctrines and tactics.

The labor and socialist movements during the Second Empire may be divided roughly into two periods: 1852-1860 and 1860-1870. During the first, labor was hesitant and timid; during the second, it reawakened and became active and militant. In the first period, both labor and socialism lacked power and organization. The cooperative societies which had been given life under the Constituent Assembly of 1848 had either perished through their own inexperience and weakness or were dissolved after the *coup d'état*.[1] The leaders had been either imprisoned or exiled. Propaganda was difficult, for the press was muzzled and the police vigilant. Proudhon's *Philosophie du Progrès* had to be published in Belgium, and, when it was transported across the frontier under great difficulty, bookdealers refused to handle it. For his *De la justice dans la révolution et dans l'église* Proudhon was sentenced to three years' imprisonment and fined four thousand francs.[2]

Labor was the object of suspicion and persecution. Except for the few mutual aid societies which were permitted to reorganize, workers' associations were dissolved. Combinations formed to force a rise in wages or a decrease in the working day felt the heavy hand of the government. From 1852 to 1860 there were no less than 728 coalition cases before the courts, resulting in the punishment of 3,847 persons.[3] While the government was proceeding with these prosecutions, it, nevertheless, permitted employers to organize syndical chambers and to federate them into the National Union of Industry and Commerce. During the period of repression, moreover, no attempt was made by the government to restrict the labor of women and children or to limit the working day. The law on the hated *livret*, which facilitated the supervision and control of the workers, was not only maintained, but was also extended to include women.[4]

But the policy of rigid restraint could not be continued, for a rapidly expanding capitalism was making the workers increasingly restless and resentful. Beginning in 1860, the labor movement assumed a vigorous aspect despite the restraint of the law. Credit societies were founded in order to form the nucleus for producers' cooperatives, and parallel with them, resistance societies (sociétés de résistance), the forerunners of the later syndicats, were organized. Labor delegations, sent to international expositions, tended to group and awaken the workers, while labor's participation in poli-

2

tics after 1863 helped to strengthen the opposition to the Empire. Faced by this new power, the Imperial Government tried to conciliate the workers. It tolerated coalitions; it did not interfere with the organization of producers' co-operatives and of credit and mutual aid societies; it did not persecute the International during the early years of its existence in France; and it subsidized the labor delegations sent to international expositions.

The reports of these delegations are interesting, because they give expression to some of labor's views. Those published by the delegates to the International Exposition in London in 1862 contain frequent mention of the superior condition of the British workers. Reference was made to their higher wages, to their trade unions, and to the struggles of the latter against the employers. All the reports deplored the low wages, the long hours of labor, and the high cost of living in France, and thirty-eight of the fifty-three reports expressed the hope that syndical chambers might be organized.[5] The desire dominating all others was for freedom to combine and to organize, for upon it depended the realization of all of labor's other demands: the limitation of the working day; the fixing of the wage scale; the regulation of apprenticeship; the development of a system of professional training; the creation of all kinds of mutual aid funds.[6] At the same time many delegates affirmed that they would resort not to the strike but to mixed commissions of employers and employees in order to determine the wage scales.

That the labor movement was raising its head was made evident not only by the reports of the delegates of 1862, but also by labor's growing interest in politics. Under the leadership of Henri Tolain, a Parisian worker, two labor can-

3

didates were nominated in Paris in the election of 1863. Though most of the workers voted for the opposition candidates and assured the success of liberalism, the attempt on the part of a few labor leaders to separate the workers from the bourgeois parties was indicative of a new trend in the labor movement. This trend became more definite in the Manifesto of the Sixty, published in February, 1864, on the eve of Parisian by-elections, and signed by sixty workers representing various trades. The document, though moderate in tone, was a trumpet-call to the workers to seek direct representation in the *Corps législatif*. "It has been repeated to satiety," said the signers, "that there are no classes, that since 1789 all Frenchmen are equal before the law. But we who have nothing but our hands, we who are subjected every day to the legitimate or arbitrary regulations of capital, we who are living under exceptional laws . . . which hurt our interests as well as our dignity, we find it difficult to believe this assertion." The workers, the Manifesto went on to say, were deprived of the opportunities of education. Their children were compelled to go to work at an early age, and their family life was ruined because their wives had to desert the home for the factory. The workers did not demand agrarian laws, or the equal division of wealth. They wanted "freedom, credit and the right to unite"; but no deputy raised his voice to formulate their aspirations. Hence, it was imperative that labor be directly represented.[7]

The Manifesto caused considerable comment in the bourgeois press. While reactionary and catholic newspapers read socialism into it, the liberal and democratic organs said that in France there was neither caste nor class. Only the *Opinion Nationale,* a newspaper edited by Guéroult, a former Saint-Simonian, defended it. Among the workers there was

4

divided opinion concerning the document. In answer to the Manifesto of the Sixty, there was published the Manifesto of the Eighty in which the signers claimed that the earlier document expressed the opinion of only a small minority of the workers. They, the Eighty, opposed the idea of independent labor candidates, because it would tend to raise a social question at a time when the political question had to be solved.[8] Proudhon hailed the Manifesto of the Sixty as a reawakening of socialism [9] and made it the theme of one of his best works.[10]

The elections of 1863, the Parisian by-elections of 1864, as well as the reports of the delegates of 1862 breathed new life into the labor movement. The result was an increase in the number of credit, resistance and cooperative societies, and the formation of coalitions in defiance of the law.[11] The government, sensing the growing restlessness of the workers, decided to make concessions. In 1864 it modified the law on coalitions. The new law authorized coalitions of employees, but it punished interference with the freedom of labor through violence, threats or fraudulent means.[12]

The weaknesses and dangers of the law were only too apparent. "What the legislator gave with one hand he took away with the other, for he replaced the misdemeanor of coalition with the misdemeanor of attack on property. . . . Besides, it was difficult to determine where . . . violence, threats and fraudulent means began and ended. Moreover, the law was incomplete on the right to assemble and combine." [13] The result was that from 1864 to 1870, 984 persons were hailed to court and 893 of them were either fined or imprisoned for interfering with the freedom of labor through coalitions and strikes.[14]

But strikes were not the method generally desired either

by the workers or by their leaders. The followers of Proudhon opposed strikes, the reports of the delegates of 1862 stated that they would not resort to them,[15] and a commission of labor delegates to the Exposition of 1867 studied the method of avoiding them.[16] What many workers desired was the right to organize syndical chambers by means of which they hoped not only to avoid labor conflicts but also to effect an improvement in their economic condition. The workingmen's syndical chambers, composed of syndics elected by the workers of each trade, would, in the words of the delegates, have it as their aim "to pave the way for the coalition of employers and workers, while safeguarding the interests of all; to tighten the bonds of solidarity among the workers of each trade; to promote the organization of insurance against unemployment, sickness, infirmity and old age, and the formation of producers' cooperative societies as well as others; to promote inventions in each industry; to organize modern and professional education through lectures or practical courses." [17]

In 1868, the government decided to yield somewhat to the demands of the workers. In that year it declared that it would tolerate workingmen's associations and assemblies in the same manner as it tolerated employers' unions. But the labor associations were prohibited from infringing on the freedom of commerce and industry and from developing into political organizations. This law, which introduced the period of toleration for labor, remained in force until 1884. The change of policy on the part of the Imperial Government caused from fifty to fifty-five syndical chambers, which had existed secretly, to come out into the open.[18]

The workingmen had been organizing even before the introduction of the period of toleration. In 1860, the Parisian printers had formed a society whose membership had become considerable in the succeeding years. During the same period, the resistance society of the lithographers waged a strike, causing its membership to triple. Even more successful than the lithographers were the workers in the bronze industry, whose society, organized in 1864, came into conflict with the employers. Out of a struggle in 1867, in which it was assisted by other labor organizations as well as by the International, the organization came out victorious, with a membership of 6,000. Resistance societies were formed not only in Paris, but also in Lyons, Limoges, Roubaix, and several other industrial centers' of France. In general, the societies organized from 1860 to 1868 pursued moderate policies. They were for the most part interested in professional education, in the training of apprentices, and in unemployment and sickness benefits.

In 1868, the Parisian syndical chambers, encouraged by the law of toleration, united into a Federation of Workers' Syndical Chambers which soon became involved in long and costly strikes. It was during that year that the workers' organizations were drawn into the revolutionary movement which preceded the Franco-Prussian War and the Commune.[19]

While the workers were forming their resistance societies and syndical chambers, the cooperative movement was spreading its influence. Cooperation, during the second half of the Second Empire, was receiving encouragement from three sources: from capitalists and bourgeois economists; from the government; and from disillusioned utopians and Proudhonians. To the first, cooperative societies appeared not only as a check to socialism, but also as a means of winning for the party of the opposition a strong following among the masses. Thus, rich bankers and industrialists like Casimir Périer and Augustin Cochin, and economists like Anselme Batbie and Léon Say endeavored to spread cooperation through the press and platform, and through a bank founded in order to aid the establishment of cooperative societies.[20] To the second, i.e., to the government, cooperation was a method of flirting with the workers, of drawing them away from politics and from revolutionary agitation. In his speech before the Corps législatif in 1864, the Emperor declared his sympathy with the cooperative societies "destined to improve the condition of the working classes," and in 1866 he subscribed 500,000 francs to a Bank of Cooperative Societies. The excessive guarantee required by the bank alienated most of the societies, and its influence on the cooperative movement was extremely limited.[21] To the third, the utopians and Proudhonians, cooperation appealed as a means of emancipating labor, of elevating the worker through association. In the Sixties, just as in the Seventies, labor leaders inclined more toward producers' than toward consumers' cooperation, because in the first type they saw a profound social significance, and in the second only an immediate utility. Starting with the credit society formed by the syndical chamber through a system of regular dues paid by the members, the workers would create a producers' cooperative. In 1863, there were already in existence, particularly in Paris, numerous credit societies; but their activity was limited and isolated. In that year, Beluze, son-in-law of Etienne Cabet, together with former Fourierists and Proudhonians, established a central bank, La Société du Crédit au Travail, which soon extended its influence throughout France and became a sort of central cooperative exchange, giving advice and information, and extending credit.

8

According to its founders, it was to be "a savings bank for the workers, a mutual credit society among the members and a credit and discount bank for the cooperative societies." Some of its aims were "to extend credit to existing associations of workers, and to assist in the formation of new cooperative societies and in the development and propaganda of the principles of mutuality and solidarity." [22]

Aided by Orleanists and liberals, and by radicals and revolutionists, and advertised by the liberal newspapers, the bank prospered from the very start. Five years after its founding, it boasted of a membership of two thousand individuals, had a capital of over a million francs and did a monthly business of three million francs.[23] In 1864 it founded a monthly review, *L'Association,* and, when this disappeared, it replaced it with *La Coopération.* Through the influence of the bank, cooperation received a great stimulus. Societies were founded in Paris, and in the provinces where they were aided by institutions analogous to the *Crédit au Travail.*[24]

When the cooperative movement seemed to be in the full swing of prosperity, it suffered a great disaster. In 1868, the *Crédit au Travail* failed; and with it collapsed all the societies which owed their existence to it, as well as the cooperative banks founded in the provinces. The effect on the workers was profound. The cooperative movement was greatly weakened and the workers turned their efforts to politics and to trade-union action.

2. Socialism

The recrudescence of the labor and cooperative movements after 1860 was one phase of a general protest against conditions in the second half of the Second Empire. Parallel with these movements and often guiding them was the activity of republicans and socialists whose attacks on the despotic government and on the advancing capitalism were gaining a following. Republican and socialist leaders and journalists met in cafés of the Latin Quarter and Montmartre, where they discussed their doctrines. They published small papers in which they criticized the existing institutions; they held large meetings—the law of 1868 permitted them, providing the question of politics was omitted —where various socialist doctrines were exposed; they participated in strikes and demonstrations, and organized conspiracies for the overthrow of the government. Radicals revived an interest in the French Revolution and praised either Danton or Robespierre. Others extolled the violence of the Paris Commune of 1793 and admired the names of Pache, Hébert and Chaumette. The cultivation of the Jacobin tradition which was later present in the Commune of 1871 was already in full swing in the 1860's.[25]

Allied with the latter-day Jacobins of the Second Empire, both by their anticlericalism and by their cult of 1793, were the socialists who drew their doctrines and guidance from Blanqui and Proudhon.

Louis Auguste Blanqui, born in 1805 of a middle-class family in the southwest of France, and educated in Parisian schools, where he attracted attention by his rare intelligence and extraordinary memory, was a product of the revolutionary ferment in France from the days of the Restoration to the Commune. From the Carbonari, with whom he became affiliated in his early days, he learned the technique of secret organization and conspiracy which he practiced in the period of the Bourgeois Monarchy and the Second Empire. Through Buonarotti, the friend and associate of Babeuf and the author of the *History of the Conspiracy of the Equals*,[26] he became acquainted with a revolutionary theory and method which, with singleness of purpose and an indomitable will, he endeavored to utilize during his long revolutionary career.

Blanqui's life, replete with suffering and struggle for human emancipation, alternated between long terms of imprisonment and secret political activity during the years of freedom. Disappointed by the outcome of the Revolution of 1830, he participated actively in the life of the secret societies during the Louis Philippe Monarchy, which he tried to overthrow by an insurrection in 1839. The *coup* failed; he was given a death sentence, later commuted to life imprisonment. The Revolution of 1848 liberated him; but the revolutionary note in his language, and his prominent rôle in a demonstration against the Constituent Assembly, led to his incarceration and to a ten-year prison sentence. After an interlude of two years of freedom, during which he carried on secret propaganda, he was again imprisoned in 1861 in Sainte-Pélagie, and later in a prison hospital where he made contact with revolutionists of various tendencies and where he formed the nucleus of what was to be the Blanquist party. In 1865 he escaped to Brussels. From this city he corresponded with his lieutenants in Paris and directed his followers, and from it he made frequent flying visits to the French capital in order to attend important meetings and to review his disciplined troops. Back in Paris during the Franco-Prussian War, he, at the head of a handful of men, tried to seize the military barracks on the Boulevard de la Villette, and with the captured ammunition to overthrow the government. As in 1839, the attempt failed.

During the period intervening between the fall of the

Empire and the establishment of the Commune, Blanqui played an active rôle in the revolutionary movement. He edited a paper, *La Patrie en Danger,* in which he criticized the military policies of the Provisional Government, exposed its weaknesses and indecision, demanded the requisitioning of food and men, the rationing of necessities and an offensive against the enemy, and called on all patriots to rush to the defense of the fatherland. On the eve of the revolt of the Commune, he was imprisoned and shut out from the world for nine years. His liberation in 1879 after his election to the Chamber of Deputies left him two years of complete freedom to live among his admiring friends. He died in 1881, the symbol of revolutionary tactics which had become obsolete.[27]

In Blanqui one finds three main currents of thought: the rationalist current of the eighteenth century; the Jacobin current which found its ultimate expression in Babouvism; and the communist current of the nineteenth century which culminated in scientific socialism. His rationalism became manifest through his implicit belief in education and enlightenment as the real agents of revolution. It was his boundless faith in the efficacy of education to crush the forces of social and economic evil that caused him to write: "There is no durable revolution without light! There is no emancipation without intelligence for a foundation! Liberty means instruction! Equality means instruction! Fraternity means instruction! Teachers, books, the printing press, these are the true revolutionary agencies." [28] Education, he said, was of greater value to man than fifty Californias.[29] It was ignorance, fostered by the church, the army and the capitalists, that made the worker "the docile tool of the privileged." [30] It was this ignorance which only a revolutionary dictatorship would dispel, by destroying the agencies which kept man enslaved.

Blanqui's trust in a dictatorship showed that he was in part the intellectual descendant of the Jacobins and the Babouvists. Like his forerunners, he espoused a dictatorship with Paris as the center. Paris, he wrote, was "responsible for France";[31] it was not merely "a municipality, shut up in its personal interests; it really represented the nation."[32] Like the Jacobins and the Babouvists, he was a patriot who, during the Franco-Prussian War, gave vent to the most stirring patriotic emotions,[33] and like them, he was an enemy of the catholic church. In the matter of religion, however, Blanqui was more extreme than the Jacobins and the Babouvists, who were generally deists. Unlike them, he was an atheist who drew his inspiration not from Robespierre, whom he hated for sacrificing to the Supreme Being, but from Hébert, "the defender of the weak and lowly," "the soul feverish with thirst for justice."[34]

Living at a time when the industrial proletariat was only beginning to emerge and to become separated as a class, Blanqui could not very well consider the proletariat as a revolutionary force. Hence he looked to the bourgeoisie to supply him with the leaders of the revolution, to the thousands of the élite who "live in conditions of extreme misery. . . . These *déclassés,* invisible agents of progress, are to-day the secret ferment which sustains the masses and prevents them from sinking to a condition of impotence. To-morrow they [*déclassés*] will be the reserve force of the revolution."[35] Blanqui depended upon this small disciplined minority to seize the political power. Like the modern communists, he aimed to establish a dictatorship in the interests of the proletariat.

Blanqui once outlined a policy which was to be pursued after the seizure of political power. He would not appeal to universal suffrage, for that could have only one of two sad results: "to nullify the vote by compulsion, or to bring back to monarchy." Instead, he would establish a dictatorship, introduce free education, restrict the freedom of speech and press, abolish the public debt, the standing army and the magistracy, place taxes on inheritance and incomes, confiscate the property of the church and of the religious orders and make it a part of the national domain, and form a national militia by a general arming of the workers and the republican elements. The employers of industry and trade would be ordered to keep their business going and to maintain their personnel and wage scales. At the same time, various assemblies would be convoked to deal with questions of credit, exchange, industry, mines, and labor associations. Recalling the experience of 1848, Blanqui urged prudence in dealing with the peasant. Thus, the decree regarding the land would have to respect the small and middle-class landowners.[36] Blanqui, therefore, would permit the existence of private ownership after the establishment of the dictatorship.

Blanqui did not expect a sudden transformation on the day after the revolution. Men and things, he said, would remain the same as before. But the nation would be free, with an immense horizon opening before it. Two parallel routes, running side by side, would be followed: one leading to universal education, the other to an organized social system. The clergy, the army, the capitalists, the three great obstacles in the way of social emancipation, would be crushed.[37] Just how long it would take for communism to evolve, Blanqui did not know. But he was convinced that it would be the

14

result of education.[38] Communism and education were like Siamese twins; "the one will not come without the other." [39]

Though Blanqui, like Babeuf, taught the necessity of a revolutionary dictatorship in the interest of the proletariat, he differed from his revolutionary forebear in two important respects. In the first place, he saw the golden age not in the past, as Babeuf did, but in the future. To Blanqui it was an absurdity to allege that communism was the form of society of primitive man. Progress, he maintained, was from individualism to communism which was to be the ultimate end of association.[40] In the second place, Blanqui never outlined the mechanism of the communist society as Babeuf did. Of any prepared social system, Blanqui, the man of action, was very critical.[41] "The morrow," he said, "does not belong to us, and does not concern us. Our sole duty is to prepare good material for the work of organization." [42] He was engaged in conspiring to overthrow an absolute government, and his economic program for the day after the revolution was very limited; we must, therefore, accept Engels' estimate of him as "an essentially political revolutionist, and only a sentimental socialist, sympathetic with the people's sorrows." [43]

Blanqui nevertheless attempted, however ineffectively, to refute the theories of the classical economists. Wealth, he said, is created by intelligence and labor. But the social order founded on conquest has enslaved labor. Capital is sterile by itself; it is made productive only by labor.[44] Capital is money, withheld from circulation. It is a prevention of labor. Interest is an evil, for it tends to upset the fundamental principle of economic life, which is the exchange of equal values, measured by labor. However, equality will result not from the abolition of money, but from the substi-

15

tution of associative for individual ownership.[45] Private
property has divided society into exploited and exploiters.
It will be replaced by a communist régime.[46]

Blanqui was critical both of the utopians and of the advocates of cooperation. To the former he said that a new
social order could not be improvised by any single individual;
that it would necessarily be the work of all and the product
of experience gradually gained.[47] To the latter he declared
that cooperation had the same basis as that of the commercial companies; namely, *laissez-faire, laissez-passer;* that it
was illusory to hope for the emancipation of labor by means
of small societies created through the contributions of workers; and that cooperation would deprive the workers of their
best leaders.[48]

Blanqui was more sympathetic with the strike than with
cooperation. The strike, he said, was intelligible to all because it was a simple idea and because it meant resistance to
oppression. Cooperation, however, was a complicated idea
which could seduce only the intelligent. Thus he wrote: "To
the one, the general mass; to the other, some rare exceptions. Is not the flag which rallies the mass preferable to
the one which attracts the few?" [49]

For Proudhon, Blanqui had a profound admiration,
chiefly because his contemporary was an outspoken anti-
clerical and a merciless critic of interest and unearned income
as basic evils of economic life. He urged the advocates of
communism and Proudhonism to cross the river together instead of wasting their energies in disputes about what lay on
the other bank. "Proudhonism and communism, fife and
drum," he once said. "The two instruments scarcely re-
semble each other, but they marry together very well and
can make society dance very agreeably." [50]

In the agitation which seized Paris in the 1860's the followers of Blanqui, drawn mainly from students in the Latin Quarter, played their part. They participated in demonstrations against the Empire, and they tried to spread their ideas through the press; but they could not keep alive their ephemeral *Candide* for more than eight numbers.[51] The Blanquist party, which never numbered more than 2,500 members, was a secret organization which was so constituted that a spy could never betray more than ten members.[52] It was a disciplined body under the command of Blanqui who had among his lieutenants Eudes, Granger, Tridon, Protot, Rigault and Da Costa, all of whom were to play leading rôles in the government of the Commune in which they would find themselves opposed by the followers of Proudhon.

Pierre Joseph Proudhon, born at Besançon in 1809, was the son of a cooper and brewer and was forced to earn his living at an early age. The section in which he was brought up was almost entirely peopled with artisans, small tradesmen and small landowners, whose psychology and ideals Proudhon so imbibed that they became the basis of his system of thought. Through the kindness of a friend, the young Pierre gained free admission to the *collège* of his native town where he pursued his studies brilliantly and manifested an insatiable thirst for knowledge. Forced to terminate his formal education at nineteen, he obtained employment as a proof-reader; but during intervals, the diligent reader and student found time to study the ancient languages. In 1836, Proudhon became part-owner of a printing shop. After two years, the small business failed, and the unfortunate experience made its impression on the development of his later ideas. He applied for and won a triennial pension from the Academy of Besançon, went to Paris to pursue his studies, and there, in 1840, published his first important book, *Qu'est-ce que la propriété?* on the first page of which appeared the startling statement: "Property is theft." The book, which was a destructive criticism of property, had an immediate success,[53] but it involved the author in difficulties with the Academy of Besançon. Two more essays, intended to complete his ideas on property, soon followed, for one of which Proudhon was hailed to court where, after amusing and astonishing the jury with his ideas, he was acquitted. In 1846, appeared his *Système des contradictions économiques* in which he tried to apply Hegel's dialectics to a criticism of economic phenomena.[54]

The Revolution of 1848 drew Proudhon into politics. He became editor of a paper, published pamphlets, and was elected to the Constituent Assembly where he presented a plan for the reduction of rent and interest and for the reorganization of credit,[55] and where he made numerous enemies by his violent and mordant language. The following year he was condemned to three years' imprisonment. It was during the revolutionary period that he proposed to solve the social and economic problems by means of a Bank of Exchange.

During the period of intellectual calm which followed the *coup d'état,* Proudhon's prolific mind continued to pour out ideas. In 1851, he published his *Idée générale de la révolution au XIXᵉ siècle,* maintaining that there was sufficient reason for a revolution and that its tendency would be to substitute an economic for a governmental régime. Seven years later appeared one of his most comprehensive works, *De la justice dans la révolution et dans l'église,* which was an attack on the church and an idealized development of the reign of justice. For this book he was condemned to three years'

18

imprisonment and fined 4,000 francs. He fled to Belgium. Between the time of his return in 1862 and his death in 1865, he wrote several books of which the best known to-day are: *Du principe fédératif* and *De la capacité politique des classes ouvrières.*[56]

Proudhon was one of the most brilliant polemicists of France during the nineteenth century. An original and forceful thinker, he astounded his opponents by the fertility of his ideas, by the sweep of his imagination and by the ease with which he passed from metaphysics to dialectics and from theology to history. But Proudhon, like most self-taught controversialists who gather their knowledge hurriedly, was incoherent and diffuse in his thought. In his ideas one meets with paradoxes and apparent contradictions. The man who proclaimed that property was theft was not averse to private ownership. He who constantly used the word revolution and advocated a social revolution proved himself to be an evolutionist and a reformer. The socialist who attacked the utopians of his day became the enthusiast of a scheme, utopian in nature, by which the problem of exchange would be solved and mutualism introduced. The individualist and lover of liberty was not willing to extend freedom to women, and the seeming enemy of religion was basically profoundly religious. However, despite the maze of his doctrines two permanent ideas stand out: liberty and justice, both of which he fused into his idea of mutualism.

If Blanqui claimed that he spoke in the interest of the *déclassés* and the proletariat, Proudhon believed that he voiced the aspirations of the workers, independent artisans, shopkeepers and small landowners, among whom he was raised and in whose ideals he was steeped. Declaring himself the savior of these liberty-loving classes, to whom the problems of credit and exchange seemed more vital than the question of production, Proudhon strove for a peaceful social revolution from which would slowly emerge a system of society in which property would be owned in more or less equal parts, the problem of credit would be solved, labor would receive its full product and government would become superfluous or would at least be reduced to a form of political federalism.

Throughout his writings, Proudhon reveals himself as a strong individualist and lover of liberty. This liberty would be the principle of the new social organization which he strove to establish. It manifested itself both in nature and in history, and all progress consisted in its realization. In the name of liberty he attacked an order of society based on force. He, too, he said, desired order, "as much as and more than those who disturb it by their so-called government; but I desire it as a result of my will, as a condition of my labor and as a law of my reason. I shall never bear it when it comes from a will strange to me and imposes upon me slavery and sacrifice as preliminary conditions." [57] Again in the name of liberty, he referred to the utopian socialists of his day in harsh terms. Their systems would enthrone authority and crush liberty. "Communism," he said, "does not mean science, but annihilation." "It means the negation of nature and of the spirit, the negation of the past, the present and the future." It implied organization, and any organization which damaged individual freedom would "perish through individual freedom." [58]

Proudhon's notion of liberty had a close resemblance to that of the classical economists whom he had read. Accordingly, he endeavored not to suppress the prevailing economic forces, but to preserve them by resolving the conflicts among them through an equilibrium. These economic forces, "division of labor, collective force, competition, exchange, credit, property and even liberty," brought to an equilibrium, would result in equality.[59] Competition was necessary to the formation of "constituted value," and freedom of contract was the "supreme law" lying at the basis of the organization of the economic forces.[60]

But liberty, left unrestrained, would become egoism. Hence, Proudhon introduced the idea of justice which he said was innate in man, "his rule and his sanction." [61] Justice was "immanent and real," "the first and most essential of our faculties." It made us conscious of our dignity and, consequently, caused us "to desire it and to defend it in others as well as in ourselves." Through justice each one "feels that he is at the same time a person and a collectivity, an individual and a family, a citizen and a people, a man and humanity." Hence, justice implied liberty, fraternity, unity and reciprocity. Man could not be free in society without the sentiment of justice which was the basis of society and its cohesive force.[62]

Justice, to Proudhon, was the principle and force of progress, a constant striving toward perfection.[63] It caused society to move forward despite the prevailing inequalities. It gave direction to history, created an equilibrium between struggling forces, that is, between opposing liberties.[64]

This element of the conflict of ideas, borrowed from Hegel, Proudhon wove into his theory of progress. By placing the thesis and the antithesis against each other, he, moved by a preexistent idea of equality, tried to create a synthesis, a new concept, by means of which justice would be possible. Thus he endeavored to unite into a synthesis both value in use and value in exchange. These two values, he said, were in inverse ratio to each other, for as value in exchange fell on account of increased production, value in use rose. There was an antinomy or a contradiction which would resolve itself into a synthesis. This synthesis, called by Proudhon "constituted value," would be nothing more than the expression of the relations among the products composing wealth, a relation which depended entirely upon the labor expended in the making of each product. The new form of value, based exclusively on labor, would be, in the opinion of Proudhon, the best measure of utility and exchange, a principle of justice and equality.[65] "Constituted value" would result in the equivalence of wages and products. Proudhon, the idealist, saw in history the constant striving toward the realization of justice arising from a perpetual struggle of opposites which resolved themselves into one superior to either of the other two.[66]

But how to realize liberty, equality and justice in the economic world? Proudhon arrived at his formula by placing property and communism in opposition to each other. Property, he said, rested on no solid foundation. It could not be defended either by the doctrine of natural right, or by the social contract theory. Moreover, its consequences were disastrous. The proprietor, producing nothing, drew an unearned income, and deprived the worker of a part of his product. Property inflated the value of products and caused poverty and tyranny. It was incompatible with political and civil equality.[67]

Communism, like property, received harsh criticism from Proudhon's pen. Communism, by making labor obligatory, made it odious. It resulted in the loss of liberty, spontaneity and genius. If property was the exploitation of the weak by the strong, communism was the exploitation of the strong

22

by the weak. Communism meant servitude, the violation of equality.[68]

If communism was the thesis and property the antithesis, then what was the synthesis? Property based on labor. The worker would be the proprietor of the value created by him.[69] Property would be preserved, while the unearned income would be abolished. Such property would lead to liberty and justice.

The new form of property could be attained not through the organization of labor, which would enthrone authority, but through the organization of credit and exchange, which would bring liberty and order in anarchy. In his *Contradictions économiques* Proudhon asked himself what should be the formula of equation among all the economic contradictions; and his answer was: "It must be a law of exchange, a theory of mutualism, a system of guarantees which would resolve the old forms of our civil and commercial societies." "This theory of mutualism, that is, of natural exchange . . . is, from the collective point of view, the synthesis of two ideas, property and communism." [70] Equality would exist only when money and interest were abolished, for "constituted value" would not be realized unless products were exchanged for products in proportion to the quantity of labor expended. Free credit would put an end to interest. Hence, Proudhon proposed, in 1848, the establishment of a Bank of Exchange, an institution, which, founded without any capital, would lend paper money that would serve as a medium of exchange among the members of the new bank. The bearer would be certain that this money was always exchangeable as if it were cash, for it would be guaranteed by the goods in trade. [71]

This extraordinary institution would cause a social revolution. Interest would disappear, unearned incomes would become impossible, products would be exchanged for products, labor would receive the full value of what it produced, and class distinctions would disappear. Government, too, would be superfluous, for capital and labor would become identified. There would be neither weak nor strong, but only workers who would be at the same time private owners, for property would not be abolished, but would be owned in more or less equal parts. Government would be replaced by free contract, or anarchism. It was no wonder that Marx called Proudhon "the petty bourgeois, tossed about constantly between capital and labor, between political economy and communism." [72]

The bank was never established, but Proudhon did not cease to hope for a peaceful social revolution which would substitute free contract for authority.[73] In 1851, he maintained that there was sufficient cause for a social transformation. The Revolution of 1789 had two tasks to complete: to destroy the old régime and to found a new one, on the principle that "every negation in society implies an affirmation subsequent and contradictory." [74] But it completed only the first task and forgot the second. Politics alone held the stage; the economic question was thrown into the background.[75] Thus the new society which the French Revolution should have constructed was still to be created. Moreover, in economic life society was tending toward increased misery. The division of labor was causing the impoverishment of the worker; competition, denied to the workers, was the privilege of only a few; and credit was monopolized by the "financial power." [76] Where did the remedy lie? Not in association, for it was neither "a directing principle," nor "an industrial force." [77] It was by nature "sterile, even injurious," for it impeded the freedom of the worker.[78] Neither did the remedy lie in authority, for the tendency of social evolution was away from Rousseau's idea of the social contract and toward the negation of government, toward "the anarchic idea," or free contract, "the only moral link acceptable to free and equal beings." [79] The solution lay in a social revolution, peacefully conducted. It would lead to the liquidation of vested interests, and to the dissolution of the state into economic functional groups. The revolution would be economic, effected not from below, but from above. The state was to transform the Bank of France into an institution of public utility which would proceed to reduce the rate of interest to one half or one quarter per cent. The general rate of interest would steadily drop. Since credit would be cheap, the state would convert, and with the saving on the interest, amortize the public debt. Similarly, individuals would be able to clear their personal debts and the mortgages on their properties, and acquire the complete ownership of their homes and farms. Cheap credit would also lead to the construction of more houses; hence, he believed, rent would gradually fall until it disappeared. Workers could obtain credit almost without cost and become independent of the capitalists. Thus "constituted value" would become possible.[80]

The social revolution would be world-wide in its significance. It would mean: "the cessation of exploitation by capitalists and landowners; the abolition of the wage system; the guarantee of equal and true exchange; the constitution of value; the assurance of a good market; a change in the principle of protection, that is, the market of the globe opened to producers of all countries; the placing of the police, justice and the administration under the control of the producers;

the substitution of economic organization for the governmental and military régime, in the colonial possessions as well as at home; and finally the free and universal communication of races under the single law of contract. That is the revolution." [81]

Thus to Proudhon, the ideal society was anarchy, based on the freedom of contract, in which liberty, equality and justice would prevail. Several years later, however, he adopted a form of political federalism, destined to balance authority and liberty. The basis of federalism would be contract, that is, "an agreement by which one or more heads of families, one or more communes, one or more groups of communes or states are mutually and equally obliged to each other for one or more particular objects whose care falls exclusively upon the delegates of the federation." [82] The government of the federation would be organized on the principles of local autonomy and division of power, so that authority would be circumscribed and liberty maintained. [83]

Proudhon considered federalism only as a consequence of mutualism, which was the term he applied to the basic idea of the social and economic order of which he dreamed. [84] It has been shown how he attempted to apply Hegelian dialectics to human progress and to economics in order to show that humanity was constantly advancing toward liberty, equality and justice. It has also been shown how he hoped through the Bank of Exchange, and later, through an appeal to the government, to begin the dissolution of the old order into a new one based on mutualism. His own scheme remained on paper, and the government paid no heed to his warning that society was tending toward a social revolution. But that did not cause Proudhon to abandon his mutualist idea. In his last work, which he left unfinished, he appealed to the working class to avoid the path of other political parties, refrain from entering parliament,[85] form an alliance with the declining middle class[86] and be guided by the idea of mutualism; in other words, " to become a power or nothing." [87] It was in the name of liberty and justice, the two fundamental principles of mutualism, that Proudhon criticized the law on coalitions and opposed strikes.[88]

What was this mutualism which became the catchword of a large section of the labor movement in the 1860's? It was a political and particularly a social and economic idea. From its realization there would ensue a system of society, "the most perfect and the most convenient" one which would guarantee the complete freedom of the individual. Applied to credit, mutualism would lead to the abolition of interest and of unearned income. As the guiding principle of labor, it would take the form of the exchange of products on the basis of the quantity of the labor content. The mutualist idea would reform and breathe new life into the cooperative societies. Its application to government would result in reconciling individual liberty with national unity by contract, which was the basis of federalism.[89] In Proudhon's own words mutualism was "a formula of justice . . . in virtue of which the members of a society—whatever be their rank, fortune and condition, whether they be corporations or individuals, families or cities, engaged in industry, agriculture or public service—promise and guarantee to each other service for service, credit for credit, pledge for pledge, security for security, value for value, information for information, good faith for good faith, truth for truth, freedom for freedom, property for property. . . ." [90] Among workers mutualism took the concrete form of mutual aid societies, credit societies and cooperative societies which Proudhon extolled in his last years.[91]

If Blanqui's followers were drawn from the students of the Latin Quarter, those of Proudhon came, according to Weill, from "the intelligent workers," [92] who produced such leaders as Tolain, Fribourg, Chemalé, Malon and Varlin.[93] Proudhonians were active in the mutual aid and credit societies, in the cooperative movement and in the syndical chambers. Many of them were signers of the Manifesto of the Sixty, and several were not without influence among intellectuals and students. Proudhonians not only contributed to republican papers, but also published their own. The *Courrier français,* edited by Vermorel, popularized the ideas of Proudhon, and had such contributors as Georges Duchêne, Henri Tolain, Yves Guyot and even Jules Guesde, a future Marxist of France.[94] The *Ecoles de France* and the *Rive Gauche,* both edited by Charles Longuet, future son-in-law of Marx, also taught the doctrines of Proudhon, and boasted of such contributors as Vermorel, César de Paepe, the Belgian socialist, and Paul Lafargue, another future son-in-law of Marx.[95] The activity of the Proudhonians, however, was to a large extent connected with the International in which their ideas were dominant during the first four years of the life of the association.

3. *The International*

The idea of establishing an international understanding among workers was not new in the 1860's. Utopian socialists both in Great Britain and in France had dreamed of liberating all of humanity through their schemes. The Chartists had shown sympathy with the revolutionary struggles in other countries, and revolutionary exiles in England helped to give life to the international idea. In fact, attempts were made in England to create an international association of workers; but the results were two ephemeral organizations: the Fraternal Democrats, formed in the Late Forties; and the International Association in the Mid-Fifties.[96]

Between the end of the International Association and the organization of the First International only about five years elapsed. During this brief period, the Civil War in the United States helped to impress upon English and French labor leaders and workers the idea of international economic solidarity. Moreover, the International Exposition of 1862 brought French and English workers into close and friendly relations which did not cease with the Exposition. Thus, when a meeting was organized in St. Martin's Hall in September, 1864, in connection with the Polish Question, three French delegates attended and helped to lay the foundations of the First International.[97] Toward the end of the year, the *Address and Provisional Rules of the International Workingmen's Association,* drafted by Karl Marx, were adopted and sent to the various sections of the organization.[98] More than twenty thousand copies of the preamble and rules were distributed in France.

In Paris, a bureau of the International was opened at 44 rue des Gravilliers in a small room which during the day served as Fribourg's workshop. The association soon received the adherence not only of workers, but also of physicians, journalists, civil servants and even of Jules Simon and Henri Martin. From the very beginning, the correspondents, Tolain, Fribourg and Limousin, had to contend not only against material difficulties, but also against attacks from republicans and Blanquists who were spreading the news in labor circles that the organizers were in secret relations with the government. To reassure the labor leaders, the founders of the International in France invited them to a meeting where it was definitely asserted that the International would not mingle in politics, but that it would strive to organize the workers. In typical Proudhonian fashion, Tolain and his colleagues said that it was more important to spend the time on study and education than on conspiracies.[99] "The society," Fribourg announced emphatically, "will absolutely refuse to meddle in the political affairs of France; it is a study society, not a revival of Carbonarism."[100] The correspondents profited by the occasion to interest the leaders of the workers in the association by increasing the membership of the bureau from three to twenty.

Though its funds were limited, the International gradually spread its influence in France. It established branches in the provinces, and sent delegates to towns in order to prevail upon the labor organizations to affiliate themselves with it. Under its direction were formed mutual aid, credit and resistance societies, and consumers' and producers' co-operatives. It did not favor strikes. As one of its leading members said, "it never advised the workers to strike. On the contrary, many were the occasions when it prevented strikes from breaking out."[101] Despite the efforts of the leaders, the International won only about five hundred adherents in the first seven months of its existence.

The congress scheduled to meet in Brussels in 1865 was replaced by a conference in London. The four French delegates favored the exclusion not only of members of the professional classes, whose influence would tend to inject politics into the association, but also of women who would be drawn away from their natural duties as mothers and housekeepers.[102] The Polish Question caused discord among the members of the conference. The French and Swiss maintained that the association should limit itself to social and economic problems; but they were outvoted, and the question remained in the program of the International.[103]

The opinions of the French delegates at the London conference indicated that the International in France was being swayed by Proudhon's doctrines. However, for a fuller understanding of the extent of Proudhonian influence we must examine briefly the ideas expressed by the French delegates at the Geneva Congress held in 1866, from which the Blanquists were expelled.[104]

After listening to the General Council's report written by Marx, the French delegates presented theirs. In it Proudhon's ideas were easily recognizable. The workers, they said, still lacked the intellectual and political competence to emancipate themselves. Thus it was "the aim of the International to lead the proletariat scientifically—and peacefully, if possible—to its emancipation." Labor was the source of all wealth, and capital was accumulated labor. Interest was unjust; the organization of mutual credit would abolish it. The real education of the child would be best accomplished by the family and not by the state, for the first developed the individual, while the second modeled him according to a single type. To preserve the family, the best school for the child, the mother was to be freed from workshop and factory. Mutualism in education would supplement the work of the family. Cooperation was good, because it meant "contract freely entered into for a single aim, determined and defined in advance"; because it was "the collectivity organizing itself in order to furnish the individual with all the means of increasing his freedom of action,

and in order to develop his individual initiative." Strikes
were bad; they led to a reduction in consumption, hence to
more unemployment. The causes of struggle between capital and labor resided in their existing relations; these could
be transformed through a system of exchange based on reciprocity and through the reform of education. It was impossible under prevailing conditions to effect a radical modification in taxation; but until such a change was made, direct
taxes were to be substituted for indirect taxes. Standing
armies were not only injurious to production, but also destructive of freedom. Sections in which the French delegates disposed of free trade versus protection as a quarrel
among capitalists, and declared religion a useless subject
of discussion and the Polish Question out of place in an
economic congress, completed the report,[105] which was favorably received by the Swiss and by a majority of the English delegates.

Proudhonism extended its authority beyond the French
section of the International. Its influence was marked not
only at the Congress of Geneva, the resolutions of which
displayed the stamp of mutualism,[106] but also at the Congress
of Lausanne where resolutions were adopted favoring the
establishment of producers' cooperatives with the aid of mutual credit, and declaring that the social transformation
could be accomplished by methods which were "in conformity with reciprocity and justice." [107] But the Lausanne Congress which was a sweeping victory for mutualism also heard
César de Paepe advocate Colinsian collectivism,[108] and saw
it defended by the German, English and Flemish delegates.
Moreover, one of the resolutions contained the following
sentence: "The social emancipation of the worker is inseparable from his political emancipation." It was evident to

many that the International was turning to a new doctrine. At the Congress of Brussels, held the following year, collectivism won a victory over mutualism.[109] The hold of the Proudhonians on the International was lost. Thereafter the stage was occupied by the followers of Marx and Bakunin.

In the meantime, the French branch of the International was forced to adopt policies which brought upon it the heavy hand of the French government. Despite the International's hostility to strikes, it was drawn into labor conflicts. Through its adherence to the League of Peace and Freedom, a political and republican organization, it was forced into politics. Moreover, on November 2, 1867, it participated in a demonstration near Manin's grave in the cemetery of Montmartre and in another on November 4th to protest against the reoccupation of Rome by French troops. The government decided to act against the organization which it had been tolerating since its foundation. In March, 1868, a court ordered the dissolution of the association, and fined each of fifteen arrested members of the Parisian commission. When a new commission was formed under aggressive leadership the government instituted a second trial. This time the leaders were sentenced to three months' imprisonment and fined one hundred francs each.[110] The International in France was decapitated. Only the revolutionists remained faithful to it.

But the International in France soon assumed new life under the direction of its revolutionary labor leaders. With its headquarters on rue de la Corderie, in the same building where the Federation of Syndical Chambers met, it was in a favorable position to spread its propaganda among the labor organizations. Its participation in strikes and demonstrations gave it popularity in labor circles, a popularity which

33

was enhanced when the failure of the *Crédit au Travail* blasted the hope of many of the workers in cooperation and caused them to turn to the International for guidance. The result was a rapid increase in its membership.[111] The government became alarmed and brought the International to trial for the third time. Many of the leaders were sentenced to terms of imprisonment; but the activity of the International was not entirely paralyzed, for the revolutionary movement had made too much headway. No one can predict what direction this movement would have taken if it had not been diverted by the Franco-Prussian War.

The International, after the trial of 1868, fell under the control of militant leaders; but Proudhonism was still dominant within its ranks, at least in the Parisian sections. Though it was forced to abandon its antipolitical and peaceful policies, though many of its leaders professed to be either collectivists or communists, the economic and social views of many of them were still basically Proudhonian. Thus, the manifesto of March 23, 1871, in which the Paris Federal Council gave support to the Commune, was an expression of Proudhonian thought. The document established a connection between "contract" and "social equality," advocated communal autonomy, and made the political question subordinate to "the organization of credit, exchange and cooperation, to assure to the worker the entire value of his labor." [112]

Despite its rapid growth from 1868 to 1870, the International had a fluctuating membership and was not a well-knit organization. Its sections, poorly disciplined, followed more or less the dictates and views of their respective leaders. This loose organization was reduced to a mere shadow by the events following September 4, 1870. It, therefore, could not and did not assume leadership in the critical situation which Paris faced on the morning of March 18th, culminating in the revolt of the Paris Commune.

4. The Commune [118]

The Paris Commune did not spring from the socialist movement which had made headway during the last years of the Empire. Despite the fact that revolutionary clubs, journals and societies were allowed to multiply in Paris after September 4, 1870, despite the socialist character of the pronouncements of many of the leaders, the Commune arose from causes other than socialistic. In the first place, there was dissatisfaction in Paris with the Government of National Defense for its lack of initiative and aggressiveness in the face of the enemy. In the second place, the election of a monarchist National Assembly which ratified the Treaty of Frankfort struck a blow at the republican sentiments of the Parisians and injured their vanity and patriotism. They who wished to continue the war to the very end, were instead subjected to the insult of seeing a part of their city occupied by German troops. In the third place, a five months' siege had fatigued the capital, had disorganized industry and had driven many to the verge of starvation.

To these aggravating conditions the National Assembly added irritating laws. Small shopkeepers were faced with ruin when a law was passed providing that payment on notes which had matured could be demanded by the holders after March 13th. Workers were thrown on the mercy of their landlords by a law ordering the immediate payment of back rents under threat of eviction. Another law suppressed the daily allowance of a franc-and-a-half to national guardsmen and deprived many of the workingmen of their sole means of support. Among these irritated masses of Parisians, the radical clubs, newspapers and revolutionary leaders spread their vague and diverse doctrines, and fanned the smouldering embers of revolt. And when, on the morning of March 18th, Thiers attempted to disarm Paris, which he feared as the hotbed of radicalism, as an obstacle in his relations with Germany, he found his regular troops opposed by the national guardsmen. During the next two months Paris was in open revolt against Versailles.

From its very beginning the Commune had a patriotic, republican and proletarian character. It was a protest against the capitulation to Germany and an attempt to regenerate the country.[114] The Commune was as republican as it was patriotic; but the word republic had several meanings. To some Communards, it meant "peace and labor," and "social regeneration." [115] To others it signified the beginning of a vigorous policy against the enemy, the centralization of France, national defense and a reawakening of "the daring and boldness, the self-sacrifice and the triumphs of the Great Revolution." [116] The Commune was also in part a proletarian movement. It had the support of the workers, who formed the bulk of its forces, and for whose benefit the government of the Commune was obliged to decree reforms. In that government there were many labor and socialist leaders whose mission and aim were to defend the interests of the proletariat and to attempt to solve the social question.

The Commune was not a government of one party or group. Within its governing circles, Blanquists, Jacobins and Proudhonians elbowed one another without knowing or understanding one another. The Blanquists, partly Jacobin, partly socialist, were seconded by Jacobins who harked back

36

to the revolutionary traditions of 1793 and 1848. These two groups, the majority in the government of the Commune, formed the party of the dictatorship which tried to replace the National Assembly by the Assembly of Paris as the government of France. The exponents of the revolutionary tradition of centralization, they believed that the Commune was "the continuation of the old Commune of Paris of 1793."[117] In imitation of it, they created a Committee of Public Safety,[118] revived the revolutionary calendar, and appealed to the people in the name of Liberty, Equality and Fraternity. In the attempt to set up a dictatorship, they made arrests wholesale,[119] and adopted repressive measures against newspapers.[120] The Blanquists and Jacobins formed the party of force in the Commune.

Opposed to them were the Proudhonians, most of whom were members of the International. These were enemies of centralization and dictatorship, against which they advocated autonomy and the free and open discussion of the actions of the representatives. It was for this reason that they, the minority in the government of the Commune, protested, but without effect, against the creation of the Committee of Public Safety,[121] and against the tyrannical policies of the Prefecture of Police[122] which was at one time dominated by Raoul Rigault, a young and enthusiastic Blanquist. The Proudhonians, who claimed to speak in the name of the working class, concerned themselves during the Commune with the social and economic life of the people. While Blanquists and Jacobins were making blunders in the military operations and in the police department, the Proudhonians turned their attention to the problems of labor and education, so that whatever concern with social reform was exhibited in the Commune was attributable to them.

The members of the International formed a minority in the government of the Commune; yet, it was they who were blamed for organizing in Paris the party of the revolution, which took the lead on March 18th.[123] The strength of the International was stated to have been tremendous, and the number of its adherents was calculated to have been about 800,000 in France and about 200,000 in Paris.[124] It was accused of having set fire to public buildings [125] and of having aimed at a bloody uprising to realize its social and egalitarian program.[126]

But these accusations in no way tally with the facts. It has been shown that the events after September 4th reduced the strength of the loosely organized association and rendered it unfit to take aggressive action.[127] Furthermore, the evidence of those who had first-hand knowledge of the work of the International as well as its own records prove that it was powerless to lead the revolution of March 18th, and that almost all of its members were opposed to violence. M. de Molinari, who was well acquainted with the Parisian socialist movement at the time of the uprising, claimed that the International took no part in it.[128] Tolain, one of the founders of the International in France, made a similar observation before the committee investigating the causes of the insurrection.[129] In a pamphlet published in London in 1872 against the International, several ex-Communards stated that the International was nothing but a shadow "to which public credulity alone lent existence." [130]

One need only consult the minutes of the Paris Federal Council to see how weak the association was, and how little it was responsible for the uprising. The "rich" organization with its "vast" membership could not found a paper for lack of funds.[131] On January 19th, a delegate affirmed

38

that the sections were "ruined, and their members scattered." [132]   At the meeting of February 15th, Frankel said: "Since the 4th of September, events have dispersed the International. . . . We have a moral force, if not in France, at least in Paris; we lack material force for want of organization. Many members do not understand the aim of the association." [133]   On March 17th, one day before the uprising, a member, writing to Gambon who inquired about the Federal Council's attitude to the Versailles Assembly, expressed the irresolution of the group when he stated: "The Federal Council of the International Workingmen's Association is, like you, very much embarrassed by the obscurity of the political situation. What is to be done? What does the people think deep down in its heart?" [134]   At another sitting of the Council, a member declared: "The revolution of March 18th is entirely social, and the newspapers throughout France state that the International has seized power. We know that it is altogether different." [135]

Not only could the International not be held responsible for the uprising of March 18th, but it could not even be properly accused of the excesses committed in the last days of the Commune. Its members, most of whom were Proudhonians, were opposed to the dictatorship of the Blanquists and Jacobins, and nearly all of them voted against the establishment of the Committee of Public Safety.[136] It was the Internationalist minority which opposed the violent measures of the Communards. Theisz prevented them from burning the post-office, Camélinat the mint. Beslay protected the bank, Varlin tried to save the hostages condemned to death by the Blanquists, and Avrial did not sign any measure that might result in violence.[137]

It is not true that the International made the revolution

of March 18th which created the Commune. Rather is it true that the Commune gave publicity to the International which, during a brief period after the uprising, seemed to be spreading its power.[138]

Despite the fact that the Internationalists in the government were interested in the economic emancipation of the workers, despite the presence of socialists in important positions, the Commune "attempted nothing, planned nothing with a view to the transformation of the relations between capital and labor, which deserves to be extolled or even mentioned." [139] The social and economic changes made by the Commune were not what one could call socialistic. It separated church and state, and confiscated the property of the religious orders.[140] It remitted rents for stated periods, suspended the sale of articles by pawnshops [141] and permitted the free withdrawal of some of these articles.[142] It limited the salaries of officeholders to 6,000 francs a year,[143] took under its care the widows and orphans of those who died for the Commune,[144] provided for the relief of debtors,[145] and opened a few secular schools.[146]

In the field of labor the Commune made a few important changes. It abolished fines imposed on workers, and prohibited night work in bakeries.[147] The latter decree was opposed by certain members who believed that the government should not interfere in labor questions,[148] and was hailed by workers, of whom twelve to fifteen hundred, carrying red flags and banners, marched to the Hôtel de Ville to thank the government.[149] The Commune also instructed the workers' syndical chambers to form a commission in order to inquire into the condition of the abandoned workshops, and to report when these workshops could be put into operation, "no longer by the deserters who have abandoned them, but by the cooperative association of the workers employed there." Not wishing to alienate the bourgeois elements in the Commune, the members of the Commission of Labor, Industry and Trade, who were Proudhonians, provided for a jury to determine, upon the return of the employers, "the conditions of the definitive transfer of the shops to the labor societies, and the amount of indemnity which the societies will have to pay to the employers." [150] The scheme, which was reminiscent of the plan of Louis Blanc, was never put into operation. The Commune attacked the contract system in the manufacture of military uniforms when it authorized the Commission of Exchange to revise existing contracts and to make arrangements directly with the labor associations.[151] It further showed its interest in the workers when it adopted a plan giving labor a voice in the management of the workshops of the Louvre.[152]

Neither its social and labor legislation nor its official declarations of policy reveal that the Commune was socialistic. The work of the Commission of Labor, Industry and Trade, led by members of the International, was hampered by the fact that it had to address itself to a working class that had scarcely begun to raise its head, and to a petty bourgeoisie, "restless, frightened, whom a too vigorous stroke of the revolutionary government would certainly have thrown into the camp of reaction." Thus, the Commission which could have best translated the aspirations of labor "finally left nothing which can authorize the unlearned or the doctrinaire to say: the Commune was socialistic." [153] Furthermore, the Commune in none of its official documents presented a socialist program. The Declaration to the People of France of April 19th, its so-called program, drawn up and accepted by a minority, harped rather on a decentralized republic than on socialism. Essentially Proudhonian in doctrine, the document referred only vaguely to the reorganization of production and property.[154] The Commune said nothing about socialist ideals, because, as a socialist historian wrote, "it had little or nothing to say. It was, it must be repeated, an extremely mixed assembly in which the authoritarian Jacobin element elbowed the federalist and Proudhonian element of the International, in which few men exactly sensed the immediate situation, and still fewer had the intuition of the subsequent events which the revolution of March 18th prepared and announced. A document truly characteristic of a period or a tendency could scarcely come out of its deliberations, still less a charter helping to constitute the society of to-morrow."[155]

Nor were most of the Communards definitely conscious of the antagonism of classes. The Proudhonians may have written and spoken about it,[156] but the *Journal officiel* appealed alike to tradesmen, shopkeepers and workers,[157] maintained that the republic "must establish harmony of interests, and not sacrifice them to each other,"[158] and definitely asserted that in 1871 "the antagonism of class against class does not exist."[159] When the Commune enacted the law relieving debtors, it in no way expropriated the creditors. On the contrary, the latter were assured of eventual payment.[160] The plan to take over the abandoned shops provided for an indemnity to the former owners. Unquestionably these laws were meant to benefit the workers, but they were not prompted by class hatred.

With the exception of the Internationalists, the Communards were only vaguely conscious of any class antagonism, chiefly because social and economic classes were not yet fully developed. Large scale industry was still in its infancy in France, and, in Paris particularly, the handicraft system prevailed. A modern industrial proletariat was therefore lacking in Paris; but a proletariat there was—a proletariat with the psychology and habits of the craftsman. The Commune was proletarian and was led in part by many socialists the obscurity of whose notions about social changes was equalled by their indecision. But one cannot accept the claim of later socialists, that the Commune was socialistic because it was proletarian. Proletariat and socialism are not inseparable, and a working-class movement may be non-socialistic.

The defeat of the Commune [161] swept away most of the workers' syndical chambers, and caused a shortage in the labor supply. The Parisian Chamber of Commerce noted that, "in 1871 and 1872, hands which were not missing before are at present lacking, in consequence of the disturbance caused by the crisis through which the country has passed." [162]

The Commune also reacted on the subsequent socialist movement, not only in France, but also in other European countries. During its brief existence, it received the sympathy of socialist groups and of socialists in Europe. *La Liberté,* a socialist journal of Brussels, greeted it as a definitive break between the proletariat and the bourgeoisie, and the Communards as those "who will have opened the gates of the country to organic socialism." [163] A socialist society of Florence sent an enthusiastic address in praise of the Communards.[164] The Hanoverian socialists were no less ardent in their greetings when they said that the Communards were "the proletariat fighting for the rights of man." And the Geneva section of the International saw in the revolution of March 18th "the political accession of

43

the working class," "the beginning of the era of social re-organization." [165]   Bebel, who, together with his friend, Liebknecht, had protested against the annexation of Alsace-Lorraine,[166] expressed his admiration for the Commu-nards.[167]   Bakunin, the travelling salesman of anarchism, whose partly heroic and partly foolhardy attempt to inau-gurate a revolution in Lyons and to abolish the state ended in a fiasco,[168] openly declared his partisanship for the Com-mune, because he saw in it a bold and openly pronounced negation of the state and of religion.[169]

The revolution that was republican, patriotic and pro-letarian was being transformed into a socialistic one in the minds of foreign socialists.

The person most responsible for the transformation was Karl Marx.   Even before the writing of *The Civil War in France* he claimed the Commune for socialism.   He praised the Communards for their heroism, for their "his-torical initiative" and "self-sacrifice," and enthusiastically referred to the rising of Paris as "the most glorious achievement of our party since the June Revolution." [170] He saw in the Commune a workingmen's revolution, and therefore, according to his theory of history, a socialistic one.   Thus, he not only offered it his advice,[171] but also de-fended it after its death.

A short time after the suppression of the Commune, there appeared *The Civil War in France,* one of the most biting polemics Marx ever composed.   Every page of it breathed a spirit of hatred for the conquerors of the Commune. The Government of National Defense was a "Government of National Defection," "an assembly of ghouls." [172] Thiers appeared as a "monstrous gnome," a "lying" his-torian, a "hypocrite," "the historical shoe-black" of the first Napoleon.[173] Favre was accused of "adultery," forgery and graft.[174]

Marx pictured Paris as the self-sacrificing champion of France whose salvation the city was determined to take in hand; but it could not succeed "without the revolutionary overthrow of the political and social conditions that had engendered the Second Empire." To him the Commune was "the direct antithesis" of the Empire. It was the positive form of the "Social Republic," a working-class government which was to effect the emancipation of the proletariat.[175]

Marx saw in the Commune the expression of the dictatorship of the proletariat, because, by abolishing the standing army and the bureaucracy, and by stripping the police "of its political attributes" and turning it into a "revocable agent of the Commune," it destroyed the repressive organs of the bourgeois state.[176] But the dictatorship of the proletariat cannot be restricted to the destruction of the political functions of the bourgeois state. It also implies the expropriation of the bourgeoisie and the centralization of the ownership of the instruments of production. Which party in the Commune was prepared to carry out such a program? The Blanquists, who centered their efforts on the seizure of the state, had no economic program which pointed to expropriation; and the Internationalists, who were generally Proudhonians, were hostile to both dictatorship and expropriation. No party in the Commune was prepared to establish a dictatorship in the Marxian sense, and none did establish it. Therefore, the Commune could not "serve as a lever for uprooting the economical foundations upon which rests the existence of classes."

The Commune, said Marx, saved the shopkeepers, the

tradesmen and the merchants by its decree on debts. It would have freed the peasant of heavy taxation, given him an inexpensive government, liberated him from ruthless officials and enlightened him through education. It is difficult to find any socialism in these measures whether realized or projected. Of decrees affecting labor, Marx could mention only the abolition of night work in bakeries, the annulment of the practice of levying fines on workers, and the surrender of closed workshops and factories to associations of workers.[177] He praised the financial measures of the Commune, but failed to state that the Communards did not confiscate the funds of the Bank of France, which present-day communists criticize as a grievous blunder.[178]

Marx utilized for socialist ends the bloody defeat of the Commune. In his opinion, it heightened the struggle between classes. The Commune was "a glorious harbinger of a new society" [179] which would arrive inevitably after the victory of the proletariat over the bourgeoisie.

Thus, the Commune, arising spontaneously from conditions created by war, was stamped with a socialist seal. As a result, it became a notable landmark in the history of socialism. French socialists and communists evoke its memory, speak with reverence of its leaders and make annual pilgrimages to Père Lachaise. During the Nineties, socialists even paid it the compliment of imitation by patterning some of their bills in parliament after its decrees,[180] and regarded the manifesto, "To the Workers of the Country," as of sufficient importance to merit its reprinting in full.[181]

The defeat of the Commune had a more immediate effect on socialism in France. The Blanquism of the *coup de main* became obsolete. Developed and practiced during the July Monarchy and the Second Empire, it lost its *raison d'être* during the Third Republic. Proudhonism, too, felt the blow of the Commune. Its doctrines lost their influence on socialists during the Third Republic; but they were accepted in part by anarchists and syndicalists. Among socialists, Proudhonism was replaced by Marxism.

CHAPTER II

THE LABOR MOVEMENT AFTER THE COMMUNE,

1871-1878

1. Public and governmental attitudes toward labor

A radical movement like the Commune naturally aroused the antipathy of the conservative elements. The Commune was proletarian, and though it was not socialistic, its manifestoes and decrees with their vague expressions on social and economic equality were sufficient to instill fear in its opponents. Its hostility to the church and to the Napoleonic traditions of conquest, the friendliness shown to it by German socialists while the enemy was in control of French territory, and its defiance of Versailles only succeeded in raising against it all the forces which labored for the status quo. Its defeat was followed by a wave of reaction. Radicalism in any form was attacked, and the International was banned by law.

The International aroused fear because its strength was exaggerated by its enemies. Though most of its members had opposed violence,[1] it was made the scape-goat of all the misdeeds committed by the Communards. All parties charged it "with assassination, incendiarism and with all the inexpiable crimes." [2] Government officials and people in private life, authors and journalists, all vied with one another in traducing the International. The interest in the association became so great that most of the studies on it, to which the French reader may refer to-day, were published within a few years after the Commune.[3] At a time when the International was weakened through internal dissension between anarchists and socialists, Testut, whose books were seriously studied in official circles,[4] was warning the authorities against the impending violent revolution it was planning to lead.[5] Jules Favre, the foreign minister, appealed to foreign governments to assist him in prosecuting the organization,[6] and Thiers, who believed that it was "infinitely formidable," demanded the adoption of a law proscribing it.[7] So great was the fear engendered by the Commune and the International that a parliamentary committee was appointed to inquire into the causes of the insurrection, and a law was passed, making the existence of the International unlawful in France and affiliation with it a crime.[8]

The defeat of the Commune raised the problem as to how the workers could be pacified. Economists and social reformers had their respective solutions; but their remedies were those suggested during the Second Empire. The economists held to their faith in the *laissez-faire* doctrines, while the followers of Le Play, de Mun and Comte, and the remaining disciples of Fourier and Saint-Simon, maintained their trust in their panaceas. The Commune had only strengthened in each the belief that had his scheme been applied the great catastrophe would have been avoided. All wished to placate the workers, but they disagreed on the method.

Whether the workers should have the right to combine was a question discussed by conservatives and liberals alike, because it was pertinent to the problem of social peace. The position of trade unions was regulated by the law of 1864 which said nothing about their legality or illegality. Though the right to strike was recognized, the government reserved the right to intervene when there was interference with the freedom of work.[9] Many held the opinion that the freedom of work was conducive to social peace, and, consequently, that the existing law should be abolished. The parliamentary committee on the causes of the insurrection believed that the law encouraged false hopes and fanned the flames of civil war.[10] The Parisian Chamber of Commerce asserted that workers' combinations tended to create hostility between capital and labor and to decrease production.[11] The report of the parliamentary committee headed by Ducarre upheld the freedom of labor as an advance over the system of regulation. "The freedom of labor formulated by Turgot and decreed by the great Constituent Assembly," concluded Ducarre in his report, "is the *raison d'être* of our industrial prosperity. It allows all French citizens, workers or employers, to regulate their professional relations as they understand them. It forbids any group, whatever be its name, form or origin, to take the place of personal initiative." [12]

The reaction of the economists to labor combinations was best expressed by them when the Lockroy Bill was before the French Chamber. Introduced on July 4, 1876, it aimed to give recognition to trade unions which were, however, to deposit with the prefect the names and addresses of the members. Though the law was not passed, it is of interest to examine the opinions it evoked.[13] Michel Chevalier feared lest the bill should restrain the workers and prove prejudicial to freedom and to the public interest.[14] Another economist opposed combinations because they

50

would reduce the pay of the capable workers to the rate of the less capable. A member of the Society of Political Economy attacked trade unions, calling them a peril and insisting that their authorization would create a second parliament within the state.[15] Maurice Block, an author of several works in economics, objected to them on the ground that they would thwart the natural operation of economic laws.[16]

However, a few economists broke the monotony of opposition to labor combinations. To Joseph Garnier it appeared that social stability rested on the most complete freedom to combine. Combinations would enlighten the workers and counsel against violence; and he cited the example of England where the freedom to combine had resulted in a reduction of violence.[17] Other economists, and even some manufacturers, agreed with Garnier. They reasoned that labor organizations would help to promote peace between the classes.[18]

While nothing was done to legalize labor unions, a step was taken to improve the working conditions of children. The law of 1841, which applied only to children in factories and shops employing more than twenty workers, had had no effect, for no provision had been made for its enforcement. In 1874, the conservative National Assembly passed a law which forbade the employment of children under ten. Those from ten to twelve years of age might be kept at work only six hours; for those from twelve to sixteen years the law provided a maximum of twelve hours. Women, and children under twelve, might not be employed in underground work. But the real improvement of this law over the one of 1841 was the provision for its enforcement. Though the number of inspectors was very limited, the child-labor law was an important initial step in labor legislation.[19]

But the bourgeoisie hoped to undermine radicalism and violence by methods other than labor legislation. The economists believed that the teaching of political economy to rich and poor alike would prove effective in combating socialism. The masses were to be penetrated with the following eternal "truths": capital "is a democratic, philanthropic and egalitarian force"; "wealth is useful to all and is to be respected; to threaten it and to wish to divide it is simply to kill the hen that lays the golden egg";[20] the class struggle is "a figment of the imagination"; labor is a blessing; poverty can be escaped through "labor, saving and the credit which labor and saving bring."[21] Economics was to be taught not only through lectures, pamphlets and books, but also in the schools, on a par with Latin, history and geography. In the *école primaire,* the sons of workers were to be instructed not in "dogmatic precepts on the duties of the worker," but in "precise notions on the natural and immutable laws which govern the rise and fall of values and wages. The worker would realize the causes of his suffering, and it would be possible to reason with him."[22]

The solution of Le Play and his disciples differed from that of the economists. Deploring the sorry effect of the French Revolution on the generations which succeeded it, Le Play based his remedy on religion, property, family, labor and "the beneficent rôle of the capitalist" which he summarized under the word *patronage.*[23] People should be taught the doctrines of the catholic church in order to counteract the destructive effects of materialism on morals and religion. Property, after religion, was the chief mainstay of the social order, if it were properly diffused. A

believer in the necessity of the free transmission of property, Le Play was openly hostile to the law of equal parti-
tion, which undermined the well-being of the family. The
famille souche [24] could alone regenerate the nation after a
great catastrophe. It alone could produce "God-fearing
men trained to labor," and upon it depended the continu-
ance of social peace.[25] Labor was ordained by God, taught
Le Play; it was the basis of moral and intellectual progress. Its purpose was not to create wealth as such, but to
breed virtue.[26] The salvation of the working class could
come only from the benevolence of the employer. Hence,
the bourgeoisie should reform itself in order to serve as an
example to the workers; hence, the capitalists should assume responsibilty for their workers, encourage them to
save and to become the owners of homes, and help to
maintain the stability of the family.[27] To spread his doctrines, Le Play had organized in 1856 the Society of Social
Economy, whose membership comprised capitalists, rich
landowners, lawyers, engineers and official dignitaries.[28]
Its aim was to discuss methods to keep the workers peaceful. After the Commune, he also founded Unions of Social Peace, which were units of propaganda. They were
to undermine the influence of socialism, and "to preach
social conciliation, moral regeneration and social peace." [29]

While Le Play was founding the Unions of Social Peace,
Count Albert de Mun was organizing Catholic Workingmen's Clubs. Though the two men appealed to the benevo-
lent master, though they both pinned their hope on the catholic religion to save the social order, they differed in the
method of realizing social peace. Le Play addressed himself mainly to the bourgeoisie, for he had no faith in organized labor; de Mun went into the heart of the workers' dis-

tricts, preached the regeneration of the working classes through the church, and organized clubs to prepare mixed corporations of capitalists and workers, with a joint committee to handle common problems. Aided by sympathizers and influential persons, he formed an Association of Catholic Workingmen's Clubs which, in 1875, "boasted 130 committees, 150 clubs and 18,000 members." [30] Every important town had its local committee of members of the upper classes to found workingmen's clubs. To join one of them, one had to be a manual worker, at least sixteen years of age, and be nominated by a member. "Each club had its chaplain and its chapel. The workers were attracted by various privileges, such as libraries, cheap lodgings, money saving establishments and various amusements; all of these were carefully supervised by the directing group to which the labor organization owed obedience and respect." [31] This method of bringing together capitalists and workers seemed to the Association the best guarantee for social peace.

Like the disciples of Le Play and the followers of de Mun, the successors of Auguste Comte also preached submission on the part of the workers and benevolence on the part of the bourgeoisie. But while the approach of the first two schools of thought to the social problem was religious, that of the positivist school was sociological. After the Commune, the positivists continued the work of their master by opposing revolution and by attempting to refute socialism and cooperation. Accepting the existing economic organization, they taught that profit and interest were "indispensable and legitimate." But they also maintained that, since wealth was social in origin, capital and labor were in duty bound to cooperate.[32] Individual ownership was necessary; but property was to be used for public service.[33] The trouble lay more in human nature than in the wage system.[34] Therefore, the solution of the social question depended not only on the benevolence of the capitalists,[35] but also on education which would raise the intellectual level of the workers. The positivists, like the Association of Catholic Workingmen's Clubs, carried on an agitation among the workers. But their bourgeois following and their hostility to cooperation[36] and to the independent political action of labor[37] alienated the workers.[38]

Though Fourierism and Saint-Simonism were dead, a few men still venerated the ideas of the old socialist schools, and believed that their schemes could usher in social peace. Prominent among the Fourierists were Godin and Limousin. The first had founded during the Second Empire the *Familistère de Guise,* a form of producers' and consumers' cooperative, and had based its organization on Fourier's principles.[39] The success of his venture gave him such confidence in the regenerative force of his project that he appealed to capitalists and to the government to found *Familistères* in order to solve the problem of capitalism versus labor.[40] The second, Limousin, was a less ambitious Fourierist. He depended on producers' cooperatives, based on labor, talent and capital, to solve the social question.[41] But the capitalists should first train the workers to manage cooperatives by introducing a system of workers' participation in the profits.[42]

A few former Saint-Simonians continued to have a more or less passive interest in the workers. Isaac Pereire, a financier, advocated the abolition of the *octrois* and of other taxes on food, and offered prizes for the best studies "on the removal of poverty, on the best system of education, on the organization of credit and on the reform of taxation." [43] Guéroult appealed to the government and to the bourgeoisie to take an interest in social reforms.[44]

Thus various schools of thought made the social question the subject of inquiry. The economists held that its solution depended on the dissemination and application of economic laws. The social catholics maintained that only the catholic religion and the real benevolence of the bourgeoisie could establish social harmony. The positivists also appealed to bourgeois benevolence in order to effect social changes; but they made it subordinate to the teaching of the laws governing society. The Fourierists and Saint-Simonians were like faint echoes of a dead past. Like their contemporaries, they aimed at the same goal—social peace.

2. Labor's apathy to radicalism

The Commune made the upper classes more conscious of the social question than ever before. So disturbed were the governing circles that they forbade federations of workingmen and simultaneously introduced labor legislation. The effect of the Commune on the workers was even more profound. Gone were their leaders, dissolved were their organizations. In place of the labor organizations which had gained in strength and influence after the laws of 1864 and 1868, there were now some isolated groups of workingmen who feared to raise their heads lest the heavy hand of the government should crush them. They were apathetic to socialist and revolutionary doctrines, and aimed, instead, at improving their conditions by peaceful methods. The cooperative movement rather than revolutionary action became their means of emancipation. Revolution, they reasoned, had brought them nothing but bloodshed and suffering, and socialist theorists had diverted them from their right path. Politics had embroiled them in struggles with the government and had retarded the improvement of their economic condition. Their immediate task, therefore, was to increase their wages and with their savings to create the capital necessary to found producers' cooperatives.

The labor movement after the Commune was marked by its moderation, and by its indifference to radicalism. From the Bloody Week in 1871 to the beginning of Guesde's active influence in 1878 there was practically nothing of any significance which would indicate that labor was other than peaceful, even conservative. Strikes broke out, and the International still attempted secretly to carry on its propaganda, but the strikes were comparatively few in number, and the International's efforts proved fruitless because the workers were afraid of becoming involved in the activities of an organization which was under the ban of the law. The total number of strikes occurring during the five years from 1874 to 1878 was less than the number during the single year of 1882.[45] Labor's moment of calm was so apparent during the first few years of the Third Republic as to cause an economist to believe that "the violent conflicts between capitalists and workers are over or nearly so. The earnest workers," he continued, "have learned to their cost that strikes are a detestable way of gaining an increase in wages and other advantages to which they think they have a right." [46] The Paris correspondent of one of the organs of the Anarchist International was struck by the workers' inactivity and by their coldness toward the International; and he explained it by "the general ignorance, the lack of the necessary energy to combine

57

and by the fear which recent arrests have tended to heighten." On their attitude toward the International he said: "I have noticed an extreme prudence, an excessive care to avoid any relation with the reviled association." [47] The same want of enthusiasm on the part of the workers was observed by the correspondent of a Belgian paper, and he attributed it to "the absence of intelligent leadership." [48]

The reporters understood the situation correctly. The workers were more interested in raising their wages than in espousing revolutionary doctrines. Beginning with 1872, trade and industry were reviving. More coal and iron were mined, more machines were introduced and more railroads were being constructed. The year 1872 showed an increase in the consumption of coal; and, while the amount of raw cotton manufactured into cloth was somewhat less than in the previous year, more raw wool was imported for home consumption.[49] Industry felt the need of labor, particularly since the defeat of the Commune had resulted in the reduction of the number of hands; and some manufacturers were asking the government to free their workers from the prisons.[50] Not only was industry expanding, but the cost of living was rising, if the conclusions of Moréno Henriquès, who directed the inquiry on labor conditions in the Department of the Seine, are trustworthy. Speaking at the Society of Social Economy, he said that though there had been an increase in wages there had also been a gradual rise in prices. If, as he computed, wages showed an advantage over prices, it was because the year 1872, which he had in mind, was "one noted for activity in almost all the shops," and because there was a shortage of labor.[51] Strikes broke out in Paris, Brassac, Sainte-Florine, Puy-de-Dome, Castres, Saint-Etienne and in the coal regions of the

North and Pas-de-Calais where the strikes became violent. Thiers, who feared lest a widespread cessation of work would endanger the credit of the government, was prompt in urging the use of force. The prefect of Pas-de-Calais was honored with a message approving his repressive measures, and informing him that there were 100,000 men ready to march. "The means of repression are not lacking," Thiers wrote to his subordinate. "The republic cannot tolerate disorder, above all the disorder instigated from the outside by disturbers who wish to overturn European society." [52] In his message to the prefect of the North, Thiers, the economic liberal, and, at the same time, the strong protectionist,[53] wrote: "The workers certainly have the right not to work, but they have not the right to prohibit from working those who desire to work." [54]

Strikes were forbidden. There remained the peaceful method of cooperation. And cooperatives could best be formed through syndical chambers. Hence, to organize syndical chambers became the main objective of the French workers after the Commune. Under such leaders as Chabert, Desmoulins, Barberet, Oudin, Portalis and Pauliat, the labor movement began to take on new life.[55] Jewelers, printers, lithographers and masons were followed by glove makers, toolmakers, upholsterers, bookbinders, carpenters, saddlers, etc., in organizing syndical chambers. A few radical newspapers came to their support and even the *République française,* Gambetta's organ, striving to win support for the republic, gave its aid.[56] In less than three months a labor federation was formed with the innocuous title, Circle of the Workers' Syndical Union (Cercle de l'Union syndicale ouvrière).[57]

The outstanding leader of this early labor movement

was the journalist, Barberet. It was he who was chiefly responsible for the initial steps toward organization, and for the ideas of the syndical chambers. So influential was he among them that the term, Barberetism, can be aptly used to describe the doctrine and tactics generally held by labor after the Commune.

Barberet's ideas, drawn in large measure from early French social theorists, were best adapted to the state of siege and reaction that prevailed in France after the uprising. He compared the social question to a rheumatic condition of the social organism, and thought he had found the right prescription for its cure.[58] He warned the workers against "socialist intriguers," and cautioned them against strikes. "We can no longer be the scape-goats of the sins of others," he said. He urged the workers to be prudent. "It is our safety which is involved. No strikes! By a cessation of work we are prevented from saving," and accumulating capital.[59] Strikes, he claimed, were a danger to democracy and to the republic. Their encouragement would be "a crime of *lèse-démocratie*." Their results were negative, not only because they weakened the workers both materially and morally, but also because they caused a greater division of classes.[60] Strikes were injurious to the syndical chambers; they alienated the masses and emptied the treasury. The entire purpose was lost, because they did not improve the economic conditions of the workers. "If the labor of some workers is better paid," he wrote, "the necessities of life cost more. The increase in the price of commodities is largely caused by the rise in the cost of labor. The capitalist who pays more for his labor sells his manufactured articles more dearly. On whom, therefore, does the high cost of manufactured articles finally fall . . . if not on the workers who are the great number, the mass of the consumers?" [61]   He, therefore, condemned the strike as "nonsense" and as a "utopia." [62]

The road to the solution of the social question led through the syndical chamber.   Through it labor would be peacefully organized, strikes would be avoided and the workers freed from the wage system.   "As soon as the workers grasp its mechanism," he wrote, "and the advantages they can gain from it, the social problem will be on the high road toward solution." [63]   In place of using the funds to wage strikes, the syndical chamber should utilize them to create producers' cooperatives in which all the members would have an interest according to their payments.   The cooperatives would be formed one by one, depending on the success or failure of those first established.   The workers in the successful shops would aid in creating still more cooperatives until all were working for themselves.   As the cooperatives increased in number they would form a federation of cooperative societies.   With such an organization, said Barberet, labor could defy any individual competition, however highly capitalized.[64]   Cooperation, he claimed, would change the entire aspect of the social question.   "Strikes would lose their *raison d'être,* for the workers would be producing for themselves without making profit from or exploiting any one." [65]   The middleman's profits would go to the workers, for the products would be exchanged in the "social bazaar" or "common store" of the cooperatives.   Steady and regular work would result, the economic life of the worker would be improved, and the problem of poverty would be solved.

The social transformation dreamed of by Barberet was subordinated to the organization of the syndical chambers

61

which, it has been shown, had begun to federate. It was the aim of their leaders to keep them moderate and to direct them into peaceful channels. Consequently the rules of the Circle of the Workers' Syndical Union stated that the organization aimed to pursue the improvement of the workers' conditions "through study, harmony and justice," and to serve as a training school for the syndical chambers. The Circle planned to open courses in design, science and commercial subjects for the benefit of the members, and expressly forbade the discussion of politics. It openly opposed strikes and favored the formation of boards of arbitration to settle disputes between the employers and their workers. Naturally its chief goal was to establish producers' cooperatives.[66] Socialism was disowned by Barberet and his friends for the discreet and moderate method of cooperation.

Even such moderation and discretion were too much for the government which had made the International illegal in France. Testut, who always saw red, wrote that "it is under the name of Union of Syndical Chambers that the International is destined to continue its work." [67] The prefect sent for the secretary of the Circle and notified him that meetings of the organization would no longer be permitted. When three members were delegated to inquire why the Circle had been suspended, they were given the following reasons: (1) the members had smiled when they voted the article which forbade political and religious discussions in their midst; (2) pressure had been used for the organization of cooperatives; (3) the syndical chambers might be dangerous in the future. Despite the protest of the delegates that their organization was an exact copy of the union of the employers' syndical chambers, the order was given to dissolve.[68]

The suspicions and fears of the authorities retarded, but did not stop the growth of syndicats and cooperatives. Other workers soon organized, so that by 1875 there were about 135 syndicats in Paris.[69] Some leaders even planned to replace the Circle with another organization bearing a still more harmless title, but the project was abandoned.

Labor agitation found an outlet in the question of the reform of the *Conseils de Prud'hommes*.[70] In 1873, there was to be an election to these Councils, and a committee of labor delegates was formed to acquaint the workers with their purpose and functioning. After ten lengthy discussions it was found that the workers' delegates were usually foremen, and that employers exercised an undue influence during elections. The chief reason why workers were not elected was that councillors were not paid during the performance of their duties. The committee appealed to the Paris municipal council to reform the institution, and that body consented to pay delegates for attendance at meetings. Workers were elected in place of foremen. "It was a valuable success for the syndical chambers," [71] and a stimulus to their further organization.

The movement toward cooperation also struggled on. A few producers' cooperatives were founded to add to the list of those which had survived the stormy days of 1871. Saddle makers, tin workers, leather workers and tailors organized cooperative workshops, and some arranged to sell directly to consumers. Consumers' cooperation, which was at this time important only in so far as it served to promote the development of producers' cooperation, was beginning to show some progress, and to win the sympathy of the workers, due to an increase in the cost of living. In 1875, there were twenty-three consumers' societies in the

63

Department of the Seine, nearly all of which were founded during the three preceding years.[72] The suburbs of Paris had seven societies, each of which was recording growth in membership, business and profits.[73] In 1873, an increase in the cost of bread led to the organization of a cooperative bakery under the leadership of Barberet. It was, however, short-lived.[74]

To propagate the cooperative idea, a group was organized under the presidency of Tolain, a Proudhonian, to study various phases of cooperation.[75] The meetings of the organization very soon deteriorated into vague discussions about questions alien to cooperation. The purpose of the group was lost, and it silently disappeared.

Cooperation had its sympathizers not only among labor leaders, but also among politicians of the radical republican stamp. Some of them, municipal councillors and deputies, had either formerly taken an active part in the cooperative movement of the last years of the Second Empire, or were still members of cooperative societies. They were interested in maintaining the workers' attachment to the republic and in steering them into peaceful channels.[76]

The cooperative ideal had not only its exponents, but also its opponents, the staunchest of whom were the positivists. These disciples of Comte, it has been shown, were attempting to carry their influence among the workers. To them they were saying that the solution of the social question through cooperation was an illusion. It could never benefit all the workers, and the few who would profit could never rise above the position of the small employer. Cooperation would only tend to make the workers lose their position as workers, but it would in no way improve their moral condition. Cooperation, they said, took no cognizance of agriculture. Moreover, it did not end the struggle between large concentrated industry and the small cooperatives. If cooperation were successful in abolishing the individual employer, it would destroy all competition, and every bit of the independence which was so beneficial to society. In place of the individual capitalist, there would arise one more oppressive and less responsible, because "association neither destroys nor changes human nature. . . ." [77] The solution of the social problem lay not through cooperation, but through the moral regeneration of man. Once that was effected, all other beneficent changes would follow.

The positivists brought their opposition to cooperation before the first labor congress.[78] There, Finance, painters' delegate and a convinced positivist, made a long speech against it. "We believe," he said, "that social science, like all the other sciences, is based on knowledge of the natural laws, independent of any human or divine will, laws which are not invented, but which can be discovered." It was the duty of all to help in their discovery and development, and to apply them to society. The social question could be solved only through the proper understanding of these laws.[79]

It was utopian, Finance thought, to hope to counter the influence of capital with the savings of the workers. The wages were too meagre for such a gigantic task. The capital of the industrialists had been accumulating for centuries. How many centuries would the workers need to reach their goal?[80] Though certain industrialists had given their blessings to cooperation, and had even advanced the necessary capital to create consumers' cooperatives for their workers, he saw no reason for being grateful. He attributed their action to trickery. It was their aim, he said, to distract the workers' leaders from demanding higher wages, from protesting against abuses and from participating in politics. The cooperative movement had lost its social character and had become "essentially bourgeois and conservative in the bad sense of the word." From the time of the Second Empire, the cooperatives had been encouraged in their efforts by the emperor and the capitalists. " 'Emancipate yourselves,' directed to the proletariat, has become the exact counterpart of 'Enrich yourselves,' directed by Guizot to the bourgeoisie of 1830." [81]

As a positivist, Finance offered no substitute for cooperation, for it was unscientific to advocate a formula which was not based on study and observation. "Thanks to Auguste Comte," he said, "we know that the social and industrial phenomena are subject to natural laws which can be discovered through experimentation and the study of the facts." Since social science, Finance continued, had not yet succeeded in finding the road to be followed by the proletariat, it was unwise to recommend changes whose results were unknown. It was much more prudent for the proletariat to maintain its position and to organize itself, rather than to venture into cooperation. The syndical chamber could have a beneficent moral influence on the workers. It could have an elevating effect on the employers through the arbitration boards which would settle the differences between the capitalist and the worker. For Finance and his positivist friends the social problem did not mean the changing of owners, but the determination of the proper use of wealth. He would not abolish the individual owner. Instead, he would regulate the relations of capital and labor peacefully, and teach both parties the dignity and social value of their duties. Before they could hope to solve the social question, the workers would have to rise morally and intellectually. Therefore, not cooperation, but moral regeneration was the cure of the social evils.[82]

3. The labor delegations to the Vienna and Philadelphia Expositions

During the years following the Commune, the labor and cooperative movements were stimulated to organization and activity by the two labor delegations sent to the Vienna and Philadelphia Expositions. From the time of the Second Empire it had become the accepted practice to dispatch workers' delegations to international expositions. Accordingly, Tolain proposed to the National Assembly to vote 100,000 francs as a subsidy for a labor delegation to be sent to Vienna. But the memory of the Commune was still fresh in the minds of the legislators, and the international significance of the idea did not appeal to those who only a year ago had voted the law against the International. Tolain's bill was defeated by a large majority. The leaders, however, succeeded in raising the necessary funds through subscription.

The choice of the delegation and the framing of its instructions were the occasions for organization, federation and joint action on the part of the workers. After the National Assembly had rejected the bill, the masons' delegates later related, an assembly, consisting of diverse labor elements, was held, and the solidarity of the labor organizations was voted. "Our syndical chamber," they continued, "answered the call and sent a delegate to the labor commission which was to be charged with the sending of a labor delegation to Vienna. . . .

67

"Forty-five corporations had already responded when an administrative order again hampered a movement so just and so peaceful." [83]

Another assembly was convoked and a commission was appointed. One hundred and five delegates supplied with instructions departed for Vienna. On their return eighty separate reports and one joint report were submitted.

That a note of moderation ran through all of the reports was most natural. The delegates were mindful of the government's policy toward labor, and were, consequently, cautious in their language. Moreover, they had been fed on the ideas of Barberet, and of others who sought the amelioration of conditions through cooperation. Weill gives another reason for their conservatism: the delegates found by comparison that the French workers were better off than their Austrian comrades. [84]

The moderate character of the reports reveals the nature of the delegates' views on the different social and economic issues. In general, their approach to the social question was like that of Barberet. If they deplored the sad effects of individualism, they also disagreed with socialism and its methods. [85] To oppose the tyranny of the capitalist, and to emancipate the workers, they put their trust in cooperation. The tailors' delegates did not hesitate to resort to an imitation of Proudhon's scheme of mutual credit or bank notes by which the necessary credit would be found to establish producers' cooperatives. These notes, they said, would have the same value as the notes of the Bank of France, [86] for while the latter were based on gold, the former would be guaranteed by labor. Others found a different source for the capital essential to create producers' cooperatives. They advocated the founding of consumers' cooperatives which would not only reduce the workers' cost of living, but also earn enough profits to be utilized for producers' cooperatives. The former were undoubtedly important, they said, but the latter were the key to the solution of the social problem.[87]

The delegates generally deplored the introduction of machinery. This was characteristic of workers who were passing from hand to machine labor, and were feeling the impact of the new industrial force. In habits of thought and work they were the product of a period which was slowly disappearing. However, they were being faced by their enemy, the machine. In an earlier period, the hostility of the workers to the new force had found expression in machine breaking, or Luddism, as it was called in England. Since then, their leaders had been raised on the ideas of Fourier, Blanc and Proudhon. These writers had analyzed industrial society, and had pointed the way out of the evils created by it. Instead of wrecking the machine, the theory had been developed that it would be to the greater advantage of the workingmen to control it. The producers' cooperative appeared to the workers as the instrument with which to utilize the machine for their own profit. The producers' cooperative was not as far removed from the domestic workshop as was the factory, and in it a worker felt that he was producing for himself. As in the domestic workshop the profits of each would be based on his contributions and skill. The producers' cooperative was largely motivated by that feeling for individual freedom which was the prevailing spirit of the domestic workshop, but which was being destroyed by the modern factory. In a sense, therefore, it was the continuation of a system of production which had preceded it. However, the producers' cooperative was destructive of its predecessor because it was based on the necessity of association and joint effort. As such it bore a strong resemblance to the new system of production. Thus, producers' cooperation stood with one foot in the past and with the other in the present. It was a compromise between two different social and economic epochs. Its establishment and growth were possible in a country where machine industry had not yet assumed large proportions. France after the Franco-Prussian War was essentially the land where the small industrial unit prevailed and where producers' cooperation, therefore, thrived. When joined together, workers could organize a small industrial unit with a limited capital and compete favorably with small capitalist enterprises.

Producers' cooperation was not only a protest against the new industrialism, but also the means of emancipating the workers. As producers, the workingmen would no longer be under the control of the capitalist, but in an association where all were working and sharing the profits. The different cooperatives would federate, aid each other, and slowly replace the existing economic order. Capitalism would have no reason to exist, not only because the producers' cooperative would have absorbed the best workers, but also because capitalism would have lost the domestic market. The new producers' society would be a loose federation of industrial units, united by economic and social ties. Economic federalism would take the place of political centralism.

During none of the stages of the evolution of the cooperative society was there room for the interference of the state. Many delegates to the Exposition expressed fear of the state when they placed reliance on private initiative.

"We are among those who reject state socialism," said delegates from Lyons, "whether this state be monarchical or republican, and we think that the associations cannot place themselves under its protection except by surrendering their independence and sacrificing all their principles." All they asked of the state was to grant them the same liberties commonly extended to the other classes, so that they could proceed freely with their plans. Experience had taught them, they said, that cooperatives which depended on the state were doomed to failure. "What has become of the associations which received the three millions voted by the Chamber under the Republic of 1848?" they asked. "In what condition are those [cooperatives] which accepted the patronage of the Empire? They have either disappeared or will soon disappear." [88] Like the economic liberals, the apostles of cooperation said: "The state can be neither a producer nor a trader. It cannot substitute its function for that of private industry, even for the benefit of the working class, for it would throw confusion into the active sources of the country's production." [89] The interposition of the state also reminded them of the despotic Second Empire under which labor had been persecuted. Thus, the delegates from Lyons said that the state's protection, "in the matter concerning us, can be nothing but a disguise for the heavy chains which, sooner or later, it will rivet on the freedom of the citizens." [90]

Following the same logical process, some delegates arrived at the conclusion that politics was not for them. If the state was not to meddle in the affairs of labor and cooperation, then why were the workers interesting themselves in political parties and politicians? Participation in politics had resulted in disappointment and bloodshed—

71

they recalled the tragic fate of the workers in the Commune. The workers, they said, should abandon their former errors and no longer remain "the victims of parties." Rather should they expend their energy for their own cause, for their emancipation through cooperation.[91] However, the joint report of the delegation, appearing in 1876, expressed confidence in the ballot.

The delegates were unanimous in demanding the right to combine. Without the syndical chamber it would be difficult to create producers' cooperatives. Through it the workers would be disciplined and directed into peaceful channels. One of the missions of the syndical chambers would be to collaborate with the employers to fix wages, and to guarantee the pacific relations of the two parties. "Thus we shall avoid strikes," wrote a Parisian delegate.[92]

In its joint report, the delegation to the Vienna Exposition said that the workers aimed above all to establish the reign of "justice" which they vaguely explained as "the equality and perfect mutuality of the duties of citizens towards one another and towards society." This justice would be attained through the syndical chambers which would arbitrate differences between employers and workers, establish vocational training to develop a more skilled and a more dependable worker, and apply the workers' savings to the creation of consumers' and producers' cooperatives. Furthermore, the syndical chambers would found a mutual credit society in order that interest might be gradually abolished, and organize education to prepare the next generation for the cooperative ideal. "The organization of a syndicat should not be considered the last word of social reform," continued the joint report. "Otherwise it would mean the reestablishment, under a new form, of the individualism we are combating." [93]

Some of the other demands in the joint report were: a change in the law on the *Conseils de Prud'hommes;* the freedom of the press; the modification of the child labor law of 1874, so that half of the inspectors would be workers elected for the purpose; the abolition of all laws which hindered the workers either in organizing or in their relations with their employers; the restriction of monopolies.[94]

These moderate demands did not escape the criticism of the parliamentary committee then inquiring into the labor problem. Its report stated that the program of the labor delegation, "the only one at present opposed to the freedom of labor, would be disastrous for them [the workers] if it were realized." Such a program "would reduce the workers to servitude." Its demands were borrowed from economic systems which had proved costly to the workers. The report added that the profits which the workers hoped to realize from their consumers' and producers' cooperatives were "fantastic." The producers' cooperatives would never cause a reduction in the cost of manufactured articles, as the delegates promised. "To this day, the labor societies of production have given entirely different results." [95]

The sending of a delegation to the Centennial Exposition held at Philadelphia added vitality to the French labor movement. As in 1873, the syndicats collaborated to choose a delegation. Meetings were held, committees were appointed, and public subscriptions were opened to obtain the necessary fund. The Paris municipal council came to the assistance of the syndicats with a contribution of 30,000 francs, and the Chamber, which had refused aid in 1873, voted 100,000. However, the Chamber's subvention carried with it the provision that the government should participate in the choice of the delegates. When some syndicats agreed to the government's demand, a rift occurred in the ranks of the workers. The result was that two delegations left for Philadelphia, one subsidized by the government, the other supported by the fund of the Paris municipal council and by individual contributions.[96]

While the demands of the Philadelphia delegation were similar to those of its predecessor, the delegates did not hesitate to voice their ideas more boldly. Weill, who has analyzed their reports, observes that the moderate tone which predominated among the syndicats after the Commune here gives way before revolutionary tendencies. Some reports, he says, were moderate "and others almost violent." [97] This change in attitude was largely due to the turn in the political situation and to the growth of a revolutionary doctrine. It is in connection with the development of this doctrine in France that the reports will be more fully discussed.

4. Labor and the republic

The word "republic" had a magic effect on the French workers. Throughout the nineteenth century it was associated with radical movements and was uttered in the same breath with "revolution." The Communards had fought for the republic when they opposed the monarchical National Assembly. After the suppression of the Commune, the republican sentiment among the workers had in no way weakened. They were prepared to remain peaceful and suffer rather than to agitate and thus to give the monarchists the excuse to establish their form of government.

The panic of 1873 had brought temporary hardship to the French workers. "Their situation was frightful," wrote Barberet. "Despite hunger, they were silent. Why this abnegation carried to the point of stoicism? Because of the word republic! We say 'the word,' for we had then scarcely more than that. . . . It was sufficient to say to them that the republic was in danger to make them fast in silence, so profound is their love of the republican form [of government]." [98]

The word "republic" fascinated the French worker just as the phrase "universal suffrage" captivated the British Chartist. Each saw in his formula the means to strengthen the democratic institutions, and to effect the peaceful and gradual solution of the social question. Under the republic the workers expected to gain the right to combine, and to end the state's meddling in their affairs as it had during the Second Empire. The more the monarchist National Assembly prevented them from forming unions and from federating, the more were they convinced of the necessity of the republic, and of the need of moderation and peace on their part. This was corroborated by Limousin, who regularly mingled with workers. In a letter to a member of the National Assembly, he wrote: "I can tell you that during the past three years there has been effected a great appeasement of the spirit of the workers." He noted that the language used by them in the last days of the Empire differed from that used in 1875. He attributed it to the growing strength of the republic which evoked in them the hope of social and economic amelioration.[99]

It was for this reason that the workers supported the republicans. Though there were some labor leaders who warned against the influence of politicians among the work-

ers on the ground that politics concealed labor's main
objective, the workingmen were attracted by a republican
leader like Gambetta. The Paris correspondent of the
chief anarchist publication thought that the active labor
movement favored more the Gambetta type of democracy
than a socialist organization of society.[100]

That the correspondent estimated correctly was partly
suggested by the by-election in Paris in April, 1873. Against
Rémusat, Thiers' candidate, there was nominated Barodet,
a free thinker and a republican. The election attracted
wide attention because it was to be a test of the attitude of
Paris, first toward Thiers, and secondly toward the monarchist and clerical Right in the Assembly. Gambetta
joined Louis Blanc, Edmond Adam and other republicans
in addressing a manifesto to the voters, in which they linked
the election of Barodet with the cause of the republic,
democracy and social peace.[101] Barodet defeated his opponent by a large majority, and it was the workers and
small shopkeepers, "the vanquished Communards, who had
given the spur to victory." [102]

Gambetta was the republican idol of the Parisian workers. Belleville, a working class district, was his political
stronghold. This district gave the name to the program
with which he fought not only the Empire during its last
days, but also the monarchists in the National Assembly
after the Commune. His Belleville program [103] contained
nothing radical on fiscal or labor reform which would
frighten the bourgeoisie, and was sufficiently vague on the
social problem to hold out hope to the workers. During
the Commune, he had kept silent, but after its bloody
defeat he had reappeared as the "commercial traveller of
democracy" [104] to combat the church and the monarchists,

76

and to fight for free and lay education. He warned the monarchists of the appearance, in politics, of a new class, "the workers of town and country, this world of labor to which the future belongs." Gambetta interpreted this political awakening of labor as a sign that the country wanted to try the republican form of government.[105] He urged the workers to be prudent, to guard themselves against "utopias," "panaceas" and "formulas." "There is no social remedy," he said at Havre, "because there is no one social question. There is a series of problems to be solved, difficulties to vanquish . . . ; these problems must be solved one by one and not by a single formula. It is through labor and study, through association and the constant and united effort of honest men that the people are led toward emancipation. I repeat, there is no social panacea. There is progress to be made every day, but no immediate, positive and complete solution." [106]

Gambetta and his republican followers were attempting to placate the workers with the promise of such reforms as free, lay and compulsory education, the freedom to organize, and amnesty for the Communards. Their educational program became to them the basis of democracy, a method to regenerate the country, the weapon with which to fight the influence of clericalism. France had been conquered by a nation which was better educated. To strengthen France it was essential to expand education.

While the Gambetta republicans did not see in cooperation the means of emancipating the workers, they were not opposed to the freedom of the workers to organize syndicats. In these they saw a medium for spreading their political propaganda, and an instrument for maintaining social peace. Syndicats were important for arbitration, and the republicans urged the workers to unite. Gambetta's journal even suggested to them a plan of union strongly resembling the one adopted later by the *Bourses du travail* and the national federations.[107]

The republicans also proposed to end the state of siege. The amnesty of the Communards, they thought, would be popular among the workers, and they were awaiting the opportunity to make it the subject of a parliamentary debate. In the meantime, they were giving some financial aid to the families of imprisoned Communards.[108]

Among the republicans there were some like Alfred Naquet and Georges Clemenceau who, after the adoption of the conservative constitution of 1875, were not content either with the conservative republic or with Gambetta's program. The constitution showed a lack of confidence in the great mass of the French people, and the program made no appeal to the lower classes because it made no demands for social reform. "We have now a monarchy without a monarch, or rather with an elected monarch, not hereditary, it is true, but reeligible," said Naquet of the new French constitution, during the electoral campaign of 1876. "Gambetta and his friends are in the constitutional rut; let them remain there since they think it useful; let them represent the conservative republican element. But, beyond them, a democratic advance guard must be constituted. At the next elections, Gambetta's name must be left to the less advanced departments." [109] In his program Naquet inscribed not only such political demands as the revision of the Constitution of 1875, the referendum, the freedom to assemble and to associate and the separation of church and state, but also articles of an economic and social nature. He demanded that the state should take

78

over the banks, railways and mines; that it impose an income tax, give women civil rights equal to those of men, replace the standing army by a national militia, and grant amnesty to the Communards.

Clemenceau, a radical republican, was no less critical of Gambetta's conservatism. "We, the radical republicans," he said, "we want the republic for its consequences: the great and productive social reforms which it involves." [110] Like many of his radical republican friends, Clemenceau advocated cooperation among the workers.[111]

It was evident that the republicans were bent on winning the support of the lower classes. They made promises of social reform and of the right to combine, and they appealed to the sentiments of the workers by their demand for amnesty. The republicans were rewarded for their efforts in the election of 1876, when the Senate and Chamber of Deputies were elected for the first time. Independent labor candidates were presented in a few districts, but the workers did not come to their aid. They supported republicans.[112]

The republicans were grateful for the assistance of the workers. In return they voted to subsidize the labor delegation to Philadelphia, and introduced a bill giving workers the legal right to combine. The Lockroy Bill, mentioned above,[113] provided that the syndicat was to file a copy of its statutes and a list of its members with the prefecture of police. The exponents of the freedom of labor objected to the bill because, they believed, it did not sufficiently protect the individual worker against the tyranny of the syndicat.[114] The workers attacked the bill for other reasons. They saw in it a trap, and a restraint on their freedom. Their opposition to it was heard at the first labor congress which met three months after the introduction of the bill.

5. *The first and second labor congresses*

The idea of summoning a labor congress arose with the *Tribune,* a paper founded to spread the idea of cooperation. Its editor was no other than Pauliat, who, together with Barberet, had been playing an active rôle in the labor movement. When the labor delegation left for Philadelphia, the cooperative organ wrote: "What would our friends think of a labor congress which would meet in Paris . . . a few weeks after the return of the delegates, a congress at which the bases of a common socialist program would be discussed?

"We are content for the present with expressing this idea which has been suggested to us by the Congress of Bologna." [115] The proposal was favorably received and the Parisian syndicats formed a committee of organization.

The time seemed very propitious for calling a congress. The election of February and March, 1876, had resulted in a republican victory and had assured the workers the type of government they had been demanding. The republicans, who were making efforts to repay the workers for the faithful support they had rendered, would not interrupt the sessions of a congress organized by those to whom they were prepared to grant the right to combine. The workers' leaders felt that after the establishment of the republic "the working class, which had been marching jointly with the republican bourgeoisie, would have to assert its own interests, and to look for the means by which it could transform its economic condition." [116]

Since it was the first labor congress held in France, the committee naturally attached to it great hopes. They expected it "to establish among all the French workers the solidarity, the cohesion, the unity of aspirations and peaceful efforts, without which the solution of the social question will be constantly sought" but never found. The congress would acquaint all workers with the various types of association in existence and with those needed to effect the necessary social and economic changes. To avoid any possible interference from the government the committee ruled that only syndicats, cooperatives and credit societies should be represented; that no one should speak unless he were a worker; that debates should be prohibited; and that no politics should be discussed.[117] The workers were to present their point of view frankly and clearly "to show the bourgeoisie on what terms it might collaborate with the workers." [118]

The congress opened October 2, and was attended by 360 delegates who represented over one hundred and twenty syndicats and syndical chambers, and thirty-five cooperative and mutual aid societies. Two hundred and fifty-five of the delegates were from Paris while one hundred and five of them came from thirty-seven towns in the provinces. Eight questions were on the agenda: (1) women's work; (2) syndical chambers; (3) *Conseils de Prud'hommes;* (4) technical and vocational education; (5) labor representation in parliament; (6) cooperation; (7) insurance and old age pensions; (8) agricultural associations.

Many reports were presented on the question of women's work. Nearly all agreed that their competition with men tended to reduce wages, and all knew that women could not be driven from the factory. What was the solution? One suggested that women receive wages equal to those of men, and that prisons and convents be prohibited from competing in the open market.[119] A woman delegate was warmly applauded when she claimed that there was only one method by which to solve the problem of women's work: *viz.*, cooperation. "Why shouldn't the women-workers form cooperative shops," she asked, "and why shouldn't their fathers, mothers or husbands come there to purchase their necessities . . . rather than go to those places which they enrich, and where their companions are so exploited that they cannot live by their work?" The money could be procured through individual savings, through private contributions from sympathizers and through the foundation of people's banks.[120] The recommendations of the congress were merely a recapitulation of the main points presented in the reports: the immediate organization of syndical chambers of women; an eight-hour day with no wage reduction; the prohibition of night work in factories; an equal wage for equal work; the restriction of prison and convent labor; the creation of cooperatives.[121]

On no question was there greater unanimity than on the freedom of the workers to combine.[122] The delegates assured the authorities that syndicats were not centers of conspiracy. That was possible under a monarchy, but under the republic based "on the principle of liberty and equality, rebels and factious persons are met with only among those who have been deceived in their hopes." [123] The syndical chambers, the delegates asserted, were peaceful organizations. It was not their intention to attack capital, for "capital and labor have a community of interest." [124]

82

Bonne, representing the textile workers of Roubaix, pictured the absolute dependence of the employees on their employers. Their freedom in time of election was curtailed by virtue of the fact that the employers owned the homes inhabited by the workers. He maintained that the workers should have the right to combine not only to defend their interests, but also to establish libraries, consumers' cooperatives and old age pensions.[125] The freedom to combine, alleged a delegate, was not "the right of capital to exploit labor," but that "which permits the workers to treat with the capitalists on an equal footing." [126] Another delegate opposed mixed unions of workers and employers on the ground that in such unions disagreements would arise more frequently than when the two parties were organized separately. The Lockroy Bill was assailed, because it permitted the interference of the government in the affairs of the syndicats.

The *Conseils de Prud'hommes* were praised as a beneficent institution. They helped to remove industrial war, and permitted the workers to concentrate on their aim. The *Conseils de Prud'hommes* might aid in the future in solving the social question; but before they could be put to such service they would have to be reformed. The congress, therefore, demanded the increase of the powers of the councils, a fixed wage for their members, and the right to choose their own officers.[127]

The question of technical education was the occasion for the expression of the republican views of the delegates. They demanded free, lay and compulsory education in order to destroy "prejudices" and "unhealthy doctrines." They believed that education would slowly cause the disappearance of social inequalities.[128]

83

The direct representation of the proletariat as a separate class in parliament seemed necessary to the delegates. Upon it depended the freedom of the workers to unite.[129] The bourgeoisie could not represent the workers, said a delegate, for it had lost all contact with the masses. "It constitutes in our society a class apart, with its own interests which are in no way those of the worker. Formerly, the bourgeoisie marched with the people whom it needed to overthrow the nobility which dominated it. To-day, the nobility is no longer in existence; thus you see the bourgeoisie becoming more reactionary and clerical than the former nobility have ever been." He was prepared to admit that there were exceptions. Among the bourgeoisie there were many who were moved by the noblest intentions. But even they could not understand the people's needs, "by reason of their education and turn of mind." [130] Chabert, an active labor leader of Paris, who had been one of the outstanding members of the Vienna Delegation, demanded the right of the workers to representation. "When labor candidates are presented," he reminded his audience, "we are told: 'you are reviving class antagonism.' No, it is unnecessary to revive the classes, for we well know that they exist and we deplore it. But it is not our fault if it is so. Who has formed the classes? Is it we who are suffering from them? Who repeatedly says that the governing classes must continue to direct? And who adds that the hard-working and needy classes must not be forgotten? That is a very fine protectorate, but we see in it all kinds of inconveniences, and, in such a case, we prefer not to be protected." [131]

Such was the sentiment of the congress.[132] The delegates generally distrusted the bourgeoisie and its parties.

It was their opinion that only workers should be designated as candidates. They wanted no intellectuals to represent labor.

Much time was devoted to the discussion on cooperation. It was the workers' panacea for the social evils, and its advocates declared themselves for cooperation in all of its forms: producers' cooperatives by which they would receive the full product of their labor; consumers' cooperatives to reduce the cost of living; credit societies to lower the rate of interest on capital; popular libraries and technical schools to educate the workers and to train the new generation to continue the work and ideals of the founders. An important part of their cooperative program was the popular banks which were to extend credit to cooperative societies engaged in industry, facilitate their commercial transactions and handle their insurance funds. They were to serve as an important arm of the cooperative and labor movements in their march toward emancipation.[133]

The committee's report on cooperation presented certain conditions which were to govern the establishment and functioning of societies. The capital of the cooperative was to be "impersonal, indivisible and inalienable." The profits were to be divided into three parts: one devoted to redeem shares if the capital of the society had been obtained through their sale; another to form an old age pension fund for the members; a third to be employed for the extension and development of other cooperative societies. The cooperatives were to exist not for the sole interest of the members, "but, on the contrary, for the general interest of the mass." [134]

Against cooperation was raised the voice of the positivist, Finance, whose arguments against it have already been analyzed.[135] In place of consumers' and producers' societies and popular banks he demanded what he called "a moral and human education completely freed from all theology and all metaphysics." Like many of his co-workers in the labor movement he rejected the intervention of the state both in the social question and in education. All he asked was that it grant the freedom to assemble, to combine and to discuss.[136]

An integral part of the cooperative program was insurance against old age, invalidity and unemployment.[137] It was hoped that a part of the profits of the societies would be employed for the insurance of their members. In this as in other matters the state's rôle was to be a passive one, limited to removing the obstacles in the way of the syndicats and cooperatives.

The congress showed an antipathy to the state. This was undoubtedly the result of the sad experiences during the Empire, when governmental patronage and benevolence went hand-in-hand with rigid supervision and persecution. The committee on organization expressed the desire of the workers to be "free from the tutelage of the state," [138] and several delegates were no less emphatic in their desire to be left to themselves. The committee which reported in favor of the direct representation of the workers spoke of "prevailing upon the state not to concern itself with our affairs, but to suppress the numerous obstacles strewn on our path. . . ." [139]

The reports of the delegates displayed a timidity and an uneasiness about the attitude of the authorities. Though the republic was gaining ground, the head of the government and the higher officials were still monarchist or strongly conservative. There was the constant fear that the police might order the dissolution of the congress, a fear which was evidenced in the reports. On the first day of the congress a speaker said: "Citizens, you are sufficiently acquainted with the government to know that it is absolutely necessary for us to conform to all the prescriptions of the law, however puerile, otherwise we run the risk of seeing the congress dissolved at any moment. . . ."[140] The sessions of the congress were not opened to the public because the delegates wished to avoid the police regulations. Open meetings would have meant the presence of a representative of the prefecture who might have found in some allusion to politics an excuse for dissolving the congress. The sessions were peaceful. Violence was condemned, and the workers were warned against the influence of socialists, "the madmen who would like to bring us back to the past."[141] Any relation with the International was denied.

What was the effect of the first labor congress on public opinion? Conservatives expressed satisfaction with the moderate demands of its delegates. *Le Figaro* wrote that it was "led by very prudent men" and *Le Moniteur* found it "almost dull by dint of its moderation and discretion." *Le Pays* said that "affairs are going on very properly among men who are quietly discussing their interests, and who are animated with practical purposes." *La Défense* called the delegates "kind, brave and honest men."[142] Though the *Journal des économistes* thought that the reasons given for the independent political action of the workers were "absurdities," it praised the congress for its "calm and dignity."[143] It declared that "from the point of view of order, of discipline and even of parliamentary practice, the workers have made considerable progress."[144]

Anarchists and socialists varied in their estimate of the

congress. The former valued it not for the doctrines that were expounded, but "for the sole fact of having assembled the workers in a congress." [145] The Colinsists [146] criticized the congress for its mildness; nevertheless, they recognized its usefulness because "it has at least aroused public attention to questions which had been neglected too long by the press." [147]

Very different was the reaction of the Blanquist exiles in London. These former Communards reproached the congress for its timidity and moderation. In a virulent manifesto, *Les syndicaux et leur congrès*,[148] they denounced it for having repudiated the revolution, and disowned the Commune "in the town of the revolution," and only "five years after the struggle of the Commune." [149] "Under the protective shadow of the Bonapartist Councils of War," said the Blanquists, "hunting as at first the remains of the Commune, in the silence of the Versailles terror and sheltered by it, the members of syndicats have come to insult the Paris of the revolution, which they are vainly attempting to dishonor. In the usurped name of this very proletariat which only yesterday fought, with arms in hand, to overthrow a society which they want to preserve, they have come to declare that they accept this society, its institutions, its classes, its property; that it is sufficient for them to be permitted to reform it, to improve it and to adjust themselves to it as best they can. They have declared that they no longer expect emancipation through violence and battle, but through the granting of liberty [by the authorities] through universal suffrage, through the progress of ideas and customs and through the wisdom and the good will of their masters." [150]

Cooperation, "this magic word, this cabalistic formula,

this mysterious power," could never be the means of emancipation. It would merely result in the formation of a new class of small capitalists. The appeal to it as the liberating force was an indication that the spirit of the congress was "reactionary and bourgeois." [151]

The opinion of Jules Guesde was favorable. A contributor to *Les Droits de l'Homme* after his return to France, he devoted a series of articles to the congress.[152] Though he found the resolutions insufficient, he saw in the congress a fact of great political consequence. "Whether one has observed it with sympathy or with fright," he wrote in the opening paragraph of his first article, "friends and enemies have been almost unanimous in recognizing its importance.

"And how could it have been otherwise when one reflects: (1) that it was the first time that the opportunity was afforded to the French proletariat to assemble and to make its voice heard; (2) that this assembly took place scarcely five years after the May days in the Paris which witnessed the workers' revolution of March 18th; (3) that the first word of the delegates, their first act, even before . . . speaking and transacting business was to exclude from their deliberations any one who was not a manual worker or delegated by manual workers, in order to separate themselves, to distinguish themselves from all existing political parties.

"Especially in view of this last aspect, the congress constitutes an event of the first order, as threatening as [it is] instructive to all shades of our politicians." [153]

The first labor congress was an event of profound significance. Its reports and resolutions were mild and discreet. It pinned its faith on cooperation, education and the *Conseils de Prud'hommes*. It was even prepared to com-

promise with the bourgeoisie. It was an expression of Barberetism, and to some extent of Proudhonism. But were
these characteristics of the congress a fault, as the Blanquists thought? Its social and economic doctrines were a
product of the workers' milieu. These doctrines, therefore, could not be socialistic in the modern sense, for modern socialism had not yet found its way into France; nor
could they be violent, for the memory of the Commune was
still fresh in the minds of the laboring classes. The cooperative ideal, it has been shown, was most natural to
the French worker of the Seventies and Eighties because
it carried over the individualism of the domestic workshop.
Barberetism was, therefore, a truer expression of French
labor after the Commune than either Blanquism or Marxism would have been, and the moderation of the congress
of Paris was neither a fault nor a virtue. It was moderate because it could not be anything else. As the first
of the congresses of the French labor movement it remains
an event of capital importance. For the first time since the
Commune, workers, through their representatives, gave
united expression to their demand for separation from the
bourgeoisie.

The second congress was scheduled to meet the following year at Lyons. But the political events subsequent to
the 16th of May tended to obscure the labor movement,
and the congress was postponed. Once more the workers
rallied to the support of the republic and helped return a
republican majority to the Chamber in October, 1877. The
Lyons congress assembled in the end of January, 1878, and
examined the same questions which had appeared on the
program of its predecessor.[154] Like the congress of Paris,
the congress of Lyons was generally peaceful in tone and

restrained in its demands. It showed the same distrust of intellectuals and the state. But at this congress was heard a new note which jarred on the ears of most of the delegates. A few members appeared to declare that cooperation was only another form of exploitation, that the class struggle would exist as long as the means of production were in the hands of the few, and "that without collective ownership there was nothing to be done, nothing to be attempted, nothing to hope for." [155] It was evident that the collectivist or modern socialist doctrine was invading France. Just how the Lyons Congress reflected this invasion will be shown more fully later. Two months before the meeting of the Lyons Congress appeared the *Egalité,* the first Marxist journal in France, under the editorship of Jules Guesde.

CHAPTER III

THE COMING OF MARXISM INTO FRANCE

1. The International in France after the Hague Congress

Socialism, other than that which came to be called scientific, was not a new concept in France. From the French Revolution to the Commune, a host of French writers and their disciples had been theorizing about the various phases of social welfare, and had been spreading their ideas among the French workers. Socialist doctrines had played their rôle in the secret societies during the monarchy of Louis Philippe, in the Revolution of 1848, in the opposition to the Second Empire and in the Commune. Each of the doctrines had attacked the existing order and had offered a solution to the social question. Nearly all of them had left some impress not only on the social thought of France, but also on the ideas of social and economic thinkers in other countries.

The influence exerted by Proudhonism on the labor movement during the Sixties received a mortal blow through the defeat of the Commune. Former labor leaders and Proudhonians, like Tolain and Fribourg, were left without a following. If Barberet, Pauliat and Chabert, who were guided by some of Proudhon's ideas, were labor's spokesmen during the Seventies, it was not an indication that Proudhonism still had a strong hold on the workers, but rather that the other labor and socialist philosophies were even more discredited. Scientific socialism did not begin to enter France until after the Commune. By the end of the decade following it, Proudhon's influence on the organized labor movement was replaced by that of his rival, Karl Marx.

Other French socialist schools were no more than names. Godin and Limousin tried to breathe new life into Fourierism, and Pellarin had such implicit faith in the doctrines of Fourier that when Gambetta said that there was no social remedy because there was no social question, Pellarin was bold enough to assert that such a remedy had been found by his master.[1] However, the Fourierists met with no enthusiastic response. Limousin admitted the decadent condition of the Fourierist school when he wrote on the hundredth anniversary of the birth of Fourier: "The Societary School which erstwhile cast such a gleaming splendor, is now a memory; it was, but is no more."[2] Saint-Simonism, it has been shown, was dead. It had for its spokesmen only a few sentimental traditionalists who dreamed about peace and hoped for social reform.[3]

Socialism was in disgrace after the insurrection of 1871. Leaders of workingmen either denounced it or feared to discuss it. "The socialist controversy, so ardent a short time ago," wrote a publicist in 1874, "seems calm to-day and forgotten by public opinion."[4] Adherents of socialism were persecuted and imprisoned, and the organization which embodied it was made illegal. The dangers accompanying the expression and discussion of social theories were described by a journalist in 1874. "Write the words, 'societary commune,' 'domestic, industrial and agricultural association,' and you will be taken for a Communard! Speak about the free and voluntary association of capital, labor and talent, and you are looked upon as a disguised member of the International. If you dream of the greatest possible freedom in compromise and of respect for free agreements, you are suspected of drawing up secret pacts among workers or of meditating the deportation of citizens. Write again the word federalism from the point of view of the future union of European states and of universal peace, and you will be taken for the late autonomists of the Commune or for uncompromising radicals affiliated with Spanish cantonalism. May God equally keep you from philosophizing on the conditions of the moral order; you will be confused with Jesuits, white radicals or black ultramontanes." [5]

The word "socialism" was little used during the years immediately after 1871. A Fourierist like Limousin sometimes employed it, but to him it meant merely the antithesis to *laissez-faire*. In its place, the word "radical" was employed to include demands for reform and even to cover collectivist principles, because it did not bear the stigma associated with the word "socialism." [6] Furthermore, the French workers were too much absorbed in cooperation to be socialistic in the modern sense. Marxism was still unknown in French working-class circles, and therefore, could not have disturbed the peaceful tendencies of labor.

The International, which was made illegal in France, was secretly attempting to organize the workers into sections. Secret agents of the General Council tried to win adherents to the Marxist wing; but little progress was made in the organization of new groups. [7] The vigilance of the police resulted in the arrest and punishment of several leaders. Van Heddeghem, an agent of the General Council, proved to be a spy, and Dentraygues, another agent, played the part of informer at the trial of the International in 1873.[8] By 1873 the Marxist International was dead in France, and Engels wrote to Sorge on May 3rd: "All our sections are seized"; and on June 14th: "Serailler has absolutely nothing to write, because he no longer has a single address in France. Everything has been seized." [9]

The Bakuninists who were expelled from the International at the Hague Congress in 1872, competed with the Marxists to win over the French workers. In the southwest of France, near to the center of anarchist activities, they succeeded in founding a few groups. In Lyons, where Bakunin had formerly tried to abolish the state, in Saint-Etienne, Perpignan and Montpellier, there were secret sections which adhered to anarchist principles. In August, 1873, thirty representatives of the various secret and autonomous anarchist groups assembled in a congress at Lyons where they discussed methods of action and programs of organization, and drew up projects for the day after the social revolution. But the police whom they were planning to abolish interrupted their enthusiastic designs and arrested several of them. The anarchists were no more successful in attracting the workers than were the socialists.[10]

2. The French exiles

It was not in France that socialism was being preached, but abroad, by French exiles who had fled to foreign lands after the Commune. In London the Blanquists, who had fallen under the influence of Marx, were hitching to their political doctrine of revolutionary dictatorship the socialist principle of collective ownership of the means of production. In a manifesto published in 1874,[11] they not only reasserted their belief in atheism and in the use of force "to realize the aim of the revolution," but also described themselves as communists. "We are communists," they said, "because we desire that the land, that nature's riches, should no longer be appropriated by a few, but that they should belong to the community; because we wish that the workers, once freed from all oppression, and finally masters of all the means of production, [such as] land, factories, etc., should make the world a place of comfort and no longer one of poverty.

"To-day, as formerly, the majority of men are condemned to work to support the pleasures of a small number of masters.

"The last expression of all the forms of servitude, bourgeois domination, has disengaged the exploitation of labor from the mystic veils which darkened it. Governments, religions, the family, laws, institutions of the past as well as of the present have finally been revealed—in this society reduced to the simple terms of capitalists and wage earners—as the oppressive instruments by means of which the bourgeoisie maintains its domination, and holds the proletariat in check.

"Appropriating the entire surplus of labor to increase his wealth, the capitalist leaves to the worker exactly what he needs to keep him from dying of hunger.

"Held by force in this hell of capitalist production and property, the worker . . . cannot break his chains.

"But the proletariat has finally succeeded in becoming conscious of itself. It knows that it bears within it the elements of the new society, that its deliverance will be the reward of its victory over the bourgeoisie, and that, once this class [the bourgeoisie] is destroyed, classes will be abolished, and the aim of the revolution will be attained." [12]

Farther on, the manifesto declared that the bourgeoisie, as a class, would disappear when private property ceased to exist, and when all the instruments of oppression lost their *raison d'être*.

The manifesto indicated that the Blanquists had undergone a marked change in their theoretical views. Nothing so clear-cut was to be found either in Blanqui's writings, or in those of his earlier disciples. The Blanquist exiles, particularly Vaillant, had come in contact with Marx and had absorbed his theory of surplus value, his philosophy of history, and the doctrine of the class struggle, and had consequently come to believe in the inevitability of the social revolution. They had adopted the Marxian socialist program, as Engels wrote, "with its entire conception of historical materialism." [13]

While the Blanquists were coming under the sway of modern socialism, other French exiles, asembled in Switzerland, had either embraced the anarchist cause or were flirting with it. Among them were some of those who, like Paul Brousse, Benoît Malon and Jules Guesde, were to play important rôles in the French socialist movement. Brousse, a medical student, who had been engaged in southern France in propaganda for the Anarchist International, fled to Spain in 1872 and there helped found a revolutionary organ to which Jules Guesde was a contributor. Finding his way into Switzerland, he became a member of the anarchist Federation of the Jura and spoke and wrote against authority and the state. Like his brother anarchists, he dreamed of a stateless society, without authority, without laws, courts or police force.[14] The state was "useless" and "noxious," he wrote in 1873. "Having been guided by logic, science and history to the negation of the state, and its destruction having become the aim which we should pursue, we have found our criterion. The most advantageous state for us is the one which we shall be able to destroy most easily." [15] On the strength of this argument he favored the return of the Bourbons to the throne of France, because it would perpetuate the divisions among the bourgeoisie, "thus reopening for our benefit the era of revolutions." [16] Universal suffrage, he said, was a dangerous illusion for the proletariat. For the bourgeoisie, it was only another means of maintaining itself in power. The bourgeoisie would never permit universal suffrage to become an instrument of emancipation in the hands of the proletariat; it would sooner destroy the ballot and appeal to force. Consequently, Brousse advised the workers not to participate in politics.[17] During his stay in Barcelona in 1873, he, together with two anarchist comrades, founded a committee for revolutionary and socialist propaganda in southern France. In its program they said:

"The occasion is propitious, since a period of revolution has just been opened in France. From this day a moral solidarity must be established between the proletariat of this country [Spain] and the workers of southern France, in order that, everything having been prepared, it shall become real and effective and unite them on the common ground of action.

"We will make anarchism the basis of our program. . . . We are not communists because this system necessitates the establishment of a strong central power. . . . We are collectivists." [18] Brousse went to Switzerland and there continued to agitate. In 1879 he went to London where he met Marx, and the change in his ideology commenced. He eventually abandoned anarchism for socialism.[19]

Somewhat different was the career of Benoît Malon.[20] A son of poor peasants, and himself a shepherd, he did not learn to read and write until he was twenty years old. He became a member of the International, and played a notable part in the cooperative movement and in the radical agitation during the later years of the Second Empire. Active in the Commune, he escaped to Switzerland after its defeat and there became friendly with leading anarchists. Though he never embraced the anarchist cause and never joined Bakunin's Alliance of Socialist Democracy,[21] he was none the less associated with the Bakuninist wing of the International. He participated in the fight against the Marxists,[22] not because he was an anarchist, but because he favored a loose union of the federations of the International and opposed the dominating influence of the General Council. Malon's activities in behalf of the autonomists did not escape the watchful eye of Marx. In a pamphlet written for the General Council, Marx mistakenly called Malon an alliancist,[23] and accused him of laboring for the destruction of the International.[24] The struggle between the two wings seemed to Malon to have been based more on personal hatred than on a difference in doctrine, and he preached conciliation. The result was that he was, as he said, "very rudely treated by both sides. One said that I was sold to Marx, the other that I was an agent of Bakunin." [25]

The growth of republicanism in France caused Malon to question the ideas of his anarchist friends. In a letter to the Federation of the Jura, dated March 18, 1876, he definitely proposed a change in tactics. It was unwise to put politics aside, he claimed, and permit the bourgeoisie to exert an influence on the workers and peasants. It was of the highest importance to come out into the open and act. Anarchists were wrong in assuming that a republic was no better than a monarchy, for under the first it was easier to agitate and win adherents than under the second. Nor could anarchists simply say that it was sufficient to abolish the state and allow the different groups and communes to provide for their own interests. The state was more than a political organism. There had been combined with it numerous public services which it was important to reform, not to abolish. He, therefore, thought it prudent to abstain from "impotent declarations on doctrine" and to strive to rebuild the socialist movement, particularly in France.[26] Two years later, Malon was editing at Lugano a socialist review, *Le Socialisme Progressif,* in which he preached reformism in method, eclecticism in doctrine and unity among groups.[27] The integral socialism, of which he later became the chief exponent, was already reaching full development.[28]

Among the French exiles in Switzerland was one who was to become a particularly prominent personality in modern French socialism. The son of cultured middle class parents, Jules Guesde was educated chiefly under his father's direction. Through a reading of Kant's *Critique* he was turned against metaphysics and toward atheism, and from Victor Hugo he acquired a hatred of the Empire. Though a republican, he accepted a position in the Prefecture of the Seine. From 1868 to his departure into exile, Guesde took an active part in the republican movement against the Empire and against the monarchist National Assembly. Though he played no part in the Commune, he defended it in the press, because he saw in it a strong republican force. For his articles in favor of the Commune he was condemned to five years of imprisonment and to the payment of a heavy fine. Guesde preferred exile, and found refuge in Switzerland.[29]

This thin, tall, frail, bearded and long-haired young man of twenty-six, who was to be one of the spokesmen of Marxism in France, found himself abroad in the company of anarchists. Guesde's knowledge of socialist or anarchist theory was practically nil at this time. "He was," as one of his anarchist associates later said, "a simple journalist of advanced radical ideas who had written for a southern newspaper a few articles sympathetic to the Paris Commune. Having mingled in Geneva with the Parisian exiles, he had fallen under the spell of the International; but he did not know precisely what it was and what we wanted." [30] Nevertheless, he helped organize a section and represented it at the Congress of Sonvillier (1871) from which emerged the Federation of the Jura which opposed the General Council in London.[31]

Guesde was in alliance with the anti-Marxists. A circular, written by him for the congress and addressed to all the groups of the International, upbraided the General Council for its intolerance and for its authoritarian policy, and demanded that it become merely a correspondence and statistical bureau. The International was the "embryo" of the future society and should be "the faithful image of our principles of freedom and federation," said the manifesto. It could not, therefore, be based on "authority and dictatorship." [32]

In the same year, 1871, Guesde left for Italy, and it was during his stay there that Brousse was expelled from the International by Dentraygues, the agent of the General Council. Guesde, who was then friendly with Brousse, rushed to his defense. In a letter published in a Brussels paper, he denounced Dentraygues, and Calas who was partly instrumental in the expulsion of Brousse. It was claimed by Marx and the General Council that Guesde's letter put the police on the trail of other Internationalists and led to their arrest. They accused Guesde, Brousse and Malon of attempting to disorganize the International to the advantage of Bakunin's Alliance.[33] When, at the trial at Toulouse, Dentraygues revealed his treachery, Guesde sent a letter to the *Bulletin de la fédération jurassienne* in which he said: "What is apparent in the Toulouse trial, is not only the infamous rôle of the deputy of Marx and of the General Council, but also the condemnation of the system of the domineering organization of which Marx and the General Council are the props." It was the existence of a central authority which made it feasible for Dentraygues to betray to the rural police the organizers of the International in southern France.

"Let the working class in each country organize itself anarchically, according to its best interests," continued Guesde in his letter, "and Dentraygues will no longer be possible." [34]

Guesde was much nearer to anarchism than to socialism. In a pamphlet written by him in 1873, he still betrayed a vagueness in ideas. He spoke of "liberty," "equality" and "justice." These were to be realized by collectivizing the land and its products,[35] by putting education within the reach of everybody,[36] and by recognizing the worker's right "to the entire product of his labor." [37] The state seemed useless to him. Its mission, which was to maintain order, it executed very poorly. The public services which it controlled were "absolutely foreign to it," he said. In the future society they would be administered by the respective groups of producers without the necessity of a state.[38] Seven years later, Malon, utilizing this same pamphlet, asserted that Guesde had been leaning toward anarchism in his early years of association with the Geneva group. Guesde protested, and attempted to prove by a brief analysis of anarchism that he could not have been an adherent of that doctrine.[39]

The fact remains, however, that Guesde did show an inclination toward anarchism. In an article on the state which appeared in *La Solidarité révolutionnaire*, July 1, 1873,[40] he maintained that the *sine qua non* of the emancipation of the masses was "the abolition, the destruction, of the state."[41] In the same year he published another article in the *Almanach du peuple*,[42] purporting to prove that universal suffrage was a trick to deceive the workers. The history of France during the nineteenth century, he wrote, had shown that the workers' use of the ballot had always resulted in a gain for their enemy, the bourgeoisie. The workers had gained nothing from it. Under economic inequality, political equality was "nonsense." It could not result in economic and social amelioration for the working class. Universal suffrage would only hamper it in its emancipation, because: (1) the working class was too dependent on the capitalist; (2) it lacked the necessary training to free itself from its legal-minded leaders; (3) the ballot tended to divide rather than unite it.[43] There was no doubt that Guesde in this period thought like an anarchist when it concerned the state, the ballot and the future social organization. In economic theory he was still vague and uncertain.

In 1875 appeared his letter [44] to Senator Lampertico, an economist, which evinced a growth in the clarity of Guesde's economic ideas. In answer to the economist's defense of private property, he argued that its existence was detrimental to society because: (1) the owners were not interested in making their property produce to its fullest extent; (2) the small owner was incapable of doing it for lack of capital and machinery, and the large owner was prevented from doing it by his dependence on hired labor; (3) private property impeded the application of the division of labor; (4) it created a class of rentiers whose incomes were drawn from the labor of workers; (5) it divided society into "owners and non-owners" and led to the creation of the repressive forces of the state. Since private property, he said, offered neither productive nor distributive advantages, since it prevented all from living amply by their labor, he advocated its abolition. The right of property was to be guaranteed "by universalizing property." [45] Guesde's conclusions were socialistic. He arrived at the doctrine that the social and economic problems could be solved through the collective ownership of the means of production.

During the five years of active life in exile, Guesde had absorbed many ideas on political and social questions. He had discussed, read and written. He had attended congresses of anarchists, and had drawn up manifestoes. He had associated with people older than himself and more advanced than he in their doctrines. He had denounced the state and preached its destruction. He had warned the workers against the use of the ballot, because it was a dangerous illusion. He had quarrelled with the General Council of the International and had been in amicable relations with its enemies. These experiences caused him to shed many of his views. Guesde had come into exile a radical republican; he left it five years later almost a convinced socialist. In 1876 he was back in France, and soon writing for *Les Droits de l'Homme,* a newspaper owned by Yves Guyot, who was to become one of the staunchest enemies of socialism. In this organ appeared Guesde's articles on the Paris labor congress, and it was in the office of this journal that he met a number of young students who could be seen from time to time at the Café Soufflet, ardently discussing the social question.

3. The Colinsists

The Colinsian collectivists were no less enthusiastic than the students about the solution of the social problem.[46] These disciples of Baron Colins, the author of twenty volumes on social science,[47] preached the doctrines of their master with the same energy with which the positivists taught the ideas of Auguste Comte. Like the Fourierists who preceded them, the Colinsists were certain that they had found the only true social system in which poverty would be banished forever—the system of "rational socialism." They attacked the teachings of the economists, calling them "the statement of the necessity of the slavery of the masses, of poverty growing in a parallel line with wealth." [48] Free competition as preached by the *laissez-faire* school they called an illusion, for it was vitiated by social and economic inequality. Free competition could exist only when the land was not held by individuals, but was owned collectively. Poverty was the result of the individual ownership of the land. "Wherever that [individual ownership] exists," said Fr. Borde, editor of the Colinsian review, "poverty exists, and the institutions, ameliorations, associations and all the political and economic aberrations can do nothing for it, absolutely nothing." [49] All the demands of the radical republicans, such as the separation of church and state, compulsory education and the election of the magistracy, were of no importance as long as the organization of property remained the same. "The canker of poverty will continue none the less to eat away the social organization." [50] To the workers they said that cooperation would be futile in the face of the formidable association of capitalists. Victory would come necessarily to the side having the greatest amount of money.[51] Nor would the workers profit by their direct representation in parliament. If the labor members were a minority, their demands would be rejected. If they were a majority, they would turn conservative and the old system would continue. A parliament, they said, was incapable of solving social problems, because it could not make the laws of social science. Neither ballots nor bullets but reason was the essential.[52]

The Colinsists denied that poverty was a product of the wage system. If that were true, they said, poverty would be universal, "for it is impossible to conceive a social system where wages, or the reward for labor, is abolished." Poverty was caused rather by the individual ownership of the land. Not being free to refuse his labor to others, the worker was forced to compete with others in the sale of his labor to those who possessed land and capital. His wages fell to the subsistence level, and the greatest share of the wealth went to the landowner and capitalist. Only when a man was free to refuse to work for another—and that was possible only when land could be easily obtained by all—would wages be high, for no one would work for others unless he could earn more than by working for himself.[53]

The solution they offered was collectivism—the word was coined by Colins—that is, the collective ownership of the land. This would be effected gradually, within a period of twenty-five to forty years, in the following manner:

1. The right of inheritance would be limited to the direct line. Every inheritance through a will would be taxed twenty-five per cent.

2. The land, having become collective property, would remain inalienable.

3. Children would be fed, clothed, lodged and educated by the state. Education would be both practical and theoretical, and would include the physical sciences as well as ethics. When the children came of age, they would spend the next five years in the service of the state. At the end of that period they would receive a sum of money from it.

4. The public debt as well as all perpetual incomes would be abolished. Annuities, however, would be paid for fifty years.

5. The land, the dwellings on it and the material necessary for its exploitation would be owned collectively. These would be divided and rented, but everyone who leased them from the state had to exploit them. They might not be sub-let.

6. Associations of capitalists would be prohibited; those of workers only would be permitted. At the end of each year the profits of each association would be divided in proportion to the wages received.

7. The state would provide bazaars where the producers might offer their products for sale.

8. Public services would be owned and operated by the state at the lowest possible cost.[54]

Thus would the worker be freed from exploitation. He would receive the full product of his labor. Any increase in the "surplus value" of the association, or in its rolling stock, would be reflected in his share at the end of the year. The worker would be stimulated in his effort, because it would mean a larger individual reward, a fuller enjoyment of leisure and a more complete satisfaction of his needs.[55] In this manner poverty would be abolished and rational socialism realized.

In the Latin Quarter, the small group of Colinsists organized a Group of Philosophical and Social Studies to which they attempted to attract students and workingmen. They aided in the founding of the *Prolétaire,* the future organ of the possibilists, participated in the discussions on labor and social questions, and even had their doctrine presented at the second labor congress of Lyons. The collectivist amendment introduced at the congress bore the stamp of Colinsism as well as of Marxism when it referred to "the collective ownership of the land and of the instruments of labor."[56]   In the teaching of the collectivist doctrine the Colinsists preceded the Marxists whose ideas were trickling into France.

4. The introduction of Marxism into France

Marxism was little known in France before the Commune. As it has been shown, Proudhonism and Blanquism held the attention of workers and *déclassés.* Marx's polemic, *The Poverty of Philosophy,* was left unanswered by

Proudhon and continued to be unread in France.[57]   Though
The Communist Manifesto had been translated into French
before the Terrible June Days, it had no immediate influence
on the French workers. *"The Communist Manifesto . . . ,
The Eighteenth Brumaire of Louis Bonaparte, The Critique
of Political Economy,* the foundation of the International,
and even his monumental work, *Capital,* succeeded in making Marx famous only in Germany."[58]   The French people
were unaware of him and his work.[59]   On the eve of the
Franco-Prussian War and about nine months before the outbreak of the Commune, a pamphlet on the origin, aims and
methods of the International, written by one of its members
from Lyons, did not even mention the name of Marx, while
it referred twice to Proudhon.[60]   It was during the time of
the Commune, when conservative newspapers blamed the
International for causing the revolution of March 18th, that
Marx's name began to be used in France.   Thereafter, his
doctrines spread slowly in France.[61]   To his ideas the future
leaders of socialism and labor gradually turned, "and *The
Communist Manifesto* which had been left unnoticed in
France for a quarter of a century, replaced *La capacité
politique des classes ouvrières.*   The Manifesto, in turn,
became the gospel of the proletariat. Karl Marx succeeded
Proudhon." [62]

Though Marx's name was slowly becoming known in
France after the Commune, practically no one was well acquainted either with his life or work.   The parliamentary
committee on the March 18th insurrection thought that his
Poverty of Philosophy was a chapter of *Capital.*[63]   Professor Funck-Brentano, of the Ecole libres des Sciences
politiques, speaking before the Le Play Society, claimed
that Marx advised the Commune to seize the hostages, that

at the Hague Congress he was the leader of the group which favored an immediate revolution, and that, having failed, he withdrew to America.[64]

However, some attempts were made in France to examine his economic doctrines, and a few could not refrain from admiring his work, even though they were fully convinced of his errors. Maurice Block, a classical economist, and well known in his day, made an analysis of the first volume of *Capital,* and indicated the weaknesses of the theory of surplus value. But he added: "Despite the mistake on which Marx's doctrine is based, despite the hatred of the bourgeoisie which this work breathes almost in every line, and even between the lines, it is a remarkable work. By this work Marx is classed among the most eminently analytical minds, and we have only one regret: he has taken the wrong path." [65] Emile de Laveleye who wrote an article on contemporary socialism in Germany confessed the forceful effect of Marx's reasoning. "When one reads Marx's book [*Capital*]," he wrote, "and perceives himself being enclosed in the network of its inflexible logic, he feels as if he were under the spell of a nightmare, because once one has admitted the premises, which are borrowed from the least contested authorities, one is at a loss how to escape the conclusions; because, at the same time, his [Marx's] vast and sure erudition enables him to cite in support of his theses very striking extracts from numerous authors, and many striking facts drawn from parliamentary reports and from the industrial and agricultural history of England. Nevertheless, when one probes to the bottom of things and looks about, he perceives that he has been enveloped in a dexterously woven tissue of errors and subtleties interspersed with some truths. But it is not easy to release one's self from it. If one admit the theory of value propagated by Smith, Ricardo, Bastiat and Carey, he is lost." [66]

Marxian economics was also the subject of a discussion at one of the meetings of the Le Play Society, and it was a foreign economist, Professor Funck-Brentano, who was the main speaker. In answer to Marx's labor theory of value, he said: "It is not true that labor creates value. Let a scientist sacrifice his fortune and his life to the discovery of perpetual motion; the secret of the problem escapes him and all his efforts have produced nothing. Our peasants have worked an entire winter; a flood comes unexpectedly and washes away both seeds and furrows; their labor has produced nothing. The fact is that labor has no other purpose than to transform the materials which nature places within our reach. As for that which creates value, it is our needs, our desires, our passions and our vices. They alone give worth to the products of labor, raise or lower the price according to the satisfaction they find in things." [67]

Whatever the validity of their contentions against Marxian principles, bourgeois economists were helping to advertise the name of Marx and his tenets. Unconsciously they were aiding in the spread of his theories in France.

In French socialistic writings, too, reference was beginning to be made to Marx and his theories. In a study of the history and principles of the International, Malon included Marx's name among the inspirers of that association, though he placed it on a par with those of Lassalle, Becker, Bebel and Liebknecht.[68] In the same year, Malon published a volume in which he summarized the various socialist schools of thought, and to which he appended an essay on modern socialism. Here he presented a brief and incomplete account of Marxist thought, saying that Marx substituted in socialism the historical and objective for the purely logical methods of earlier socialists, and that after a study of the economic phenomena, he had concluded that collectivism was destined ultimately to dominate in production and distribution.[69] Malon went on to say that socialism, which had already passed through its period of preparation, should move on to its realization. The bourgeoisie had played its rôle and had become a reactionary force, a stumbling block in the progress of socialism. In a Marxian vein he concluded that the working class would dislodge the bourgeoisie from its privileged position and usher in the new form of society.[70]

Three years after the publication of Malon's book, there appeared the first French translation of the first volume of *Capital*.[71] The volume was published in small installments, each of which was sold at the nominal price of ten centimes. The purpose of this method of publication was expressly stated by the publisher in a letter to Marx. Its advantage, he wrote, was that it would permit "a greater number of our friends to procure your book, since the poor could pay for knowledge only with the farthing. Your end would be attained: to make your work accessible to all." Marx's answer was enthusiastic. He commended the publisher's plan of circulating his masterpiece. "In this manner," he wrote, "the work will be more accessible to the working class, and to me this consideration prevails over all others." [72]

It is difficult to determine the extent to which Marx's book was sold, or how widely it was read. But its appearance must have had some effect on the group of students who had been gathering at the Café Soufflet, in the Latin Quarter, discussing socialism. Among them were future

possibilists like John Labusquière and Victor Marouck,
future anarchists like Emile Gautier and Crié, and future
Marxists like Emile Massard and Gabriel Deville who had
been associated with the Toulouse section of the Marxist
International. Some of these young men had read Malon's
Exposé des écoles socialistes, and had studied law under
Acollas whose views on property and society bordered on
what was then known as collectivism.[73] They were not yet
wedded to any social philosophy, and their views were
necessarily vague. Though discontented with the prevailing
ills in the social order, they could offer no cure. They were,
as some of them said when they issued a call for an international congress of students, "atheists, revolutionists and
socialists." They were socialists, they said, "because there
still exist governing castes which make the law for the dis-
inherited mass; because a society in which the workers are
exposed to death from hunger, in which the subordination
of man to man is legalized by an official hierarchy, is an
illogical and unjust, not to say a criminal, society." [74]

An opportunity for action presented itself to them in the
by-election of the sixth *arrondissement,* held in February,
1876. Through their influence Professor Acollas was nominated as candidate, and a program more democratic than
socialistic was written. Their demands were a mixture of
those of the radical republicans and cooperators and contained Acollas' definition of property. These demands
were: complete amnesty for political prisoners; separation
of church and state; abolition of standing armies; removal
of all the laws against the freedom of the press and assembly; replacement of all taxes by the single tax; destruction
of all the official, industrial and financial monopolies; a
change in the property-laws "in order to restore individual

property to its only legitimate source—labor"; the organization of credit to place capital "at the disposal of him who employs it directly." [75] Acollas received only about 2,000 votes, but the program published in *Les Droits de l'Homme,* to which Guesde was a contributor, attracted notice in radical circles.

Guesde's articles in *Les Droits de l'Homme* won the attention of this small body of students. He had hailed the first labor congress as "an event of the first order," and had declared that the meeting of the delegates of workers, apart from the bourgeoisie, was "a fact of as much social significance" as the statement of Sieyès, that "the Third Estate wanted to become everything from nothing." [76] When *Les Droits de l'Homme* was suppressed and was replaced by *Le Radical,* Guesde continued his contributions. During February and March, 1877, he wrote a series of articles on the *Crisis in Lyons and the Social Order.* [77] Taking the causes of the crisis as given by economists, he contended that these causes were in themselves products of the existing social and economic organization. [78] "If the worker is not protected from accidental unemployment and from that final unemployment which is called old age," he wrote, "it is because a part, the greatest part, of the values created by him goes to others, to those who, under the pretense of having him work, deprive him of the only legitimate property, that which has labor at its source.

"In short, it is because he is robbed, robbed of the entire difference which exists between the arbitrary remuneration for his production, which is the wage, and the real value of this production, which is the product." [79] His solution was the collective ownership of the instruments of production.

Guesde had thus arrived at the rudiments of the theory of surplus value without having read anything by Marx. Though he still lacked clarity in his doctrines, he had reached the modern socialist solution of the economic and social questions. By the simplicity of his ideas, by his revolutionary assertions, and by his succinct and virulent style, he became the most influential figure in the group of the Café Soufflet and in the then limited socialist circles. Fr. Borde, the Colinsian, after reading the articles on the Lyons crisis, wrote with enthusiasm as well as with bias: "Jules Guesde is a new name in the Parisian press. But notoriety is far from being the proof of talent. Many men have been writing for thirty years, who do not reach up to his ankle." [80] Workers wrote him to ask for information and explanations. Guesde responded, went to see them, mingled with them in cafés, and thus gathered about him a few trusty followers.[81] He soon met Karl Hirsch, a young journalist thoroughly versed in German socialist literature, who had been associated with the *Volkstaat* during Liebknecht's imprisonment.[82] In his company, Guesde was brought into contact with Marxian socialism. His friendship with the young German socialist was an event in his ideological development.

The comparatively few adherents of socialism were in 1877 without a common theory. Even after the founding of the *Egalité* they scarcely knew the fundamentals of modern socialism. As Deville later wrote, "We were learning socialism while we were teaching it to our readers, and it is unquestionable but that we were at times mistaken." [83] However, they were slowly winning adherents. The International Congress of Ghent and Guesde's activities stimulated many to turn to modern socialism.

The Ghent Congress assembled in September, 1877, and was attended by forty-two delegates who were divided into two defined groups: socialists and anarchists. From the very beginning the irreconcilable differences between them came to the surface. The socialists favored the state ownership of the means of production, the anarchists opposed it. The first deemed it necessary that the workers should organize into a distinct political party, the second just as ardently claimed that the workers should abandon the political path. The socialists were in a majority, and consequently succeeded in passing resolutions favoring state ownership and the political action of the workers. One of the resolutions read as follows:

"Inasmuch as social emancipation is inseparable from political emancipation, the congress declares that the proletariat, organized as a distinct party opposed to all the other parties formed by the possessing classes, must make use of all the political methods tending to bring about the social emancipation of all its members." [84]

The defeat of the anarchists indicated that socialism was gaining ground. In France the effect of the congress on the rising socialist organizations "was considerable," wrote Malon years later, "and the revolutionary collectivist group in particular drew new strength from it. It [the group] gained valuable recruits among the workers . . . and believed itself sufficiently strong to create a weekly organ." [85] This organ was the *Egalité*.

When *Le Radical* disappeared, Guesde was sufficiently free to undertake the publication of a socialist organ. Three months after the International Congress of Ghent, appeared the *Egalité*, a weekly, with Guesde as chief editor, assisted by Gabriel Deville, P. Gervier, E. Massard and E.

Oudin. For its foreign correspondents it had such well known socialists as Bebel, Liebknecht, César de Paepe and Zanardelli. Its opening number of November 18, 1877, left in the mind of its readers no doubt about its doctrines. It said: "The *Egalité* will be not only republican in politics and atheist in religion; it will be, above all, socialist. It appears to its founders that one should no longer pose as the advocate of social betterment by vaguely proclaiming one's self a partisan of dubious measures, calculated to improve the lot of the laboring classes. They [the founders] think that the time has come to study the solutions, and that several of them have already been found.

"We believe, with the collectivist school, to which belong almost all the serious minds of the proletariat of both worlds, that the natural and scientific evolution of humanity is inevitably leading it to the collective appropriation of the land and of the instruments of labor." [86]

On the very same day on which the *Egalité* appeared, the *Bulletin de la fédération jurassienne,* the anarchist organ, reproached Guesde for having changed his convictions and for appealing to universal suffrage to maintain the republic. Its reproach was all the more forceful when it quoted arguments against the use of the ballot from Guesde's article in the *Almanach du peuple,* written in 1873.[87] This reminder of his former ideas, however, did not prevent Guesde from adding to the title, *Egalité,* the sub-title, *Journal républicain socialiste.*

The *Egalité* was the first French paper to propagate modern French socialism, and, like many radical journals, was hampered in its publication by the governmental authorities. The police paid visits to the homes of the members of its editorial staff; and the printer, "more or less terrorized" by the government, refused the use of his press.[88] Since the money deposit, required by the government as security for the payment of fines, was higher in Paris than in the other towns of France, the editors had their paper printed outside of the capital. Edouard Drumont pictured the hardships of these young idealists. "The editors," he wrote, "were obliged to leave in the morning for the printing-office, having only the exact amount needed for the trip and not eating anything the entire day. On Saturday mornings, they used to go to the station to fetch the copies and carry them on their shoulders to the rear of a wine merchant's shop where the distribution was organized." [89]

For these ardent socialists who had begun their political careers as republicans, the glamour of the republic had not worn off. The events which followed May 16, 1877 helped to lend a republican touch to their socialist organ. Though the republicans had been victorious in the elections of October, 1877, the monarchist ministry of de Broglie did not resign until November 19th, and the moderate republican ministry of Dufaure did not take office until December 13th. Thus the first number of the *Egalité* expressly stated that the socialists were too conscious of their interests not to understand that it was important for them to cooperate to the very end with the liberal bourgeoisie against the common enemy. It was not because they believed that the republican form of government would settle once and for all the social and economic questions of the country. "We know very well," they said, "that the republic does not exclude the exploitation of the great number by the small. We know very well that the republic does not impair the development of the principle of authority, that it does not prevent the wage-earner from being the prey of covetous

118

employers, that it is perfectly contented with laws destructive of liberty. We know very well that under the republic as many people are imprisoned, deported and shot as under no matter what monarchy. But the republic is the last word of the purely political or governmental evolution, and leaves room only for an economic and social revolution, substituting for the nominal equality of rights the real equality of things." It was for this reason that the *Egalité* was "delighted" with the republican victory in October.[90]

However, it was socialist first and only secondarily republican. Every one of its numbers was devoted to the dissemination of modern socialism. The various events of the day were turned to socialist ends. Marshal MacMahon could continue to rule against the national will, it said, because he had the support of hundreds of thousands of officials whom it was necessary to maintain in order to defend the "economic privileges" of the bourgeoisie.[91] If the liberty of the press did not yet exist, it was because the republican bourgeoisie did not want to grant it. The republic in its hands could not serve "as the instrument of political and economic emancipation." Only a social revolution could realize that.[92] The bourgeoisie would support a *coup d'état* which menaced its political liberties, "rather than find itself on the side of the revolution which imperils its economic rule."[93] Nothing could be expected from the bourgeoisie even though it was republican. The new form of government could not relieve the workers from their poverty, for "the source of the evil does not lie . . . in a political organization which, however defective it may be, is only the effect, the resultant, of the social organization . . .

"As long as the interests of each and all have not been harmonized and made responsible to all by an equal distribution of social burdens and privileges, as long as an organized force has to intervene between the 'haves' and the 'have-nots' in order to impose peace, this force will be in a state of permanent conspiracy against the public tranquility, no matter what it is and no matter to what hands it is entrusted." [94]

The state, said the *Egalité,* was an instrument of oppression, wielded by the owners of wealth against the non-owners. The former, to maintain their possessions and privileges, were obliged to organize such "repressive services" as the police, the magistracy, the clergy and the army.[95] It mattered little whether the state was tyrannical, monarchical or republican, for its power was always being used to exploit the lower classes.[96]

To put trust in universal suffrage as the means of emancipation was to mislead the workers. Neither as a producer, nor as a consumer, nor as a taxpayer had the worker seen his burdens reduced through his use of the ballot. Far from ameliorating his condition, universal suffrage had served only to strengthen the domination of the "ruling caste." How?

"1. By dividing the workers who until then were united, welded to each other, so to speak, by their very exclusion from any participation in the government; by causing them to fight among themselves for the choice of their political masters.

"2. By alluring them with the false hope of a gradual, peaceful and legal emancipation, springing from the ballot-box which they can fill with their ballots, but of which the bourgeoisie is master in two ways: with its capital and with its education.

"3. By imparting a semblance of legality to a state of

things which has been and can be nothing but the product, the expression, of force." [97]

Thus far Guesde reasoned much as he did during his early years of exile. But since then he had changed his tactics. After 1877 he and his followers opposed the anarchist slogan of abstaining from politics. They maintained that a milieu of political freedom was necessary to organize the proletariat and to discipline it for the social revolution. To prepare for this revolution, the workers should resort to all forms of struggle, "and, for want of any other effective means of combat, to the electoral struggle which, in France, during these last times, has been the only one possible." [98] The worker, said the editors of the *Egalité,* should try to break all the chains which kept him enslaved. He should free himself not only from the economic hold of the capitalists but also from the political mastery of those who controlled the wheels of the government. The worker should not abstain from politics, for even if the political struggle was useless, it was difficult to understand how abstention would be more productive of results than participation in politics. "Would abstaining from politics permit the worker to escape the oppressive yoke of the employer?" they asked. That was impossible, they answered, for "the social emancipation of the workers is inseparable from their political emancipation." Consequently, "to assure the triumph of the social revolution" it was absolutely necessary for the proletariat to form itself into a political party. [99] The existence of the government was a fact to be reckoned with. [100]

The socialists who contributed to the *Egalité* did not expect important results from the separate representation of the proletariat in parliament. The capitalist class "will never allow the Fourth Estate to become a majority in the

Chamber of Deputies . . . We will say more! Should the workers who constitute the great majority of the electoral body succeed in becoming the majority in the elected assembly—to suppose what is impossible—the social revolution would not make a single step forward." Parliaments could sanction a new economic order, but they could not create it.[101]

If egalitarian society was to be the result of a struggle and not of universal suffrage, why then did Guesde and his group of followers urge the workers to use the ballot? Simply because it was a potent agent in grouping the workers on a class basis, and an effective method of disseminating socialist ideas. The editors of the *Egalité* openly acknowledged that they saw in the organization of the working class into a political party "a means of propaganda and agitation whose revolutionary value has been determined by many and many an experience." [102]

The *Egalité* believed that it was continuing the revolutionary tradition of the French workers, manifested in the Conspiracy of the Equals, in the Lyons insurrection of 1831, in the June Days of 1848 and in the Commune. It consequently printed studies on these revolutionary movements, and long pages from the writings of Blanqui.[103] In a truly international spirit it sent an address to the German socialists meeting at Gotha, assuring them of its "sympathy" and "fraternal cooperation." "It is you," it wrote to them, "who to-day have the honor of serving as a target for the slanders of all the combined reactionary forces just as eight years ago it was we whom they pursued with their insults and bullets. And just as in 1871 you did not hesitate to declare yourselves, through the voices of Liebknecht and Bebel, adherents of the vanquished Commune, no more hesitant are we in accepting and claiming the most complete solidarity with your social democracy, whose coming and inevitable victory will be ours. . . .

"To-day we are with you in spirit, just as to-morrow we shall be with you in person when you judge that the hour has come to answer force with force." [104]

The collaborators and friends of the *Egalité* waged war on the social and economic theories taught by Barberet. The workers, they said, should organize syndicats, but these were not to be considered as the aim. The syndicats might at times check the employers in the abuse of their privileges; they could be only moderately valuable for the improvement of the workers' condition. The syndicats were not an end, but a means of grouping the workers for revolutionary action. [105] The proletariat should not expect to end the system of exploitation through peaceful methods. Just as the workers had to be collectivist in aim if they hoped to reap the full product of their labor, so was it necessary for them to be revolutionary in method, because "without the revolution all the cooperative societies, together with all the syndical chambers, will be powerless to make them [the workers] the owners of the capital which they lack." [106]

Guesde and his friends denounced cooperation as sterile in results and delusive in its effects on the workers. Producers' cooperatives were formed chiefly in those industries in which hand labor prevailed. They could not be applied to those branches of industry in which modern methods of manufacture were introduced. The tendency in modern production, they said, was in the direction of concentration. Furthermore, the cooperatives had to resort to "bourgeois capital" on which they had to pay a "tithe similar to the one levied by an employer on his workers." If the co-operative associations were a success they were trans-formed into bourgeois companies with their wage earners. Cooperatives were a means of "pooling the poverty of the workers." Were they to become general, they would only disguise the abuses of capitalism. "This varnishing of the existing social order would lengthen its life."

The credit societies were no less illusory, Guesde con-tended. The working population of the large factories needed no credit to buy raw material and to do business. Only those engaged in small industry, that is, "the petty bourgeoisie," could profit by these associations. The work-ers could not save anything from their wages, which repre-sented simply the amount necessary for subsistence.

The consumers' cooperatives had their advantages, but they were not to be over-estimated. The chief difficulty for the worker was not that he had to overpay for his goods, but that he was underpaid for what he produced. He suffered primarily as a producer. Thus the social problem was to be attacked not from the consuming but from the producing end. The consumers' societies had their limita-tions. If they became widespread, the cost of living would be lowered and wages would fall, for less would be needed to maintain the worker and his family. "The iron law of wages, as it is called, would be applied." [107] Since the pov-erty of the workers arose from the fact that they were "robbed" of the difference between the values created by them and the wages received, the solution of the problem lay in the collective ownership of the means of production. The proletariat was to separate itself from the liberal and republican bourgeoisie and form its own party.[108]

From its very inception the *Egalité* was harassed by the

government. Its publication was interrupted, and it could not appear from November 25th to December 16th. On March 26th its offices were searched by the police who took with them a number of manuscripts and letters. Guesde was accused of being secretly associated with the International. On July 12th the manager of the paper was fined 1,000 francs and condemned to one year in prison. In its last number (July 14, 1878) the *Egalité* announced that the heavy fine imposed on it was too great a burden, and that it had to suspend publication.

The first *Egalité* was short-lived. However, its thirty-three numbers appearing during the eight months of its existence played a decisive rôle in the early history of modern French socialism. "The words 'labor party' and 'collectivism' which are to-day a part of our political language," wrote a member of its staff five years later, "were, one may say, little known; the ideas they represented had in France only a few advocates, without a tie and without any possibility of joint action. It was the newspaper, the *Egalité*, founded toward the end of 1877 on the initiative of Jules Guesde and directed by him, which alone gave the impulse to the present revolutionary socialist movement." [109]

The influence of the propaganda of Guesde and his friends was displayed at the second labor congress which met in Lyons in 1878 while the *Egalité* was still appearing. Dupire, who claimed to adhere to the doctrines of the *Philosophie de l'Avenir* and the *Egalité*,[110] told the delegates that "the existing society is divided into two irreconcilable and hostile camps: on one side, those who possess without working, and on the other, those who work without possessing." [111] This division into classes would continue, he said, as long as the tools of production were controlled by a few individuals, and as long as the masses were deprived of the benefits arising from the increase in social wealth.[112] The solution lay in collective ownership. He warned the bourgeoisie that the proletariat would have its 1789, which, having come, would not be "local and regional," but "universal." The workers were not to depend on the bourgeoisie, but to take charge of their own affairs, "for it is certain that the emancipation of labor can be effected only by the worker himself." [113] Dupire, and Ballivet, an anarchist delegate, succeeded in introducing an amendment to the resolution on trade unions, which embodied the ideas of collectivism. It read:

"Whereas, the economic emancipation of the workers will be an accomplished fact only when they enjoy the full product of their labor;

"Whereas, to attain this aim, it is necessary that the workers shall be in possession of the elements useful to production: the raw material and the instruments of labor;

"Consequently, the congress invites all the labor associations to study the practical means of applying the principle of the collective ownership of the land and of the instruments of labor." [114]

Though the amendment won only eight votes,[115] it was a sign that modern socialism was invading the labor circles to combat the cooperative ideal.

How was the Congress of Lyons, which was as moderate as the Congress of Paris held two years earlier, but which heard an exposition of the collectivist doctrine, judged by non-socialists and by socialists? The *République Française,* Gambetta's organ, was pleased that "the partisans of the reactionary régime of the common ownership of property, presented for some time by certain misguided people as a

sort of a social panacea, found themselves opposed at
the Congress of Lyons by animated individuals of the most
genuine, good French sense." [116] In the *Journal des Economistes,* Charles Limousin, the Fourierist, took exception
to the statements of several delegates that there was a
"divergence between the interests" of the bourgeoisie and
those of the proletariat. The speakers who had developed
this thesis were guilty, he thought, "of absolutely false
assertions and of really unjust accusations." In these unjust attacks he detected a fear on the part of the orators
that the "abominable" bourgeoisie was capable of doing
something for the workers, "which would compromise the
opinion that the workers alone ought to undertake the
work of the revolution." [117] Malon, who was still in exile,
regretted that the Dupire-Ballivet amendment was rejected. "The workers," he said, "are too much preoccupied
with what the bourgeoisie will think and say about them.
It is wrong. Petty considerations, said Voltaire, are the
grave of great things. If the members of the local assemblies of 1789 had concerned themselves with appearing wise
in the eyes of the nobility, the clergy and the bourgeoisie
of the robe, there would never have resulted from their
deliberations those immortal bailiwick *cahiers* which made
the Great Revolution." [118] The *Egalité,* which followed
attentively the sessions of the congress of 1878, concluded
that its decisions were nothing but a reediting of the resolutions of the Paris Congress of 1876. The same journal,
however, prophesied that at the next labor congress, scheduled for the following year, cooperation would be driven
from its stronghold by collectivism.[119]

It predicted correctly. Several events between the end
of the Lyons Congress in 1878 and the opening of the Con-

gress of Marseilles in 1879 gave added stimulus to the socialist movement and hastened its victory over cooperation.

Before adjourning, the Lyons Congress commissioned the syndical chambers of Paris to organize an international congress in September, 1878, on the occasion of the universal exposition of that year. Meetings of labor delegates and of representatives of social study groups were held and arrangements for the congress were made. But Dufaure was then at the head of the ministry, the same Dufaure who was the author of the law against the International. Consequently, the Prefecture of Police informed the organizers that the international congress would not be tolerated. The organizing committee of syndicats thereupon ceased its preparations, but Jules Guesde and his friends determined to defy the government. He became the central figure of the opposition to the interdiction. In a protest drawn up by him the undersigned said:

"Whereas the working class, like the other classes of citizens, has interests of its own which it must defend, and whose defense cannot be limited or hampered by national and political frontiers;

"Whereas in availing themselves of the exposition to receive the workers of other countries and to discuss with them certain questions of common interest, the French workers in general, and the Parisian workers in particular, are only following the example of the men of letters who met two months ago in an international congress, and of the merchants and industrialists whose congress, equally international and organized by the chambers of employers, was held at the same time at the official palace of the Trocadero;

"Whereas the frontiers, lowered and abolished for the capitalists, cannot be raised arbitrarily and exclusively against the workers, without the republic's making itself guilty of one of those denials of justice which even a monarchy would hesitate to commit;"

The undersigned "declare . . . : (1) that they cannot take into account a verbal prohibition dictated by interests of caste and stripped of every juridical basis; (2) that the International Socialist Labor Congress will take place on the dates previously fixed, that is, from the 2nd to the 12th of September." [120]

The socialists, in receiving the foreign delegates, considered themselves as the official representatives of the French workers. The syndical chambers, encouraged by the boldness of Guesde and his friends, asked for cards of admission to the congress. When the delegates arrived at their meeting place on September 4th, thirty-nine of them (French) were arrested.[121] Guesde wanted nothing better. The opportunity was offered to him to present the socialist cause in the court room. The defense made by him in the name of his arrested comrades created a deep impression, "while the congress, if it had been held, would have undoubtedly passed unnoticed." [122] After recounting the events which led up to the arrests, he asserted that the government disregarded the fundamental rights of the citizen in its treatment of the accused. The bourgeoisie, he said, were the first to trample on "bourgeois legality" as soon as they found it necessary to do so. There were only two ways of maintaining order. "Either society is founded on justice, on the equal division among all of the burdens and privileges and on the equal satisfaction of the needs of all; and then order exists of itself, through the equal interest

which all have in maintaining it. . . . Or society is founded
on monopoly, the monopoly of education, wealth, etc. . . . ,
and on the exploitation of the great number by the few.
. . . In this society which a minority alone is interested
in maintaining, order is a question of force." The socialists
and labor leaders were being pursued, he asserted, not for
illicit association—that was only a "pretext"—but for "the
socialist and revolutionary opinions professed by the large
number among them." That they entertained such views, he
and his comrades were prepared to affirm openly. "Yes," he
continued, "we are of those who are pursuing a social revolution, who believe in the necessity and, at the same time, in
the inevitability of a workers' 1789. And, gentlemen, do
you know why?

"It is because we can stand up before the present society
with the same list of grievances as was previously formulated against the old régime by the Third Estate; because,
in support of the demands of the Fourth Estate, we can
invoke the same arguments, the same rights which were
cited by the Third to support its demands ninety-one years
ago." And just as the bourgeoisie destroyed the privileged
position of the old orders, so did the working class aim to
put an end to "this outrage . . . which consists in robbing
society's greatest number for the benefit of the smallest, in
order to satisfy the idleness of a few." [123]

Most of the thirty-nine arrested were only fined; but
Guesde, Deville, Massard and several others received
prison terms in addition. The effect of Guesde's defense
was enormous. He became known among the workers, and
his ideas as they were presented in the court room were discussed by them. As Guesde's biographer says: "Never
since the first pursuits directed against the First Interna-

tional, did a trial have such a reverberation. In the factories and dockyards the new doctrine is discussed. Workers, who yesterday were still ignorant of the word, now proclaim themselves collectivists. Subscriptions are opened to pay for the expenses of the trial and to secure the publication of the plea pronounced by Guesde. Had the congress been held, it would not have had an equal effect." [124] Guesde became a prominent figure in the labor movement and was to exert a profound influence upon it.

Modern socialism was injecting itself into labor circles, largely due to the zeal of its advocates. Unlike the leaders of the syndicats and the cooperatives, the socialists were aggressive, prepared to go to prison in order to advertise their theories and to win the admiration and support of the lower classes. They taught the irreconcilability of classes and the hopelessness of reform in a bourgeois society. They openly proclaimed that the road to the end of their troubles lay through a social revolution for which the proletariat should prepare itself by organizing itself professionally and politically. How different these tenets were from those of the Barberetists!

After the trial of the thirty-nine, Guesde knew that socialism was slowly winning followers, and, though in prison, he was determined to maintain the interest of the workers and of others in his ideas. From Sainte-Pélagie, where they were kept, he, Deville, Chabry and their friends addressed a manifesto to the workers, peasant proprietors and small employers outlining the bases on which to found a political party. Their appeal, called *Program and Address of the French Social Revolutionists,* was circulated and was signed by more than 500 sympathizers in eighteen towns of France.[125] After ascribing the evils of society to private ownership, it made certain demands which its authors knew would not be granted by the republican government. They were: cultural and vocational education for all children, together with maintenance at the expense of society; the full freedom of the press, of assembly and of combination; social ownership of the land and of the instruments of production.

To the industrial and agricultural workers the manifesto said that poverty was caused by the fact that the "major part of their product" went to the "idle proprietor" who hired them for wages. Collective ownership would alter their entire life. Instead of being mere tools, they would become men, owners of the entire product of their labor, as happy and as rich as they were wretched under individual ownership.

For the peasant proprietor the manifesto painted his poor lot. He toiled on his bit of land which was mortgaged, he was deprived of his hard earned money through taxation, and he was in danger of having his property taken away from him by the large landowner. The nationalization of the land, he was informed, would solve his problems, for to him it would mean more land and no "levies" on his labor.

The manifesto also addressed itself to the small, independent manufacturer, and to the petty merchant. It told them that the competition of big business and of large scale industry tended to throw them into the ranks of the proletariat. Only the collective ownership of all the tools of production could save them. "From producers for the gain of others," it said to them, "that is, from the wage-earners that all of you are destined to become with the progress of the existing order of things, the new society at which we are aiming and which we are inviting you to establish with us will transform you into producers for your own account, into free producers, by leaving you the entire profit, the entire return of that part of the common capital which will have been the object of your efforts." [126]

Thus the manifesto endeavored to group three sections of French society against the capitalists and large landowners. It promised that the social revolution once accomplished would benefit each, for it would safeguard "all the legitimate interests" of those who worked and produced. The Marxian formula of the concentration of wealth was utilized in an attempt to convince the small producer that his economic status was only temporary, and that he was doomed to be reduced to the state of the worker. An appeal was made to the peasant, because the writers of the manifesto, who had recalled the sad fate of the Commune, knew that any revolution in France which did not have the support of the peasantry would end in defeat. This attempt to reconcile the interests of three different social and economic sections of French society later resulted in reformism. But in the meantime the manifesto, read by many, helped to make the new doctrine known.

The agitation of Guesde, Deville and their followers was not the only solvent of the old economic concepts of workers and intellectuals. There were other forces which helped to undermine the notions on labor and capital current among the syndicats. In Switzerland, Malon, by an extensive reading of socialist literature, had been grounding himself in socialist theory. In January, 1878, he founded a review, *Le Socialisme Progressif*,[127] in which he preached the unity of socialist forces on the basis of eclecticism. His opinion of Marx had grown more favorable, and he could write admiringly of him, saying that "by his crushing criticism of orthodox political economy, by his introduction of the historical and critical method and by his irrefutable theory of value," Marx became one of the masters of socialist thought.[128]   In his correspondence with Jean Lombard and Antide Boyer, labor leaders who achieved fame at the Congress of Marseilles, Malon was endeavoring to prove to them that "outside of the socialization of the productive forces there could be no emancipation for the workers." [129]   Malon's review had many readers in southern France.

Another publication, grouping a number of prominent labor and socialist leaders and having a wider influence, was the *Prolétaire*.   Its first number appeared one month after Guesde had delivered his much discussed defense. Unlike the *Egalité* which treated socialist theory, this journal dealt essentially with events of the moment.   It was a labor organ, founded in response to the demands made at the Congresses of Paris and Lyons.   A cooperative society was organized to issue the paper, and on November 23, 1878, a specimen-number appeared, in which it was said that the labor organ was not attached to any one idea on social reform, but that it would open its columns to all doctrines.   "The spirit of exclusion in social and political economy," it declared, "has only resulted in hindering the search for truth, in preventing discussions and in creating and maintaining hatred among men.

"Moreover, scientific truth belongs to-day to no one school. . . . The solution [of social questions] can come from the united effort of the partisans of the different systems." [130]

The *Prolétaire* was prepared to fight vigorously against

every form of oppression, and to be "the indefatigable defender of all those who suffer: of the worker who is being crushed by capitalism; of the woman whom the laws and customs place in an inferior position; and of the child in whom the future man is not sufficiently respected.

"From the point of view of social economy, the *Prolétaire* claims that the exploitation of man by man is a monstrous and revolting injustice; that the moneyed aristocracy is no less bold than the landed aristocracy; that it is high time that labor should be more justly recompensed." [131]

Various representatives of schools of social thought contributed to the paper. The mutualists demonstrated the advantages of cooperative societies to the workers, and pointed to the possibility of creating a system for the exchange of products.[132] Delaporte expounded the Colinsist solution of the social question,[133] and Prudent-Dervillers set forth the theories of the revolutionary collectivists. This labor leader and journalist, a tailor by trade, had been inspired by Marxian socialism. Like Guesde, Prudent-Dervillers divided society into two classes—those who owned the means of production and those who were hired to operate them. The first class not only lived on the labor of the second, but also controlled the state whose forces were utilized to maintain its possessions.[134] He told the workers not to cherish any illusions about social reforms. "A society like ours which sweats injustice through every pore is not improved; it is transformed. Put aside your emollients and have recourse to strongly caustic substances." [135] Universal suffrage, he said, could have no real meaning to the workers as long as their economic and social emancipation was not reailzed.[136] Parliamentarism he condemned as a "lie" and as "a masterpiece of hypocrisy," for the bourgeoisie would never "deliberately decree its own downfall." [137]

In general, however, the *Prolétaire* was neither as revolutionary in its language, nor as theoretic in its discussions as was the *Egalité;* nor was it as completely dominated by a single social philosophy as was its contemporary. If Prudent-Dervillers was a revolutionary collectivist, A. Lavy, a co-editor, was an adherent of private property and opposed the use of violence. [138] Even positivists and anarchists had their representatives among the contributors. [139] In its columns one found demands for the revision of the Constitution of 1875 [140] and advice to the workers to separate themselves politically from the bourgeoisie, even from the radicals led by Clemenceau. [141] On the question of the independent political action of labor there was a wide disagreement. Those against it claimed that since parliaments had never done anything for the working class, the revolutionists should strive to destroy parliaments. If the workers succeeded in electing some of their number, they would discover that their representatives were in a "pernicious" milieu, "prisoners" of the bourgeoisie and, therefore, "lost to the revolution." [142] On the other hand, those who favored the independent political action of labor contended that elections and the presence of labor leaders and socialists in parliament would help to popularize the socialist program and to strengthen the socialist party. [143]

While the *Prolétaire* was disseminating various social theories, many able propagandists were delivering numerous lectures on socialism. Men like Guesde—he was released from prison on account of his poor health—Prudent-Dervillers, Chabert, Lavy, Marouck, Paulard and Lombard took the platform to expound their doctrines. Not only

Paris, Lyons, Marseilles and Bordeaux, but also Troyes, Béziers and Nîmes were invaded, and an impulse given to the revolutionary movement. The debates among the various theorists, such as those between the anarchists and the socialists, [144] and between the Marxists and the Colinsists,[145] helped to create an interest in the new movement.

The economic and political events were additional stimulants to the revolutionary movement. Modern industry continued its invasion of France,[146] causing a sharpening of the struggle between capital and labor. In 1879 strikes broke out among the silk weavers and the bronze-moulders, and among those engaged in the building trade of whom about 20,000 were affected. While strikes had been comparatively few in number and generally peaceful during the five preceding years, they were beginning to increase both in number and in violence after 1879.[147] The labor disturbances afforded an excellent opportunity to socialist agitators. In January, 1879, the senatorial elections resulted in a victory for the republicans. President Mac-Mahon, having found himself opposed by two republican houses, resigned toward the end of the month, and was soon replaced by Jules Grévy, a republican. But the new government not only made no attempt to deal with the social question, but even refused, despite the constant demands of labor leaders and radicals, to grant full amnesty to the former Communards.[148]

The clamor for amnesty found expression in the candidacy of Blanqui at Bordeaux. The campaign of this "jailbird" and revolutionist, still a prisoner at Clairvaux, was conducted by the youthful enthusiast, Ernest Roche. Meetings were held, money was subscribed, appeals and addresses arrived from Communards abroad, one even from

Garibaldi. On April 20, 1879, he was elected. Upon the Chamber of Deputies' refusal to seat him, the agitation for his release became so strong that the government had to yield, and liberate him from prison.[149] After the invalidation of Blanqui's election, Prudent-Dervillers and other revolutionary collectivists gleefully indicated that the action of the Chamber merely corroborated what they had been saying. There was nothing to be expected from bourgeois parliaments. The ballot could not be a lever with which to transform the wage earner into "the free owner of his labor power." [150]

Despite the campaigns, lectures, revolutionary newspapers and strikes, the French workingman did not readily accept the new doctrines. He remained indifferent to it and at times hostile. In 1878 a Parisian worker defined a socialist as "a humbug who exposes to us his beautiful theories, but who is not present when it is necessary to apply them." [151] So slowly were the workers drawn to socialism that up to the middle of the same year one of the most aggressive socialist groups, the one which published the *Egalité*,[152] succeeded in winning over to its doctrines only six small labor organizations and one consumers' cooperative society.[153] According to Malon, the socialists were largely responsible for the slow march of their ideas. Instead of uniting on a program, the groups remained divided, each with its own philosophy, its own interpretation and its own formulas. The result was that listeners and readers were more confused than convinced.[154]

The coldness of the workers to socialism was best illustrated by their attitude to the *Prolétaire* and to socialist candidates. They did not support the labor organ, and, on several occasions, the editors had to appeal to them to keep the paper alive.[155]   In the municipal elections of January, 1878, a socialist candidate, Emile Chausse, himself a worker, was nominated in a workers' district in Paris.   His program was socialistic and contained such demands as: (1) the abolition of all privileges and monopolies; (2) the collectivization of the land and the instruments of labor in order that the worker should receive the full product of his labor; (3) communal autonomy; (4) the extension of the elective principle to all public offices; (5) complete and free education for all children; (6) the freedom of the press and of assembly; (7) the replacement of the standing army by a national militia; (8) complete separation of church and state; (9) complete amnesty.[156]   Chausse received 391 votes against his opponent's 2,862.   It was evident that the traditional ideas had too strong a grip on the workers to be readily supplanted by socialism.

Nevertheless, the advocates of collectivism were not discouraged.   During 1878 and 1879, Guesde published three pamphlets which urged the workers to trust only to themselves, and to organize themselves into a political party, distinct from all the bourgeois parties.[157]   The establishment of the republic, said Guesde, was only the beginning, the first step of the working class toward emancipation. The change in the form of government did not mean an improvement in the material situation of the workers.   On the contrary, said Guesde, strikes were becoming more numerous and the poverty of the workers was increasing. The needs and demands of the workers were no more considered under the republic than under the monarchy, and the social question still remained to be solved.   Consequently the workers were to continue to struggle against the bourgeoisie in order to overthrow it and to abolish the wage system.[158]

Neither the republic nor the prevailing social and economic theories would help to solve the social question. Communal ownership, said Guesde, was replete with danger, for it would lead to quarrels between communes over certain natural resources, and would encourage them to prevent people from other centers, less favored by nature, from settling in their territory.[159] The corporate ownership of the means of production was no less risky; it might result in monopolies dangerous to society as a whole.[160] Producers' cooperation would not alter the workers' conditions. Its dependence on borrowed capital meant that a part of the workers' product would go to the money lender. The worker would still be deprived of the full product of his labor.[161] Consumers' cooperation would not reduce the workers' cost of living. Competition from cooperatives would compel the large stores to reduce their labor force, the labor market would be overflooded, wages would fall and the workers would be reduced to their former subsistence level.[162]

Neither communal ownership, nor corporate ownership, nor cooperation would improve the workers' condition. Nothing would do it except the expropriation of the owners of the means of production.[163]

By revolution Guesde meant not "insurrection for the sake of insurrection, without preparation, without any chance of success, and almost without any aim," but "force used in the service of justice." For a century, he said, the workers' blood "had flowed only too freely with no gain to them and for the sole profit of the divided bourgeoisie. . . . It is time to put an end to these useless bleedings."

The advent of a social revolution, he claimed, was dependent on two conditions: (1) the creation of a proletariat determined to gain its right to capital; (2) the organization of the proletarian forces into such combative labor agencies as syndicats, societies for the defense of labor and even consumers' cooperatives, "provided that they, instead of being considered the aim, are held to be what they really are, that is, simply a means of grouping." [164]

Added revolutionary propaganda came from two newspapers founded in 1879. Besides *La Révolution Française,* which was founded in Paris and to which Guesde and Deville contributed, there appeared at Geneva *Le Révolté,* copies of which were smuggled into France.[165] This anarchist organ advocated the revolutionary method to destroy the state and existing property relations in order to give free rein to the development of the federation of communes and of anarchist communism.[166] During the struggle between modern socialism and cooperation, preceding the Congress of Marseilles, the anarchists sided with the former.

That the revolutionists were exerting an influence was shown by the joint report of the French labor delegation to the Philadelphia Exposition, which was published during the eventful year of 1879. While the report of the Vienna Delegation was timid and peaceful, avoiding any mention of the Commune, this one referred to the antagonism of classes, and to the "massacres" of the Commune, which could not be "equalled in barbarity." The reason for the rigorous reprisals against the Communards, said the report, was "that the bourgeoisie had understood that from the communal revolution in Paris would result a program demanding the universalization of property." The report

demanded that the proletariat should separate itself completely from the bourgeoisie from whom it could expect only
"shooting and deportation," and that it should form a labor
party and prepare for the accession of the Fourth Estate.[167]

Thus the revolutionary collectivist doctrine was spreading among the workers. It was combating the theory that
the labor problem could be attacked through cooperation.
Nourished by arrest and persecution, and disseminated
through the platform and the press, it won a victory over
its rival at the third labor congress held in Marseilles in
1879.

5. The Socialist Labor Congress of Marseilles, 1879

The organizing committee of the congress was appointed
during the excitement which accompanied the trial of
Guesde and of his associates. Its first circular appeared in
February, 1879. From it one could see that the committee
was more than favorably disposed to modern socialism.
"The bourgeoisie," it said, "possesses the materials, the
instruments of labor—the productive utilities of which we,
workers and proletarians, are regularly despoiled. Propped
on a frightful militarism, on senseless stockjobbing . . . ,
on an immoral system which an erroneous science, political
economy, aspires to justify, it [the bourgeoisie] makes the
precious independence of men more and more impossible." [168]
It was decided to open the congress not only to syndicats,
but also to the clubs for social study, many of which had
been organized since 1878 under the stimulus of socialists.
In order to overcome the influence of the syndicats and syndical chambers, most of which were wedded to cooperation,
it was decided to give representation to the unorganized
workers. This meant that socialists were usually delegated

as the representatives of this disunited mass. It was also agreed to place on the calendar five questions which the two previous congresses had omitted: the wage system, property, taxation and income, free trade and protection, and the social question.[169] The report and the program as well as the banners and decorations foretold that a new spirit would prevail during the sessions. On the walls of the hall there appeared such slogans as: "Liberty, Equality, Solidarity"; "No rights without duties, no duties without rights"; "The land to the peasant, the tool to the worker, labor for all." [170]

The new name adopted by the congress was symbolic of the resolutions it would pass. On a motion from Jean Lombard, secretary of the organizing committee, the congress called itself "The Socialist Labor Congress of France." [171] This worker and littérateur of Marseilles was most active in organizing the congress.[172] He had been in correspondence with Malon to whose review he contributed, and had been at the Lyons Congress where he spoke for the independent political action of the workers.[173] In his inaugural report at the Marseilles Congress his socialism was even more pronounced. "There exists," he said, "a doctrine which, under the name of socialism, tends to continue the revolutionary tradition and to place society on rational and scientific bases. This doctrine, embraced by millions of human beings of all classes, chiefly by the proletariat, brought about the labor movements of 1831, 1848 and 1871. At present, it stirs the spirit, rouses the conscience and stands up with its anti-authoritarian negations and with its scientific and socialist affirmations against the old world, the old theories and the old ideas. We demand the overthrow of the economic structure by which the producers have been burdened through a thousand centuries of poverty. We desire the end of human suffering, the equality of all beings, freedom for all." He said that the socialists aimed to establish a society in which the workers were the ruling class. To attain this aim, he advocated the formation of a labor party "distinct from all other political parties." [174]

The congress was opened on October 20th, and the delegates listened to reports on the condition of the labor organizations in the various towns. Three days later a discussion took place on the syndical chambers. Ernest Roche, who had come to the congress fresh from his victorious campaign in favor of Blanqui, rose to say that the workers had nothing to expect from the bourgeoisie, and were not to let themselves be intimidated by it. They were to take the offensive. "The syndical chambers have only one rôle to play: to be the hotbed of the revolutionary idea." [175] Finance, the positivist, opposed the collectivists as he had opposed the advocates of cooperation. It was useless to speak of the new society, he contended, without admitting that it was necessary to have "a long period of socialist education," in order to permit the infiltration of the new doctrine. The syndical chambers were, therefore, to concern themselves first with such problems as the increase of wages, the relations between the workers and their employers and the reduction of the working day. "Of what use would it be to declare war," he said, "if the workers were not prepared, and especially if they did not know what to do on the day following the victory?" [176] Eugène Fournière, a young man of twenty-one, who represented the group which had published the *Egalité,* combated those who reserved for the syndicats a peaceful rôle. Like

Ernest Roche, he maintained that the syndical chambers should be centers of propaganda, "in order to cause the revolution in ideas which must precede the social revolution." [177] The resolution voted by the congress stated that the syndicats were to organize "lectures to acquaint the poorer classes with the just claims of the working class," and "to study in a practical way the program of the future congresses." [178] The syndicat was to be an agent of socialist propaganda.

The positivists and the collectivists found themselves in agreement in their opposition to cooperation. The cooperators were outvoted, and the following resolution was adopted:

"Whereas it appears from the speeches of the various speakers

"(1) That the worker cannot balance his budget with his wages;

"(2) That, since any saving is absolutely impossible, he cannot, through repurchase, attain his social aim—the possession of the instruments of labor, whose value is more than 150 billions;

"(3) That the producers' or consumers' cooperative societies can ameliorate the lot of only a small number of privileged persons, and only in a limited proportion;

"The congress declares that these societies can in no way be considered a sufficiently effective means of emancipating the proletariat; however, they can be useful agents of propaganda to spread collectivist and revolutionary ideas." [179]

During the debate on the wage system, Fauche, a delegate from Paris, and Jean Lombard from Marseilles, repeated the arguments developed by Guesde in his pamphlet,

145

La loi des salaires et ses conséquences. The iron law of wages prevented any improvement of the condition of the workers. The remedy lay only in the collective ownership of the means of production. The worker would then receive not a minimum of subsistence but the entire product of his labor.[180] The resolution passed by the congress embodied the theories of the collectivists. It said:

"Whereas the wage system, which represents progress over serfdom and slavery, is above all a progress for the wealthy whose capital has become more productive under the system of free labor . . . ;

"Whereas there is no relation between the remuneration of labor and the product of this labor, since the production of the worker can be increased a hundredfold by such new discoveries as the machines . . . without improving the condition of the workers, and since the wage of the worker is not the price of what he produces, but that which permits him to live and to reproduce;

"Whereas this wage will fall below the necessary sum if he finds a means of remuneration in addition to his labor; or if, without injuring the interests of the capitalists, the surplus of hands causes the population to decrease, on account of its poverty, to the number indispensable to industry;

"For these reasons, no serious amelioration can be effected in the condition of the proletariat without a complete transformation of society, that is to say, without the abolition of the wage system itself."

The wage system, the resolution continued, was inherent in a society which was divided into two classes. It would be destroyed only when the workers received the full product of their labor, that is, when capital, "ceasing to be individual," became "collective, impersonal and inalienable." [181]

On the question of property, Finance again separated himself from the collectivists. He defended individual ownership as "necessary to the independence and dignity of the citizen, necessary to the march of human progress." Impersonal or collective ownership would lead to tyranny and to injustice. "The individual owner," he said, "can still be accessible to pity, to justice and to shame; the corporate owner is without feeling and without remorse." The collectivist system would result "in the most complete negation of the independence of the individual"; it would mean the oppression of the minority by the majority, the tyranny of the state. The workers' condition, he said, would improve not through collective ownership, but through "encyclopedic education and human perfectibility." [182] To this the collectivists answered that without collective ownership no real education and no individual freedom were possible. The question of property would be solved only when the workers were "in possession of the land, machines, buildings, instruments of labor, capital, etc." [183] The resolution, adopted by the congress, was favorable to the collectivists. [184]

The congress not only declared itself in favor of the collectivist ideal, but also determined to organize the proletariat on a class basis and to separate it from the bourgeoisie. Consequently it voted for the formation of a socialist party. This will be the subject of a new chapter.

The congress came to a close on October 31st. As its resolutions indicated, it was a victory for the revolutionists. Leadership in the organized labor movement was passing from the hands of the cooperators to those of the collectivists.

In summary it may be said that during the three years intervening between the Congress of Paris in 1876 and the Congress of Marseilles in 1879 important events took place which were causing a change in the attitude of organized labor. Marxian socialism was slowly making its entry into France. Guesde was clarifying his ideas after his return from exile, and together with a number of young students was conducting an agitation among the workers. Their attempt to hold an international congress in the face of the government's prohibition was deemed an act of heroism and self-sacrifice by workers and intellectuals. That, and Guesde's defense of himself and of his arrested associates, aroused discussion of the revolutionary socialist doctrines among the workers, and won the sympathy of many of them. Between 1877 and 1879, a number of newspapers were founded to disseminate the new ideas. The *Egalité,* edited by bourgeois intellectuals, discussed socialist theory, while the *Prolétaire,* which was directed by workingmen, dealt essentially with current topics. *La Révolution Française,* published in Paris, *Le Socialisme Progressif* and *Le Révolté,* appearing in Switzerland but also read in France, helped to stimulate the revolutionary and socialist movement which Guesde and his friends were endeavoring to spread from the platform and by means of the social study clubs.

During this agitation the change in the political situation left the syndicats free to concern themselves with their own labor problems. The republic became secure after January, 1879, and the political question which had been overshadowing the economic demands of the workers was removed. The workers, left exposed to the influences of the revolutionists, were being slowly won over, particularly since the republic, which they had hoped would show solicitude for their economic difficulties, did not heed their complaints. And producers' cooperation, by means of which the labor leaders after the Commune were aiming to lead the workers to their emancipation, was not developing. In fact, several societies formed after 1873 did not receive the hoped-for support, and failed.[185] Socialism which had not been tried seemed alluring. The contentions of its leaders that nothing could be expected either from the bourgeoisie or from cooperation, that the solution of society's problems would spring only from collective ownership, convinced some workers and intellectuals. The Congress of Marseilles discarded cooperation for collectivism, and voted for the organization of a socialist party.

The congress was naturally condemned by the conservatives. The *Economiste Français* called the revolutionists a "handful of ignorant, presumptuous and rancorous demagogues who call themselves 'the socialist democracy.' " [186] The *Journal des Débats* referred to the delegates as "infuriated adversaries," "madmen" and "fanatical sectarians who in very good faith fancy that they have discovered an incomparable system of social organization." [187] Paul Leroy-Beaulieu said that had the delegates obtained precise information about the fundamental principles of cooperation, instead of talking about equality, they would perhaps have hastened the solution of the social question. While the congress did not frighten him, it did not leave him with "a lofty idea of the reforming capacity of the delegates." [188]

Socialists and anarchists were elated over the outcome of the congress. A. Le Roy, a contributor to the *Prolétaire,*

149

claimed that through its resolutions the congress had regained "all the ground which had been lost after the crushing of the Commune and the terrifying reaction which followed it." [189] Another writer of the same labor and socialist organ said that by its vote on collective ownership "this parliament of labor has done in twelve days for the cause of the proletariat more than all the more or less disguised agents of the capitalist tribe in twelve centuries." [190] And Guesde wrote that "this time the geese of the capitalist class are fully justified in their cries of alarm." [191] The anarchists hailed the decision of the congress in favor of collective ownership of the land and of the instruments of production, and praised its rejection of peaceful methods. But they maintained that the workers would waste their strength and resources "in futile electoral struggles." In order to attract voters, "the workers would be forced to be silent on expropriation." [192] The anarchists were to be disappointed. Several months later, Guesde returned from London with a program for the socialist party organized by the Marseilles Congress.

CHAPTER IV

THE PARTY AND ITS PROGRAM

1. The formation of the party

The separate representation of the proletariat as a class in parliament had been demanded in France long before the Marseilles Congress. It was the principal theme of the composers of the Manifesto of the Sixty of 1864,[1] who saw in labor candidates a means of presenting labor's demands before the legislative body. The first Labor Congress of Paris took up the theme of the labor movement of the Second Empire. Like the labor leaders during that period, the delegates of the Labor Congress urged the necessity of sending labor candidates to the legislature in order to present labor's demands, and to win "the political liberties necessary for the amelioration of our lot." And like their predecessors in the time of the Second Empire, these same delegates showed no open defiance of the bourgeoisie, used no language that might be interpreted as revolutionary. "Let us show the governing classes," read the proposal of the committee on the separate representation of the proletariat, "that we can find among us citizens who are capable of defending in parliament, with voice or with pen, the interests of the workers, just as they could defend with arms, if need be, the republic if it were in peril and the country if it were in danger."[2] The Congress of Lyons, the second labor congress, heard many expressions in favor of the separation of the proletariat from the bourgeoisie,[3] and finally voted that:

"Whereas the direct representation of the proletariat in parliament is almost universally considered as one of the most effective mediums for our just demands . . . and will enable us to present the *cahiers* of the proletariat;

"Whereas, moreover, the results once gained, however trivial they may be, will be . . . a great step toward the emancipation for which we are striving;

"The congress affirms the principle of the direct representation of the proletariat in parliament." [4]

The moderate resolutions of the first two labor congresses did not disturb the middle class. The delegates demanded separate representation, but did not express the desire to form a labor party. So long as labor candidates were nominated in certain districts and were sponsored by local committees, there was nothing to fear, for those committees were neither guided by a definite program, nor controlled by a larger organization striving to wrest political power from the hands of the middle class. Consequently, the resolutions of the first two congresses were commended by the bourgeoisie for their wisdom. But the reaction to the third congress, that is, the Marseilles Congress, it has been shown, was anything but friendly. And one of the principal reasons was that this congress voted to organize a socialist party, distinct from all other political parties.

The socialists in their campaigns of propaganda were harping on the necessity of grouping the proletariat into a political party and of participating in elections on a distinct class basis. They were urging the workers to throw off the influence which republicans and radical republicans had over them. Furthermore, socialist leaders were receiving encouragement from their German comrades who had succeeded in 1875 in organizing the Social Democratic Party which polled in the election of 1877 almost 500,000 votes and won twelve seats in the Reichstag. Karl Hirsch, a student of Marxian socialism, who enjoyed the personal confidence of Marx, had often been in the company of Guesde, had helped to clarify the latter's ideas and had contributed articles on scientific socialism to the first *Egalité*.[5] The French socialists were told that they had nothing to expect from the republicans and radical republicans who, "without exception, had behaved in a rascally manner toward the Commune." Instead, they were advised to draw away further to the Left and form an independent political organization.[6]

This the Marseilles Congress resolved to do. The committee reporting on the question expressed itself frankly and boldly. In its resolution, adopted by the congress, it demanded that "before everything else, the proletariat should separate itself completely from the bourgeoisie . . . intellectually, juridically, politically and economically." The resolution, moreover, defined the duties of the socialist representative. He "should participate in all the demonstrations in which he will be able to defend the interests and rights of the proletariat. He should demand the liberties necessary for the reforms which the labor party has inscribed in its program, and should abstain from any form of compromise with the [other] political parties represented in the various elected bodies of the country." [7]

While it was generally agreed that it was necessary to form a political party, the various elements of the congress differed on its composition. The moderates desired to have it composed exclusively of syndical chambers. Others proposed an organization of three distinct federations: the syndical chambers, the cooperative societies and the socialist clubs. The socialists wanted neither the one nor the other, for the adoption of the first plan would check their influence within the party; and if the second plan were followed, the socialist federation would be outvoted by the other two which were actuated by common ideas. Consequently, the socialists demanded an organization which, while it retained the federative ideas cherished by many, would fuse the labor and socialist groups of a locality into one integrated unit. They won.[8]

The Marseilles Congress called its new political creation the Federation of the Party of Socialist Workingmen of France. As may be gathered from its name, the party was founded on the basis of the federative principle. France was mapped out into six geographical regions: Paris or the Center, Lyons or the East, Marseilles or the South, Bordeaux or the West, Lille or the North and Algiers or Algeria. Each region was to organize its own party-federation which was to hold its own regional congresses and administer its own affairs. The annual national congress of the party was to appoint a general executive committee of nineteen members whose duty it was to execute the resolutions of the congress.[9]

After the Congress of Marseilles, meetings were held in five of the six regions to form party-federations. The Federative Union of the Center (Union fédérative du Centre) with Paris as its capital, organized in March, 1880,[10] faithfully reflected the decisions of the Marseilles Congress. Under the influence of the *Egalité* group, the federation published its statutes in June of the same year,[11] and, at its congress held in July, 1880, adopted the principle of the collective ownership of the means of production.[12] The Federation of the East with Lyons as its capital, though not as completely centralized as the Parisian Federation, decided on February 29, 1880, to adhere to the labor party "on the bases indicated by the Congress of Marseilles." At its congress held in July, the federation accepted the revolutionary collectivist principles.[13] On the other hand, the Federation of the South, organized in April, 1880, was from the very beginning under the influence of anarchists.[14] In July of the same year, it rejected the use of the ballot for the spread of propaganda.[15] The Federation of the West, founded at about the same time as the Federation of the South, held its first congress in June. A majority of the delegates objected to the words "revolutionary socialist," and passed resolutions of a purely reformist nature, strongly resembling the demands of the first two labor congresses.[16] A similarly reformist trend was observed in the Federation of the North, which had been organized in April. At a congress held four months later, the federation rejected the terms "class struggle" and "socialization of the means of production," and adopted a moderate program which indicated a strong attachment to producers' cooperation.[17] During the early and critical period in the life of the party, no party-federation was created in Algeria. Thus the socialists succeeded in gaining the support of only two of the five organized party-federations.

2. The formation of the program

The young socialist party was in danger of being stillborn. On the one hand, the revolutionary language of socialists and anarchists frightened away many; on the other hand, the cooperative ideals had too strong a grip on many of the workers to be weakened by the socialist resolutions passed at Marseilles. It seemed that the party would be divided into four fragments: the cooperators, the social reformers, the collectivists and the anarchists.[18] Was the enthusiasm of the workers, awakened by the electoral campaign in favor of Blanqui, to be permitted to die down? Were the local labor groups and federations which had embraced modern socialism to be left to their own initiative to combat the opposing doctrines? Socialist leaders felt the need of a program which would unite socialists under a single emblem, rally the workers to the socialist doctrine, wean them from the radicals and serve as a platform during the coming elections. "A new program is like a banner that is hoisted before the eyes of all," wrote Engels.[19] And such a banner the French socialists were planning to raise before the French workers.

It is interesting to note that the period between the organization of the socialist federations and the writing of the socialist program witnessed a further spread of modern socialist ideas in France. In January, 1880, there was founded the first *Revue Socialiste* which carried on a campaign in favor of modern socialism. In its numbers appeared articles by Lafargue, Malon, Kautsky, Guesde and de Paepe, a part of Engels' answer to Dührung, under the title, *Socialism, Utopian and Scientific*,[20] and a questionnaire on labor conditions drawn up by Marx and widely circulated among labor organizations and socialist clubs.[21] During the same month which saw the birth of the *Revue Socialiste*, Guesde revived the *Egalité* to which Lafargue was one of the main contributors. In its columns the editors analyzed the theories of historical materialism and of surplus value, made frequent reference to the names of Marx and Engels, and in a clear and simple style, marked with a touch of satire, were making Marxian socialism palatable to the reader.[22] They also reprinted the major part of Marx's *Poverty of Philosophy*.

At the same time French socialist literature was being enriched by new publications. In 1879 Guesde wrote his famous propaganda pamphlet, *Collectivism and Revolution*, and Malon published his *History of Socialism*, showing by a rich documentation the progress of socialist thought from the earliest times to his own day, and devoting numerous pages to long excerpts from the works of Marx, Engels and Lassalle.[23] In 1880 there appeared Malon's translation of Lassalle's *Capital and Labor* and of Schäffle's *Quintessence of Socialism*, both of which were rendered into French at the request of a rich German socialist in order to spread the socialist doctrine in France.[24] In the same year, Lafargue's translation of Engels' *Socialism, Utopian and Scientific* was published as a pamphlet by the *Revue Socialiste*. "The effect in France was enormous," wrote Engels to Sorge. "People are too lazy to read thick books like *Capital;* the influence of a thin pamphlet is so much quicker." [25] The infiltration and spread of Marxian doctrine was preparing the way for the socialist program which Guesde brought with him from London.

To write this program Guesde, after having reached an understanding with several French socialist leaders, crossed the Channel to consult with Marx and Engels. Malon wished to be present during the discussions, but he received no invitation from Marx.[26] And Brousse, who was then living in London and shedding his anarchist views, would also have liked to attend. But Guesde objected; and his former friend and later enemy did not participate in the framing of the program.[27] In the presence of Engels, Guesde and Lafargue, Marx dictated the preamble of which Engels gave a succinct summary in a letter to Bernstein:

"The worker is free only when he is the owner of his own instruments of labor. This ownership can assume either the individual or the collective form. Since individual ownership is being abolished from day to day through economic development, there remains only the form of common ownership, etc." [28]

The remaining parts of the program were then discussed. A disagreement arose between Guesde and Marx over the article demanding a legal minimum wage, which was in direct contradiction with Guesde's theory of the iron law of wages, but which Guesde deemed important in order to attract the French workers. Marx objected to the article and said: "If the French proletariat is still so childish as to need such bait, then *is it not worth while drawing up any program whatever.*" [29] But Guesde was determined, and the article remained. Nevertheless, Marx thought that the program was a great step forward, for he believed that by it he "pulled down the French workers from their nebulous phraseology to the basis of reality." [30]

Guesde returned to Paris with the program to have it adopted by the different groups and by the French socialist party. For this purpose the support of Malon, who was still residing abroad, was enlisted. In a letter addressed to him by Lafargue he was made acquainted with the document. "There is the program on which Marx, Engels, Guesde and I have collaborated," wrote Lafargue from London. "Brousse knows it and approves of it. Your task is to examine it and to have it accepted. Guesde contends that it is preferable that you should present it as your own work." [31] Guesde knew that the program would have a better chance of being accepted if it were known that it emanated from a Frenchman rather than from a German. Malon examined the document and, as he later said, "found the draft too short." But he hoped that it would be completed by the groups during their discussions, and that it would be preceded by a manifesto on the history and philosophy of modern socialism and on economic conditions in France.[32] When he learned that socialist leaders like Lombard, Prudent-Dervillers, Achille Le Roy and Dumay had accepted the program, he began to use his influence in its favor. However, Malon later said that he did not present the program as his own work, "but as the result of a collective elaboration achieved with the cooperation of Marx, Engels, Guesde, Lafargue, Dervillers, Dumay and Lombard." [33] Within a short time more than fifty syndicats and about thirty socialist study groups adopted it,[34] and it was printed in the three chief socialist organs of France.[35]

The program read as follows:

"Whereas the emancipation of the producing class is that of all human beings, without any distinction in sex or race;

"Whereas the producers can be free only when they are in possession of the means of production (land, factories, ships, banks, credit, etc.);

"Whereas there are only two forms under which the means of production can belong to them:

"1. The individual form, which has never prevailed

generally, and which is being more and more eliminated by the advance of industry;

"2. The collective form whose material and intellectual elements are being constituted through the very development of the capitalist class;

"Whereas this collective form can issue only from the revolutionary activity of the producing class—or proletariat—organized into a distinct political party;

"And whereas such an organization must be sought for by all the means which are at the command of the proletariat, including universal suffrage, thus transformed from the instrument of dupery, which it has been, into an instrument of emancipation;

"The French socialist workers, stating that the aim of their efforts in the economic sphere is the return to society of all the means of production, have decided, as a means of organization and struggle, to participate in the elections with the following minimum program:"

The program then enumerated political and economic demands which were outgrowths of conditions in France after the Commune. The political demands were: the abolition of all laws hindering the press, assembly and combination, and particularly of the law against the International Association of Workers; the abolition of the *livret* and of all articles in the Code which kept the worker in an inferior position; the suppression of the religious budget and the nationalization of the property of the religious orders; the general arming of the people; the control of the administration and of the police by the commune.

The list of economic demands was somewhat longer. It contained the following: a six-day week and an eight-hour day for adults; the prohibiton of the labor of children under fourteen and a six-hour day for those from fourteen to eighteen; a minimum wage law; equal pay for men and women; a scientific and technological training for all children; full control by the workers of the administration of their insurance funds; the responsibility of the employer in case of accident; workers' participation in the regulation of the shop; the termination of the employers' right to fine their workers; the abrogation of all contracts which alienated public property, and the exploitation of the factories of the state by the workers employed therein; the abolition of all indirect taxes, and the imposition of graduated income and inheritance taxes.

This electoral minimum program was evaluated by the socialist press in various ways. Guesde's paper greeted it as "the natural and necessary cap-stone of the revolutionary collectivist campaign begun in 1877 by the first *Egalité*." The program not only stated the aim, but also provided for the organization of the force necessary to realize it. It would help separate the workers from the "bourgeois politicians," and by proving that it was impossible to abolish exploitation under the existing economic order, it would "liberate them from their last illusions about reforms and convince them of the impossibility of dispensing with a workers' 1789." [36] In the columns of the *Prolétaire*, André-Gély urged the workers to accept the minimum program and to organize apart from the radicals,[37] and Achille Le Roy saw in the program "an important step toward the future." But the latter also saw its deficiencies. He thought that a few additional articles should be added and that the preamble should be less scientific, because, as he said, "the masses are still little versed in the social sciences." [38] Malon, writing from abroad, was less critical of the document. In a letter to Le Roy he said that the draft fulfilled, at least in a general way, the principles proclaimed by the Congress of Marseilles, and as such deserved to be defended before the various groups. To the objection that the preamble was "too scientific," Malon answered that that fault was due to the "admirable conciseness" of the document. However, he assured his friend that the scientific rigidity of the language would be tempered and mollified by the manifesto on the evolution of French socialist thought, which he hoped to place at the head of the program.[39] In a more detailed analysis, published more than two weeks later, Malon said little about the preamble, for he again placed his hope in the manifesto which would "develop the spirit of the program." Among the reforms demanded, he pointed to the two most important: the reduction of the working-day and the conquest of the municipalities. The latter, he said, would not only endow socialists with administrative experience, but would also lead to the introduction of municipal reforms which, if they were multiplied and extended, would mean a revolution, but without bloodshed.[40]

3. *The adoption of the Marxian program*

The Marxian minimum program, elaborated in London and commented on in France, found adherents in labor and socialist circles. In July, 1880, it was submitted to a regional congress of the Federation of the Center, where it was warmly opposed by the anarchists. It was at this congress that a separation was effected in France between socialism and anarchism.

The struggle between the two opposing doctrines was no novelty. The First International had witnessed the same struggle and had proved unable to bear the strain. After the Hague Congress, the anarchist wing founded its own international organization which held its congresses' up to 1877.[41] Five years after the split at the Hague Congress, a handful of socialists and anarchists again battled against one another at the Universal Socialist Congress of Ghent. Again a resolution was adopted, favoring the political action of the proletariat, and again the anarchists were defeated.[42] But this time, in 1877, they were without a forceful leader and without a following. The Federation of the Jura, which had been the center of the anarchist movement, was disintegrating, and its chief publication, the *Bulletin de la fédération jurassienne*, ceased to appear six months after the Congress of Ghent. "Of the seven delegates, all members of the Jura Federation, who had visited Verviers and Ghent as representatives of France, Italy, Germany, Russia and the Jura," wrote Guillaume, "only Brousse and I resumed our places in the ranks of the Jura socialists. As far as the five others were concerned, a chapter in their existence had closed."[43] The various anarchist leaders left for different countries, and some even repudiated their anarchist faith.

The anarchist strength in France was almost negligible after the congress of 1877. In Paris in 1878 there were not twenty anarchists "to carry on the movement," according to Kropotkin, "not two hundred openly to support it. At the first commemoration of the Commune, in March, 1878," continued the anarchist theorist, "we surely were not two hundred."[44] Outside of Paris, their

163

number was not much greater. Yet, these few rebels carried on an active agitation for abstention from politics and for collectivism in the means of production. Between 1876 and 1880 several pamphlets appeared, urging citizens to refrain from voting.[45] "Declare a strike of the voters," said a pamphlet of 1880. "Universal suffrage," it continued, "has been and still is for the bourgeoisie only the means of making the exploited sanction the social privileges." [46] At the Congress of Lyons, an anarchist, Ballivet, not only joined Dupire on the collectivist amendment presented at the congress, but also introduced one in which he rejected "the principle of the direct representation of the proletariat in parliament as ineffective in solving the social problem." [47]

Beginning in 1879, the anarchist movement took on new life. In that year Kropotkin founded *Le Révolté*, which was smuggled into France,[48] and in the same year he presented at an anarchist congress his program of anarchist communism, according to which there was to be not only the collective ownership of the means of production, but also complete communism in the enjoyment of the articles of consumption.[49] In that year, also, anarchists were beginning to come out into the open. During 1879 and 1880, Paris, Lyons and several other towns in France were witnessing an agitation which reacted on anarchists. The fight for full amnesty and the return of many Communards, the labor congresses, the tireless activity of the *Egalité* group and the open meetings and discussions—this open expenditure of energy for the working class affected the anarchists who, too, wished to play their rôle among the discontented. Two anarchist groups were founded, where men like Emile Gautier and Jean Grave held sharp discussions with Guesdists and Blanquists.[50]

Indeed, anarchists and socialists were at this time (*i.e.* 1879) mingling freely and even belonged to the same groups. The socialists, even those of the *Egalité* group in which Guesde was the dominant figure, had not yet defined their ideas, and used language which at times made it difficult to distinguish them from anarchists. Socialists and anarchists fought together at the Marseilles Congress against mutualists, reformists and positivists, and appeared on the same platform to attack the existing economic order. "We were then [*i.e.* at the time of the Marseilles Congress] separated from the anarchists by a very thin, purely ideal or rather verbal distinction," recalled Fournière many years later. "At the Congress of Marseilles I received from their best qualified representatives, particularly Elisée Reclus and Kropotkin, the fraternal rebukes which we have seen the *Libertaire* address during these days to Gustave Hervé.[51] Even in the *Egalité* group there were anarchists up to and during 1880: Jeallot, Maria, Jean Grave, superintending with me the making of the wrappers, the folding and forwarding of the paper of which I was the manager."[52] The anarchists did not completely separate themselves from the socialists until it was decided by the regional congress of the Federation of the Center, held in July, 1880, to adopt the minimum program which Guesde had brought from London.

The year 1880 was particularly favorable for anarchist propagandists. A general amnesty, voted by the Chamber and the Senate, was supported even by Gambetta, who had been opposed to it six months earlier, but who was compelled to assent to it by popular demand, expressed in the election of a Communard to the municipal council from the very district he represented. The exiled and imprisoned were returning to France in large numbers, and among them the anarchists were attempting to spread their doctrines.[53] In addition to *Le Révolté,* which had a large number of readers in France, there were founded *Le Droit Social* in Lyons and *La Révolution Sociale* in Paris—the latter with secret funds from the Prefecture of Police.[54]

Anarchism found its adherents in countries where the development of capitalism was backward, where the prevailing handicraft system bred the individualism on which anarchism fed. Consequently, it found followers in Italy, Spain, Switzerland and France. In the last country, it was also favored by the utopian dreams of early socialists, and by a long revolutionary history which offered examples of the successful use of the *coup de force* and of insurrection.[55] It was a Frenchman, Proudhon, who was the first to use the word anarchy to describe a state of society without government,[56] and it was his ideas that inspired the French members of the First International. The strongly centralized French state also helped to breed its opposite, federalism, among those who dreamed of individual liberty.

The anarchists were not a party, united either by common tactics, or for that matter, by a common aim. Among them were anarchist communists, anarchist collectivists, autonomists and mutualists. Of all the anarchist schools, the best known were the anarchist communists, and it is to them that our attention will be directed.

Society was to be freed from the yoke of government and private property, they said. On the day after the revolution, the state and all its organs of oppression would be abolished. They would be replaced by the producers, freely organized "from the simple to the complex, according to mutual needs and tendencies." [57] Government, the anarchist communists contended, was not needed in education, in defense or in any human activity. To perform these vital social functions, free federations of individuals would spring up to take the place of the modern state. [58] Private property and the authority of the capitalist would also be abolished, and the producer would be emancipated from the yoke of capital. Production would be carried on in common, each producing according to his capacity and consuming according to his needs.

Not man, but his milieu, would be changed with the revolution. In place of the society based on individualism and the struggle for existence, man would be in a society "based on the solidarity of interests," where he would be assured of the satisfaction of all his needs, having only to supply his share of labor in return. Man was not egoistic, but generous and capable of self-sacrifice and of self-denial. His faults were not innate; they were the product of a bad education and of a "corrupt society." Under a system of society where work was attractive, the individual would perform his job with joy, for work would be "a relaxation." [59] "To act, to work," wrote Kropotkin, "has become a need for the vast majority of mankind." [60]

The revolution, said the anarchist communists, would also lead to a change in conceptions of morality, to "emancipation from religious morality" and to the evolution of a "free morality without compulsion or authority, developing itself from social life and becoming habitual." [61] Like the eighteenth-century philosophers, these

167

anarchists believed that nature was the best moral guide. Mankind was perfect, and all that was necessary was to study it, compare one's own artificial life with it, and discard the unnecessary garments of law, authority, religion and capitalism. Nature was good, true, moral, beautiful, but it was corrupted by institutions. Remove these institutions to permit the noble sentiments of man to express themselves, and, under the stimulus of favorable conditions, they would be directed toward mutual aid. "Let us create circumstances," said Kropotkin, " in which man shall not be led to deceive or exploit others, and then by the very force of things the moral level of humanity will rise to a height hitherto unknown. Men are certainly not to be moralized by teaching them a moral catechism: tribunals and prisons do not diminish vice; they pour it over society in floods. Men are to be moralized only by placing them in a position which shall contribute to develop in them those habits which are social, and to weaken those which are not so." [62]   If the anarchists, like the Marxists, believed in the imminence of the revolution, they were opposed to the seizure by the proletarian state of all the means of production and distribution. This would lead, they said, to despotism which they hated in any form. Against state control the anarchist communists placed the free federations of groups for particular needs, federations which would dissolve when those needs had been satisfied. [63]

The revolution once begun, the anarchists would utilize it for the realization of their idea. Profiting by the disorganization of the machinery of the state, they would not proceed to set up the dictatorship of the proletariat, for that would be only another form of government—and revolution was "precisely the opposite, the very negation of government"—[64] but they would transform the existing property relations by expropriating the owners of all the means of production, including land, houses, etc., and by organizing production and consumption in common in each group and commune. The introduction of collectivism in any one place would be an instrument for the propaganda of the idea and the most powerful motor in those localities where the worker was still backward. For the success of the revolution, the revolutionary period would have to continue many years "in order that the propaganda of the new ideas should not be limited to the large intellectual centers, but should penetrate into the most isolated hamlets, . . . and in order that the new ideas should have time to receive a subsequent development necessary to the real progress of humanity." [65] "The struggle will be long and painful," they said. "It will end only with the destruction of the last vestige of private property and of the last vestige of authority on earth." [66]

Just how this revolutionary period could be maintained without a directive force, the anarchists did not say. They merely maintained that they would prevent the creation of any new government, and keep alive the revolutionary spirit of the people who would, of their own initiative, and without any dictatorship, create the new social order. Government would be of no use for the demolishing of old institutions and for the working out of the new social organization. "The economic change which will result from the social revolution will be so immense and so profound," wrote Kropotkin, "it must so change all the relations based to-day on property and exchange, that it is impossible for one or any individual to elaborate the different social forms which must spring up in the society of the future. This elaboration of new social forms can only be made by the collective work of the masses. To satisfy the immense variety of conditions and needs which will spring up as soon as private property shall be abolished, it is necessary to have the collective suppleness of mind of the whole people. Any authority external to it will only be an obstacle, and beside that a source of discord and hatred." [67]

Any external directive force, said the anarchist communists, would be superfluous, either to regulate production or to supervise consumption. The purpose of production was to supply social needs. The individual knew his needs; and since the average person lived in some group, it would not be difficult, they said, to determine those needs. The commune would simply tally the needs of the groups or families living within its confines. The needs would then be made known to the respective branches of production, which would proceed to supply them. No intervention of any authority would be necessary, for if any individuals or groups refused to furnish their products, there could always be found others to supply them. "A task would have to be very unpleasant not to rally anyone to execute it." [68]

Thus, while socialists urged the capture of the bourgeois state in order to destroy it, and to institute the dictatorship of the proletariat or the proletarian state, anarchist communists condemned any form of authority after the revolution. Class dictatorship, they said, was a meaningless phrase, "pompous, high-sounding, sonorous words," a means of organizing the proletariat into "a blind, unconscious mass, . . . and of habituating it to act only according to the given order." [69] A social revolution through the dictatorship of a single man or group was impossible, for it would mean the setting up of a government, and revolution and government were incompatible. The anarchist communists taught that if, after overthrowing the existing government, they prevented the establishment of any other, even of a revolutionary government, the people, moved by their instinctive love of freedom, would establish the anarchist society. The socialists depended on an organized industrial proletariat born out of capitalistic development to introduce the socialist order; the anarchist communists looked to the small peasant and to the individual in the handicraft system of production. The philosophy of the former implied organization and control from a center; that of the latter, free agreement, *laissez-faire* carried to the extreme. The socialists' point of departure was the social organism, society. They said that without it the individual was nothing, that he was a product of his group, and that he had no personality outside of it. The anarchist communists, on the other hand, made the individual the center of their thought, and concluded that society was dependent on him for its existence. "Society is not an organism existing by itself," wrote Jean Grave. "Its existence is not independent of the individuals who compose it; by itself it is nothing. Destroy the individuals and there is no longer any society. Let the association be dissolved, let the individuals become isolated, they will live badly, return to the state of savagery, but they will be able to continue to exist. Therefore society has a *raison d'être* only on condition that those who form part of it find in it a greater development of comfort and autonomy." [70]

Anarchist communists were also at variance with socialists on methods of propaganda. The latter believed that elections afforded an unusual opportunity to propagate their ideas. A program, they said, was necessary to rally the proletariat, to organize and to discipline it. More than that, there had to be a labor party, distinct from all other parties, to lead the proletariat and to prepare it to capture political power from the bourgeoisie. The former, the anarchist communists, had no such faith in the efficacy of elections to win sympathizers. Opposed to any disciplined organization, they put their trust in the individual form of propaganda. In addition to the spoken and the written word, whose revolutionary force they valued, the anarchist communists, particularly in the Eighties, also urged the use of the propaganda by deed, such as the throwing of bombs and insurrection. Since the revolution was not far off, and since the revolutionary elements would soon be called on to show their devotion to the cause of the proletariat, it was necessary to awaken the inert masses which still entertained "illusions on the morality and efficacy of legal methods." Nothing was as effective as a deed in spreading the spirit of revolt. A resolution of the International Anarchist Congress of London (1881) declared that the illegal method was "the only one leading to the revolution" and that it was, therefore, "necessary to have recourse to means which are in conformity with this aim. . . .

"Since the great mass of the rural workers still remains outside of the socialist revolutionary movement," continued the resolution, "it is absolutely essential to turn our efforts in this direction, bearing in mind that the most simple deed, directed against the existing institutions, speaks more convincingly to the masses than thousands of leaflets and streams of words, and that the propaganda by deed still has a greater importance in the country districts than in the towns." [71]

The revolutionary education of the masses could be effected not through ballots, but through bullets. The ballot, the anarchist communists said, was not a panacea or an instrument of emancipation as the Marxist minimum program described it, but "an odious instrument of domination, the greatest mystification of the century." [72]

A program was as useless as it was troublesome. It would only hamper the growth of the revolutionary spirit. Instead of destroying one another in disputes about articles and in excommunications, the anarchists were to "appeal to all those who want to destroy the present society." [73]

The number of anarchist adherents was not large,[74] but they attracted notice by their activity and violent language. The socialists considered them sufficiently dangerous to launch a campaign against them. On the platform and in the press, in the syndical chambers as well as in the study groups, the socialists endeavored to prove the soundness of their own program and the necessity of participating in elections. "Our impatience can no more hasten the revolution which is advancing on the old world," wrote Malon, "than our pacific protests can avert it. . . . Let us multiply, perfect, organize our forces, let us demand the greatest number of reforms. . . . Let us know how to profit by all possibilities, for all revolutions are not made by musket shots." [75] Social revolutions took a long time to prepare. They broke out when the historical circumstances and the economic conditions permitted, and they triumphed not only through courage and devotion, but also through organization and experience. "Three proletarian Saint Bartholomews in half a century," wrote Malon, "are enough for us to learn to replace sentimental by scientific politics." [76]   Political equality without social equality was "a lie," but the political struggle by means of the ballot and the economic struggle by means of the strike were powerful methods of hastening the victory of the proletariat. Malon strove to prove to the workers that the anarchist theory was unsound. "In the existing state of affairs," he wrote, "it is not a few hundred or even a few thousand men, determined to sacrifice their lives for the revolution, who can endanger the capitalist rule, armed with all the forces of the past. One class can be overthrown only by another class which is conscious of itself and which has for its mission a social transformation in harmony with the historical and economic tendencies of the epoch." [77]

Other editors of socialist organs were no less eager to counteract the influence of anarchist propaganda. The electoral struggle, said the socialists, disciplined the masses. During elections the class struggle became manifest and showed the proletariat its real enemies. [78] To interest the workers in the ballot and to draw them to the socialist program, Lafargue went so far as to show the advantages of conquering the municipalities, even though he and his co-Marxists were then convinced that the capture of the municipal governments could never lead to the emancipation of the workers. [79]

Guesde endeavored to prove that the use of dynamite was unnecessary in a country like France. If the nihilists of Russia resorted to it, it was because the Russian milieu called for it. "The social milieu," he said, "determines the methods of struggle just as the geological and climatic milieux determine the plant growth." The socialists did not fear the state as the anarchists did; hence, there was no need to run away from it. If the state was an organ of class domination it was the function of the proletariat to capture it and to destroy it. But this grand act could not be accomplished without a long, preliminary propaganda, and without a series of revolutionary struggles.[80] Non-participation in politics, reasoned the French Marxists, led to nothing, because it in no way crippled the electoral machine. People continued to be subject to laws made by deputies they chose. Since the French worker had the suffrage, since he had become habituated to the ballot, it was expedient and practical to urge him to use it on a class basis.[81] The Marxists devoted almost the entire second series of the *Egalité* to the struggle against anarchism, demonstrating the necessity of the political action of the proletariat organized into a political party with a definite socialist program.

It was over the Marxist minimum program, brought back by Guesde from London and discussed by the labor and study groups, that the fight between the anarchists and the socialists took place at the regional congress of the Federation of the Center, which met in July, 1880, four months after the organization of the federation, and only one month after the publication of its statutes.[82] Four elements were represented: the reformists, the Colinsists, the collectivists or scientific socialists, and the anarchists. Massard of the *Egalité* group read the minimum program, quoted above.[83] Received favorably by a number of speakers, it was attacked by the reformists and the anarchists. Drouet, who voiced the views of the former, and who was delegated by fifteen syndical chambers from Havre, declared that the workers he represented were most ardently attached to the republic, and "that they expected from it the

175

most complete realization of the reforms contained in principle in the Declaration of the Rights of Man and of the Citizen." He went on to say that the French workers were not yet sufficiently well organized to face the electoral struggle alone. Prudence, therefore, dictated that they should "unite with the various wings of the republican party." He then presented a moderate program which was very reminiscent of the demands made by the first two labor congresses.[84] Needless to say, Drouet's program was unfavorably received by the great majority of the delegates who had come to the congress to vote for the Marxist program. The delegate from Havre, finding himself in a hopeless minority, protested against the revolutionary tendencies of the congress, and withdrew. But before leaving, he said:

"You want us to follow you. No, a thousand times no! We believe we are aiding in the development of theories which are practical and which are in conformity with sound reason, while you ask us to help you realize absurd and sickly utopias." [85]

After the departure of Drouet, there followed the discussion on property. All favored the collective ownership of the means of production, and a resolution, analogous to the one adopted by the Congress of Marseilles, was passed.[86]

The struggle between the socialists and the anarchists occurred over the question of participation in politics. The former naturally stood for political action, the latter for abstention from politics. Jean Grave maintained the superiority of the anarchist methods. The socialists, he said, by demanding a legal minimum wage from the bourgeois state, were recognizing its right to exist. By urging the workers to vote, the socialists were helping to turn men into sheep. The workers would follow "the first phrase-mongers," and the revolution would have to be made again.

Grave defended the anarchist method of revolution by a small minority. "It is better," he said, "to have five thousand individuals who know what they want, who are prepared for any contingency, than to have one hundred thousand, not conscious [of their action], and always ready to fall under the influence of someone." It was illusory to expect anything from parliamentary propaganda, for, as he said, "neither the peasant nor the worker reads the official journal." The only policy to follow was to prove to the people that, instead of proclaiming a new government in time of a revolution, it was necessary to shoot the one who attempted to do so.[87]

The number of anarchists at the congress was too small to prevent the adoption of the Marxist minimum program. In the resolution calling for the acceptance of the program, the socialists said:

"Whereas the loss of the political liberties hinders the social education of the people and the economic emancipation of the proletariat;

"Whereas the proletariat, determined to make use of all means in order to gain its freedom, ought to profit by the liberties already won at the cost of the blood of the last three revolutions;

"And moreover, whereas political action is useful as a means of agitation . . . ;

"1. The social emancipation of the workers is inseparable from their political emancipation.

"2. Political abstention would be disastrous in its results.

"3. Candidates for all offices must remain the representatives of their class, and must make no alliance with any faction of the old, existing, political parties.

"4. Though it uses legal methods, the proletariat will never arrive at its emancipation peacefully. The social revolution through force remains the only possible, final solution.

"5. Participation in politics will always be secondary to the socialist movement and will serve it only as a means.

"6. While participating in the struggles of the different factions of the bourgeoisie in order to combat them indiscriminately, the proletariat will maintain its own distinct organization which is only the preliminary form of the society of the future."

After making a few more remarks about the necessity of separating the proletariat from the bourgeoisie and of organizing it into a political party, the congress accepted the Marxist minimum program with only a few slight modifications.[88]

The anarchists were definitely defeated, but their separation from the socialists was not final until they were ousted from the regional congress of Paris, held the following year (1881).[89] In the meantime, a temporary rapprochement was effected at the fourth national congress held at Havre in November, 1880, where the syndical chambers and the cooperatives reappeared to contest the influence of the collectivists.

4. The separation from mutualism

The reformist and cooperative elements were disquieted by the socialists who were gradually extending their domination over the labor organizations. The elaboration of a party program along revolutionary socialist lines, dictated by foreigners, was the signal for them to bestir themselves if they expected to save the syndicats from the control of the collectivists. At the regional congress of the Federation of the Center, held only four months previously, one of their number, as mentioned above, had given expression to his admiration for the French republican institutions, and had shown his contempt for revolutionary methods by withdrawing from the sessions.[90] Moreover, a general assembly of the syndical chambers of Havre had approved of his conduct by a large majority.[91] To dam the tide of collectivism, the moderates found themselves in a key position in 1880, for in November of that year the fourth national congress was scheduled to meet at Havre where their influence was strong. Naturally, the committee on organization consisted of their own men.

The reformists and advocates of cooperation were also befriended by the radical republicans whom the third national congress of Marseilles had somewhat upset by its organization of a socialist party. Republicans of the extreme Left, members of the Paris municipal council and of parliament, were open partisans of cooperation. Louis Blanc still entertained the hope that the union of producers' cooperative societies would lead to the general emancipation of labor,[92] and Clemenceau, who was becoming the recognized leader of the radicals, demanded that the government should help found consumers' and producers' cooperatives. The formation of a labor party with a socialist program made him and his friends fear lest they should gradually lose the support of the workers. To keep it, Clemenceau outlined his own program in a speech at Marseilles on October 29, 1880, in which he advocated "social justice." By this he meant not merely political, but also

179

social emancipation. The former without the latter "would be only a snare." It was the duty of the republic, he said, "to pursue the work of social reform inaugurated by the French Revolution whose principle was the creation of an egalitarian democracy." Besides the separation of church and state and the establishment of a national system of education, he demanded the freedom to organize, the creation of cooperative societies, the extension of credit, the abolition of the *livret*, the prohibition of child labor, the reduction of the working day and the participation of the workers in the exploitation of railroads, canals and mines. These reforms, Clemenceau asserted, would modify the existing conditions, and "facilitate a better distribution of wealth." [93]

Interest in cooperation and concern for the welfare of the working class on the part of the middle classes was also manifested by a grand gesture of a philanthropist, Benjamin Rampal, who, in 1879, willed most of his fortune, about 1,500,000 francs, to the city of Paris, the income of which was to be loaned to cooperative societies at a low rate of interest.[94] The effect was to reawaken the cooperative movement. Credit at the low interest of three per cent as well as encouragement from radical republicans induced workers to organize producers' cooperatives. During the three or four years following the Marseilles Congress of 1879, which had rejected producers' cooperation as a means of emancipating the workers, twice as many new societies were founded as during the preceding decade.[95]

Such sympathy on the part of the middle classes with cooperation only tended to increase the hostility of the collectivists toward it. Article after article appeared in the socialist press, maintaining that cooperation would result only in a reduction of wages, in an increase of the working day,[96] in the growth of unemployment and poverty;[97] and that it would "prolong the political and economic slavery of the workers."[98] The socialists who had won a victory over the anarchists at the regional congress of the Federation of the Center (July, 1880), which had adopted the Marxist minimum program, were preparing to have the fourth national congress of Havre accept the same program, and thereby make it the platform not merely of one or two federations, but of an entire national socialist party. Accordingly, they organized numerous small study circles, whose membership in very many instances was not above ten, in order to swamp the congress with their delegates. The organizing committee of Havre saw the danger, and, on its own authority, modified the provisions of the third national congress of Marseilles of 1879, which had voted to admit to the congress of 1880 delegates from syndicats, cooperatives and study circles.[99] The committee at Havre specified that any circle seeking representation had to show a membership of at least twenty-five. This unauthorized procedure evoked a protest from the Federation of the Center which on September 9, 1880 addressed a circular to the different regional federations, in which it accused the committee of having designedly exceeded its powers "in order to prevent the admission to the congress of delegates from the social study circles."[100] The circular declared that the committee had forfeited its rights to organize the fourth national congress.

The moderates and reformists were also aided by certain municipal councils like those of Rouen, Marseilles and Paris, which, through the influence of Barberet, the chief of the Bureau of Professional Societies in the Ministry of the Interior, voted special funds to defray the expenses of the labor delegates. The revolutionary collectivists protested, and found another reason for attacking the committee on organization. The *Prolétaire* called its members "flunkies of the *Palais Bourbon*," [101] while the *Egalité* maintained that the admission of delegates sent at the expense of municipalities prejudiced the freedom and the very existence of labor congresses which "would become—in return for cash—a registration bureau of the whims of such and such a faction of our bourgeois rulers." [102]

The rift which had been growing wider and wider between reformists and collectivists resulted in a complete separation on the very first day of the congress, which had been assembled in a hall called the Cercle Franklin. The reformists, who were in the majority, refused to admit many delegates of the study circles on the ground that they represented fictitious organizations, or groups too small in membership. The revolutionary collectivists, consisting of socialists and anarchists, thereupon left the congress, shouting *"Vive l'anarchie!"* [103] There was just one more violent scene connected with the split. During the second session, a group of collectivists, headed by Paule Mink, a violent revolutionist, broke into the congress, took the floor without permission, and tried to read a statement denouncing the committee on organization. The chairman had to close the session to put an end to the stormy scene.

With the departure of the collectivists to hold their own congress the reformists settled down to business. They condemned collectivism as a reactionary ideal, for it would lead, they said, to the loss of individual liberty, to police regulation and to tyranny.[104] Speeches were made by positivists and by the advocates of cooperation, each school trying to prove that its cure of the social question was the only one. Moret, who represented a cooperative society of printers, pointed to the ability of the workers to administer their own enterprises, and stressed the necessity of organizing cooperatives. Finance expressed the usual skepticism about the value of cooperative societies and was hostile to pensions for workers. In the manner of a true positivist, he said: "What is necessary, is to moralize and not to legislate. Grateful and devoted children, these are the real old age pensions." [105] The majority of the speakers were in favor of the individual ownership of property. As for the political representation of the workers, it was agreed that by electing a number of labor representatives to the municipal councils and to parliament the workers would obtain the necessary reforms. However, the delegates were not averse to combinations with certain republican factions during elections.

The series of demands emanating from such a congress could not be other than moderate. Some of them were: the removal of all laws limiting the freedom to combine; the reform of the *Conseils de Prud'hommes;* a ten-hour day; abolition of night work and of the *livret;* regular labor inspection; the selection of inspectors from among the workers in the syndical chambers; abolition of the *octroi;* the single tax; the protection of the workers against fines imposed by employers; old age pensions. There were in addition such demands as: free, compulsory education; separation of church and state; the freedom of the press; abolition of the religious orders.[106]

The congress of the reformists at the Cercle Franklin, officially called the Labor Congress of Havre, was as moderate as the first and second labor congresses. Its demands were almost of the same calibre as those outlined only two weeks before by Clemenceau in his speech at Marseilles. The delegates showed a deep attachment to the republic and an unwillingness to separate from the old political leaders. Like their friends of the republican political factions, they condemned the collective ownership of the means of production.

Very different was the congress of the revolutionists who had separated themselves from the reformists. This fourth congress of French labor, officially called the National Socialist Labor Congress, held in the Union Lyrique, a hall located in another part of the city of Havre, was composed of fifty-seven delegates, almost all of whom were from Paris, representing chiefly study circles.[107] However, according to Paule Mink, the delegates also represented one hundred and two syndical chambers.[108] The question of property was discussed by several delegates. Nearly all advocated the expropriation of the bourgeoisie and the collective ownership of the means of production. Despite the moderate tone of the delegate from a syndical chamber of Nancy, who maintained that collectivism frightened the people in the country districts, the congress declared that it was necessary to introduce the collective ownership of the means of production, "as soon as and by all means possible." [109] The same resolution bore the mark of anarchist influence when it considered the period of collectivism "as the stage of transition to anarchist communism (le communisme libertaire)." [110]

The discussion on wages consumed two sessions. Cooperation was rejected as powerless to effect any change in the condition of the workers. Only through the collective ownership of the means of production could the wage system be abolished. The delegates endeavored to prove that the development of industry was causing the disappearance of the small shop and of the middleman, and was leading to the concentration of capital, to low wages and to increasing poverty. They finally declared by resolution that reforms could neither change nor improve the condition of the workers, that the only means of transforming the conditions of labor was to abolish the wage system, "this last form of slavery," and that to attain this goal, the workers had to be organized into a party, "entirely distinct from, and opposed to, the bourgeois parties." [111]

On the question of participation in politics there was a division of opinion between the anarchists and the socialists, similar to the one at the regional congress of Paris in July.[112] The same arguments which had been presented previously were reproduced by both sides. Victory was again on the side of the socialists, and the Marxist minimum program which Guesde had imported from London was again adopted. The statement preceding the program, however, once more showed the influence of the anarchists. In it the congress declared that it "will test [the value of the ballot] for the last time in the municipal and legislative elections of 1881, and, should there be no result, it will confine itself to pure revolutionary activity." Moreover, the same statement, while accepting the minimum program as a basis for the coming elections, departed from the idea of having the same program for all candidates. It distinctly invited all the constituencies that were "prepared to have a more defined program to have such." [113]

Little did the delegates know that this latitude of action encouraged by the congress would lead to discord within

185

the party. For the time being, however, the aim of the socialists was realized. The National Socialist Labor Congress of Havre, organized by the collectivists who had separated themselves from the reformists, adopted the Marxist minimum program. Armed with it, the French socialist party was in a position to compete in elections and to attempt to rally the workers into a single political organization.

The program was short, precise—one of the most concise statements of Marxian principles ever written. As such, it was not adapted to a country like France, which was far from industrialized, and where most of the workers were still in the handicraft stage. Furthermore, the program harped on "the revolutionary activity of the proletariat"—a phrase which repelled rather than attracted many, particularly in a land where less than a decade previously a proletarian uprising had resulted in a ruthless suppression. These characteristics of the program, which struck many of its French critics, were to cause discord and ultimately a rift in the socialist ranks.

CONCLUSION

Modern socialism, or the doctrine which advocates the collective ownership by the masses of the means of production and distribution, introduced either through parliamentary methods or through the dictatorship of the proletariat inaugurated after a violent revolution—this doctrine was little known in France before the Commune. Marx's name was known only to a few, and his ideas practically to none. It was after that great disaster which took the lives of about 20,000 Parisians, most of them workers, and resulted in the discrediting of Blanquism and Proudhonism, the two socialist philosophies which rivaled each other under the Second Empire and the Commune, that Marxian socialism began to enter France. That entrance was not a glorious invasion. The new doctrine trickled in slowly, at first almost imperceptibly. It had to contend with numerous enemies and overcome many obstacles before it could become the credo of the French socialist party which the enthusiastic advocates of modern socialism were instrumental in organizing.

Prominent among these enthusiasts was Jules Guesde, who had suffered exile for expressing ideas sympathetic to the Commune, and who had been for a few years under the sway of anarchist influence. It was he who founded the *Egalité*, the first Marxist journal in France, and it was around him that there gathered the few young men who were manifesting a penchant toward Marxian socialism. One cannot accept Eugène Fournière's assertion that Guesde, under the influence of the ideas of French socialist writers, and "without any communication with Marx, arrived [independently] at the Marxian theorems with all of their mathematical rigidity." [1] It is perfectly credible that the future leader of the French Marxists was conversant with the doctrines of the French socialist writers, and it cannot be contested that by 1877 he had arrived, in a vague manner, at the rudimentary principles of collectivism. But it is difficult to determine just how much he himself had invented, how much he had retained from the writings of the French theorists, and how much he had absorbed from discussions with anarchists and with socialist friends who had read a brief analysis of Marxian socialism in Malon's *Exposé des écoles socialistes françaises*. Guesde's ideas did not begin to gain in clarity until 1878. By that time, he had met Karl Hirsch, who was thoroughly versed in German socialist

187

literature, and who had the confidence of Marx; and toward the end of that year, Guesde was reading the French edition of *Capital*. Furthermore, despite the knowledge of scientific socialism which Guesde and his socialist friends had acquired, they did not trust to their own ability to compose the program for the French socialist party. Guesde had to visit London, there to write the preamble as Marx dictated it.

Despite the predominating influence of the leaders of cooperation in workers' circles, the apostles of modern socialism were gaining a small following, particularly after 1878, and developing a socialist movement of which the central doctrine was that of Marx. As has been shown, the young party, created at the third national Socialist Labor Congress, held in Marseilles in 1879, first adopted the Marxist minimum program at the regional congress of the party-federation of the Center in July, 1880, against opposition from the anarchists, and then at the National Socialist Labor Congress which it held in November of the same year at Havre immediately after separating from the moderates. But the party which had come out victorious from its first encounters was soon after divided and weakened by the struggle which ensued over the Marxist minimum program. The schisms, occurring within the ranks of the party, were not healed before the lapse of another generation.

NOTES TO CHAPTER I

[1] Charles Gide, *Historique des associations coopératives de production,* pp. 21 *et seq.*

[2] Edouard Droz, *P. J. Proudhon,* pp. 188, 239.

[3] Office du Travail, *Les associations professionnelles ouvrières,* Vol. i, p. 40.

[4] The practice of compelling workers to present a *livret,* that is, a passbook or certificate, from their former employer to their new one was peculiar to France. It was unknown in countries like Great Britain, the United States, and Germany (except the Rhenish provinces). The *livret* was used in the eighteenth century and disappeared with the abolition of the guilds. It was reinstituted during the First Consulate. Employers were forbidden to engage a worker who did not produce the *livret* stating that he had discharged his debts and obligations toward his former master. It meant that workers who had fallen into debt with their former employer were chained to their job and that employers could take advantage of the workers' situation to lower wages.

During its existence the *livret* was useful to the employer and the state. The former found it valuable because it furnished him with a fairly stable group of workers. The latter employed it as a means of controlling the workers by regarding it as a passport within the country. During the Third Republic the *livret* fell into disuse, particularly in growing industrial centers, and it was abolished in 1890. For a summary see Georges Bry, *Cours élémentaire de législation industrielle,* pp. 84-89 (Paris, 1895). The Napoleonic law is reprinted in Albert Milhaud, *La lutte des classes à travers l'histoire et la politique,* pp. 191-195.

[5] Kritsky, *L'Evolution du syndicalisme en France,* pp. 70-71.

[6] Lagardelle, *L'Evolution des syndicats ouvriers en France,* p. 165.

[7] This interesting document is quoted in full in Albert Thomas, *Le second empire,* pp. 216 *et seq.* (*Histoire socialiste,* Vol. x, ed. Jean Jaurès) and in Proudhon, *De la capacité politique des classes ouvrières,* pp. 409 *et seq.* (Paris, 1924, Marcel Rivière).

[8] Albert Thomas, *op. cit.,* pp. 226-227. The Manifesto is reprinted in Proudhon, *op. cit.,* pp. 418-419.

[9] *Op. cit.,* p. 7.

NOTES

[10] *De la capacité politique des classes ouvrières.* Proudhon died before he completed it. The conclusion was written by Gustave Chaudey, a disciple, according to instructions given him by his master. For a good summary of the political activity of labor under the Second Empire, see A. Zévaès, *"Les candidatures ouvrières et révolutionnaires sous le second empire,"* *La Révolution de 1848*, 1932, Vol. xxix, no. cxlii, pp. 132-154.

[11] Kritsky, *op. cit.*, pp. 75-76.

[12] Lagardelle, *op. cit.*, pp. 172-174.

[13] Kritsky, *op. cit.*, pp. 77-78.

[14] Office du Travail, *op. cit.*, Vol. i, p. 49.

[15] *Cf. infra*, p. 30.

[16] Lagardelle, *op. cit.*, p. 189.

[17] Quoted in Kritsky, *op. cit.*, p. 80. See also Lagardelle, *op. cit.*, pp. 190 *et seq.*

[18] Georges Weill, *Histoire du mouvement social en France*, p. 75 (Paris, 1924).

[19] Paul Louis, *Histoire du mouvement syndical en France*, pp. 123 *et seq.* (Paris, 1907).

[20] Jean Gaumont, *Histoire générale de la coopération en France*, Vol. i, pp. 468-470, 483, 496.

[21] *Ibid.*, p. 505.

[22] *Ibid.*, p. 465.

[23] *Ibid.*, pp. 467, 557.

[24] See *ibid.*, Book vi, ch. v.

[25] Georges Weill, *Histoire du parti républicain en France*, ch. xiv (Paris, 1900).

[26] The volume was published in 1828 in Brussels and in London. In 1836, it was translated into English by the well known Chartist, Bronterre O'Brien.

[27] The best biography of Blanqui is by Gustave Geffroy, *L'Enfermé* (Paris, 1897). The following are also valuable: Maurice Dommanget, *Blanqui* (Paris, 1924), a treatment of Blanqui's ideas from the Marxist viewpoint; Alexandre Zévaès, *Auguste Blanqui* (Paris, 1920), a study of Blanqui, the patriot. See also a scholarly article on Blanqui's ideas by Edward S. Mason, "Blanqui and Communism" in *Political Science Quarterly*, 1929, Vol. xliv, pp. 498-527, and an interesting essay on Blanqui in R. W. Postgate, *Out of the Past*, pp. 24-75.

[28] Mason, *op. cit.*, p. 504.

[29] Blanqui, *Critique sociale*, Vol. ii, p. 161.

[30] *Ibid.*, Vol. ii, pp. 122, 344-345; Dommanget, *op. cit.*, p. 52.

[31] *La patrie en danger*, p. 347, December 8, 1870.

[32] *Critique sociale*, Vol. i, p. 208. See also G. Tridon, *Les hébertistes*, p. 14 (Paris, 1871).

[33] See e.g. *La patrie en danger,* pp. 9, 33.

[34] Albert Mathiez, *"Notes inédits de Blanqui sur Robespierre,"* *Annales historiques de la Révolution Française,* 1928, Vol. v, pp. 308 *et seq.*; G. Tridon, *op. cit.,* pp. 10, 19, 23, 40, 50.

[35] *Critique sociale,* Vol. i, p. 219, quoted in Mason, *op. cit.,* p. 508.

[36] *Ibid.,* Vol. i, pp. 204 *et seq.*

[37] *Ibid.,* Vol. i, pp. 203-204.

[38] *Ibid.,* Vol. i, p. 211.

[39] *Ibid.,* Vol. i, p. 201.

[40] *Ibid.,* Vol. ii, pp. 68-69, 73, 173-174.

[41] Cf. e.g. *ibid.,* pp. 113 *et seq.*

[42] *Ibid.,* Vol. i, p. 196.

[43] *"Programm der blanquistischen Kommune-Flüchtlinge,"* *Volkstaat,* 1874, no. 73.

[44] *Critique sociale,* Vol. ii, pp. 118-119.

[45] *Ibid.,* p. 126; Mason, *op. cit.,* p. 516.

[46] *Critique Sociale,* Vol. ii, pp. 121, 124. See also a citation in Benoît Malon, *Manuel d'économie sociale,* pp. 347-348.

[47] *Critique sociale,* Vol. ii, pp. 114 *et seq.*

[48] *Ibid.,* pp. 147, 150 *et seq.,* 155 *et seq.*

[49] *Ibid.,* pp. 166-167.

[50] *Ibid.,* pp. 314, 316. Proudhon also had a high regard for Blanqui. He referred to the revolutionist as "one of the most intelligent of the epoch," and spoke of his "rare penetration." *Idée générale de la révolution au XIX° siècle,* p. 99 and n. 7 (Paris, 1923).

[51] I. Tchernoff, *Le parti républicain au coup d'état et sous le second empire,* pp. 346-348.

[52] For a summary of Blanquist activity under the Empire, see Charles Da Costa, *Les blanquistes,* pp. 7 *et seq.*

[53] In 1842, Marx, who later launched his well-known polemic against Proudhon, referred to this book as "a penetrating work." D. Riazanov, *Marx-Engels Gesamtausgabe,* Section i, Part i, p. 263. In 1845, he again wrote concerning it: "Now Proudhon subjects private property, the basis of political economy, to a critical examination, which is in fact the first decisive, ruthless and at the same time scientific analysis. This constitutes the great scientific progress which he made, a progress which revolutionized political economy, and first rendered possible a real science of political economy.

"Proudhon's work, *Qu'est-ce que la propriété?* has the same significance for modern political economy as Sieyès' pamphlet: *Qu'est-ce que le tiers état?* has for modern politics." Reprinted from *Die Heilige Familie* in

NOTES

Karl Marx, *Selected Essays*, p. 172 (New York, 1926). Two years earlier, Engels was equally enthusiastic about Proudhon's book. Writing in the *New Moral World*, he said: "This is the most philosophical work, on the part of the Communists, in the French language; and, if I wish to see any French book translated into the English language, it is this. The right of private property, the consequences of this institution—competition, immorality, misery—are here developed with a power of intellect, and real scientific research, which I never since found united in a single volume." D. Riazanov, *op. cit.*, section i, Vol. ii, p. 442.

[54] The rudiments of Hegelian dialectics he acquired through long discussions with Marx, Grün, and Bakunin.

[55] Junius, *Le citoyen Proudhon devant l'Assemblée Nationale*, pp. 19-22.

[56] Concerning the life and work of Proudhon see Edouard Droz, *op. cit.* (Paris, 1909); Arthur Desjardins, *P. J. Proudhon* (Paris, 1896); C. A. Sainte-Beuve, *P. J. Proudhon, sa vie et sa correspondance* (Paris, 1872); Hubert Bourgin, *Proudhon* (Paris, 1901).

[57] *Idée générale de la révolution au XIXe siècle*, p. 203 (Paris, 1923).

[58] *Contradictions économiques*, Vol. i, p. 211, Vol. ii, pp. 281, 286 *et seq.* See also *Idée générale*, pp. 365 *et seq.*

[59] Gide and Rist, *History of Economic Doctrines*, p. 297, n. 1 (London, 1919); *Idée générale*, p. 173.

[60] *Idée générale*, pp. 202, 206.

[61] *De la justice dans la révolution et dans l'église*, Vol. i, p. 413 (Paris, 1930).

[62] *Ibid.*, pp. 414, 416.

[63] *Ibid.*, p. 233.

[64] Michel Ralea, *Proudhon, sa conception du progrès et son attitude sociale*, ch. ii.

[65] Bourgin, *op. cit.*, pp. 21-22; *Contradictions économiques*, Vol. i, ch. ii.

[66] "Whenever in the sphere of ethics, history or political economy analysis has found the antinomy of an idea, it can be stated *a priori* that this antinomy conceals a higher idea which will make its appearance sooner or later." *Contradictions économiques*, p. 116.

[67] *Qu'est-ce que la propriété?* ch. ii (Paris, 1926).

[68] *Ibid.*, pp. 325-327.

[69] *Ibid.*, p. 212.

[70] Vol. ii, pp. 410, 411.

[71] For a description of this bank, see Gide and Rist, *op. cit.*, pp. 308 *et seq.*; see also the plan of the organization of the bank and its hoped for consequences in Proudhon, *Résumé de la question sociale, banque d'échange*, pp. 35 *et seq.*

NOTES

[72] *The Poverty of Philosophy*, p. 198, tr. H. Quelch (Chicago, n.d.).

[73] For Proudhon's conception of free contract, see S. Y. Lu, *The Political Theories of P. J. Proudhon*, pp. 106 *et seq.; Idée générale*, pp. 188-189, 267-268.

[74] *Idée générale*, p. 125.

[75] *Ibid.*, pp. 126 *et seq.*

[76] *Ibid.*, pp. 128 *et seq.*

[77] *Ibid.*, p. 159.

[78] *Ibid.*, p. 162.

[79] *Ibid.*, pp. 238, 364-365. See also *Qu'est-ce que la propriété?* p. 339, for a similar observation.

[80] *Idée générale*, sections v-vi.

[81] *Ibid.*, p. 332.

[82] *Du principe fédératif*, p. 104 (Paris, 1921).

[83] For a summary of the basic ideas of Proudhon's governmental organization, see *ibid.*, pp. 121-122. For the constitution of his political organism, see *De la capacité politique des classes ouvrières*, pp. 216-217 (Paris, 1924).

[84] *De la capacité politique des classes ouvrières*, p. 207. On page 215 he writes: "The political and the economic order are one and the same order, one and the same system, established on a single principle, mutualism."

[85] *Ibid.*, pp. 261 *et seq.*

[86] *Ibid.*, pp. 101, 230-231.

[87] *Ibid.*, p. 244.

[88] *Ibid.*, pp. 386-388, 393-394, 395-398.

[89] *Cf. supra*, p. 26.

[90] *De la capacité*, etc. pp. 203-204.

[91] *Ibid.*, pp. 395-396. See Aimé Berthod's scholarly Introduction to *Idée générale de la révolution au XIXᵉ siècle*.

[92] *Histoire du parti républicain en France*, p. 493 (Paris, 1900).

[93] On Malon *cf. infra*, p. 99. On Varlin see *La vie ouvrière*, May 5, 1913, and *La Revue Socialiste*, 1885, Vol. i, pp. 415-426; 1913, Vol. lvii, pp. 514-532.

[94] Weill, *Histoire du mouvement social en France*, pp. 84-86.

[95] Tchernoff, *op. cit.*, pp. 348 *et seq.;* Thomas, *op. cit.*, pp. 286-287.

[96] On these organizations, see the scholarly discussion in Th. Rothstein, *From Chartism to Labourism*, Part i, section iii (New York, 1929). On other harbingers of the International, see Jules L. Puech, *Le proudhonisme dans l'association internationale des travailleurs*, part i, ch. ii.

[97] The three delegates were Tolain, Perrachon and Limousin.

[98] See G. M. Stekloff, *History of the First International*, Appendix (London, 1928). For the French translation of the preamble and rules, see E. E. Fribourg, *L'Association internationale des travailleurs*, pp. 14 *et seq.*

NOTES

See also James Guillaume, *L'Internationale, documents et souvenirs*, Vol. i, pp. 11 *et seq.*

[99] Puech, *op. cit.*, pp. 87-88; Fribourg, *op. cit.*, pp. 21 *et seq.*

[100] Fribourg, *op. cit.*, p. 33.

[101] Quoted in Puech, *op. cit.*, p. 92.

[102] Fribourg, *op. cit.*, pp. 42-43.

[103] *Ibid.*, pp. 44-45.

[104] Puech, *op. cit.*, pp. 113-115.

[105] The report is reprinted in Fribourg, *op. cit.*, pp. 50-86.

[106] Stekloff, *op. cit.*, pp. 84-86.

[107] The resolutions are reprinted in Fribourg, *op. cit.*, pp. 110-111.

[108] *Cf. infra*, p. 105.

[109] Guillaume, *op. cit.*, Vol. i, pp. 65 *et seq.*

[110] Weill, *Histoire du mouvement social en France*, pp. 112 *et seq.* Tchernoff, *op. cit.*, pp. 472 *et seq.*

[111] It is difficult to estimate the size of the membership. Some maintained that in 1870 the International had 70,000 members in Paris and 200,000 in all France. See Weill, *op. cit.*, p. 134 and n. 5. Thomas, *op. cit.*, p. 384, states that in April, 1870, the number of adherents was estimated to have been more than 250,000.

[112] *Procès-verbaux des séances officielles de l'internationale pendant la Commune*, pp. 145 *et seq.* (Paris, 1872) ; *Journal officiel de la Commune*, March 27, 1871, p. 66.

[113] The best general works on the Commune are: Georges Laronze, *Histoire de la Commune de 1871: la justice* (Paris, 1928), an exhaustive treatment of the judicial phase of the Commune; Louis Dubreuilh, *La Commune* (*Histoire socialiste*, ed. Jean Jaurès, Vol. xi, Paris, 1908), a presentation of the socialist point of view; Georges Bourgin, *Histoire de la Commune* (Paris, 1907), one of the best summaries of the history of the Commune; also his article, "The Commune," in *Encyclopedia of the Social Sciences*, Vol. iv, pp. 63-66, ed. Edwin R. A. Seligman. For fairness Bourgin's volume is superior to Dubreuilh's. See also Edward S. Mason, *The Paris Commune, An Episode in the History of the Socialist Movement* (New York, 1930), a scholarly discussion of the effect of the Commune on the subsequent socialist and communist movements. Good summaries of the Commune may also be found in Seignobos, *Le déclin de l'empire et l'établissement de la 3ᵉ république* (*Histoire de France contemporaine*, ed. Ernest Lavisse, Vol. vii), pp. 290-314, and in Gabriel Hanotaux, *Contemporary France*, Vol. i, pp. 158-228, tr. John Charles Tarver (New York, 1903).

[114] *Journal officiel de la Commune*, March 21, 1871, pp. 16-17.

[115] *Ibid.*, April 2, 1871, p. 128.

NOTES

[116] Georges Renard, *"Mes souvenirs (1870-1871),"* *La Révolution de 1848,* 1931, Vol. xxviii, no. cxxxvi, p. 23.

[117] Arthur Arnould, *Histoire populaire et parlementaire de la Commune,* Vol. ii, p. 83.

[118] *Journal officiel de la Commune,* May 2, p. 448; May 4, p. 459.

[119] Mason, *op. cit.,* pp. 195-196.

[120] *Journal officiel de la Commune,* May 6, p. 477; May 18, p. 602. For a list of the suppressed newspapers, see Edouard Moriac, *Paris sous la Commune,* pp. 386-387.

[121] *Journal officiel de la Commune,* May 4, p. 460; R. W. Postgate, *Revolution from 1789 to 1906,* p. 303; *Les 31 séances officielles de la Commune,* pp. 64-66, Paris, 1871.

[122] *Journal officiel de la Commune,* April 25, p. 377.

[123] See the statement of Delpit in *Journal officiel,* March 24, 1871, p. 248; *Enquête parlementaire sur l'insurrection du 18 mars,* Vol. i, p. 186.

[124] *Enquête,* Vol. ii, pp. 20, 164, 602.

[125] *Ibid.,* p. 261.

[126] *Ibid.,* pp. 222, 230.

[127] *Cf. supra,* p. 34.

[128] G. de Molinari, *Le mouvement socialiste et les réunions publiques,* p. 205 (Paris, 1872).

[129] *Enquête,* Vol. ii, p. 558.

[130] Quoted in Emile de Laveleye, *Socialism of To-day,* p. 177, n. (London, n.d.).

[131] *Procès-verbaux des séances officielles de l'internationale à Paris,* pp. 44 et seq.

[132] *Ibid.,* p. 37.

[133] *Ibid.,* pp. 55-56.

[134] *Ibid.,* p. 197.

[135] *Ibid.,* pp. 142-143.

[136] Vaillant and Frankel voted for it.

[137] Bourgin, *op. cit.,* p. 135; *Enquête,* Vol. ii, p. 560.

[138] R. W. Postgate, *The Workers' International,* pp. 71-72.

[139] *La Revue Socialiste,* 1911, Vol. liii, p. 297.

[140] *Journal officiel de la Commune,* April 3, p. 133.

[141] *Ibid.,* March 30, p. 97.

[142] *Ibid.,* May 7, p. 487.

[143] *Ibid.,* April 2, p. 126.

[144] *Ibid.,* April 11, p. 223.

[145] *Ibid.,* pp. 226-228; April 16, pp. 279-281; April 17, pp. 291-293; April 18, pp. 300-301.

[146] *Ibid.,* April 29, p. 424.

[147] *Ibid.*, April 29, pp. 411, 412.

[148] *Ibid.*, p. 418.

[149] *Ibid.*, May 17, p. 589.

[150] *Ibid.*, April 17, p. 286.

[151] *Ibid.*, May 5, p. 467; May 13, pp. 539-540.

[152] *Ibid.*, May 21, pp. 628-629.

[153] Dubreuilh, *op. cit.*, p. 402.

[154] *Journal officiel de la Commune*, April 20, p. 323.

[155] Dubreuilh, *op. cit.*, p. 422.

[156] See e.g. the manifesto of the Paris Federal Council of the International. *Procès-verbaux des séances officielles de l'internationale*, pp. 145 *et seq.*

[157] March 21, p. 18.

[158] March 25, p. 38.

[159] March 30, p. 99.

[160] *Cf. supra*, p. 40.

[161] The suppression during the Bloody Week in May 1871 was more thorough than the one during the June Days in 1848. It has been estimated that from fifteen to twenty thousand Parisians lost their lives. Bourgin, *op. cit.*, p. 183, says "at least 20,000"; Dubreuilh, *op. cit.*, p. 472, estimates it around 20,000; Laronze, *op. cit.*, p. 635, agrees with Dubreuilh; Zévaès, *Histoire de la troisième république*, p. 82, cites 30,000 as the number killed; Mason, *op. cit.*, p. 294, states that "the number killed in the streets and by court-martial exceeded 10,000 and fell short of 15,000"; Ch. Seignobos, *op. cit.*, p. 313, says that the number of the dead can never be known. He quotes General Appert's estimate of 17,000, not counting those killed outside of Paris; Gabriel Hanotaux, *op. cit.*, Vol. i, p. 225 and E. Zévort, *Histoire de la troisième république*, Vol. i, p. 246, accept General Appert's figures.

[162] Chambre de Commerce de Paris, *Enquête sur les conditions du travail en France pendant l'année 1872*, p. 17 (Paris, 1875). See also an analysis of the labor shortage in Dubreuilh, *op. cit.*, p. 489.

[163] *Journal officiel de la Commune*, April 22, p. 344.

[164] *Ibid.*, April 28, p. 410.

[165] *Ibid.*, May 7, p. 497.

[166] August Bebel, *Aus meinem Leben*, Vol. ii, pp. 194-196 (Stuttgart, 1910-1914).

[167] *Ibid.*, pp. 348-366.

[168] Georg Stekloff, *Bakunin, ein Lebensbild*, pp. 113 *et seq.* (Stuttgart, 1920); Hélène Iswolsky, *La vie de Bakounine*, pp. 258 *et seq.* (Paris, 1930).

[169] *Oeuvres*, Vol. iv, pp. 253-255 (Paris, 1910).

NOTES

[170] Letter to Kugelmann, April 12, 1871, *Neue Zeit,* 1902, Vol. xx, part i, p. 709.

[171] Franz Mehring, *Karl Marx,* p. 457, 4th edition (Leipzig, 1923).

[172] *The Civil War in France,* pp. 14, 59, tr. E. Belfort Bax (Chicago, n.d.).

[173] *Ibid.,* pp. 18-23, *passim.*

[174] *Ibid.,* pp. 17, 18.

[175] *Ibid.,* pp. 42-43, 48.

[176] *Ibid.,* p. 43. Engels concludes the preface to the third German edition of *The Civil War in France* with the following words: "Of late, the man in the street in Germany has again been frightened by the words: Dictatorship of the proletariat. Well and good, gentlemen, do you want to know what this dictatorship looks like? Look at the Paris Commune. That was the dictatorship of the proletariat." *Neue Zeit,* 1890-1891, Vol. ix, part ii, p. 41.

[177] *The Civil War in France,* p. 55.

[178] *L'Humanité,* May 29, 1927; Lenin, *The Paris Commune,* p. 18 (New York, 1931).

[179] *The Civil War in France,* p. 78.

[180] When Lafargue introduced a bill to separate church and state, he claimed that he was reviving the decree of the Commune. See *Le Socialiste,* December 26, 1891.

[181] *La Petite République,* March 18, 1895.

NOTES TO CHAPTER II

[1] *Cf. supra,* p. 39.

[2] Benoît Malon, *L'Internationale, son histoire et ses principes,* p. 5. See also E. E. Fribourg, *op. cit.,* p. 147.

[3] The best known were: Oscar Testut, *L'Internationale* (Paris, 1871), which went through three editions in one year; *Le livre bleu de l'internationale* (Paris, 1871); *L'Internationale et le jacobinisme au ban de l'europe,* 2 vols. (Paris, 1872); Edmond Villetard, *Histoire de l'internationale,* (Paris, 1872); Achille Dalsème, *Les mystères de l'internationale* (Paris, 1871); Georges Guéroult, *Les théories de l'internationale* (Paris, 1872), published originally in *L'Opinion nationale;* E. E. Fribourg, *op. cit.; Histoire de l'internationale par un bourgeois républicain* (Paris, 1873).

[4] See a review of one of his books on the International in *Journal officiel,* May 29, 1871, p. 1151.

[5] *L'Internationale,* Preface, p. vii.

[6] *Journal officiel,* June 8, 1871, pp. 1259-1260.

NOTES

[7] *Enquête parlementaire sur l'insurrection du 18 mars,* Vol. ii, pp. 2 *et seq.*

[8] For the full text of the law, see Alexandre Zévaès, *Le syndicalisme contemporain,* pp. 311-312 (Paris, 1911).

[9] *Supra,* p. 5.

[10] *Enquête,* Vol. i, p. 184.

[11] *Enquête sur les conditions du travail en France pendant l'année 1872,* p. 49.

[12] Ducarre, *Rapport fait au nom de la commission d'enquête parlementaire sur les conditions du travail en France,* p. 188.

[13] For the complete text of the bill see Mermeix, *Le syndicalisme contre le socialisme,* p. 68, n. (Paris, 1907).

[14] *Journal des Economistes,* 3rd series, 1877, Vol. xiv, p. 299.

[15] *Ibid.,* pp. 301 *et seq.*

[16] *Ibid.,* 1872, Vol. xxv, p. 484.

[17] *Annales de la société d'économie politique,* 1871-1872, Vol. ix, pp. 90 *et seq.*

[18] *Ibid.,* p. 92; *Bulletin de la société internationale des études pratiques d'économie sociale,* 1873, Vol. iv, p. 233; *Bulletin du mouvement social,* April 1, 1874.

[19] For a detailed analysis of the law, see Paul Louis, *Histoire de la classe ouvrière en France de la révolution à nos jours,* pp. 168-169 (Paris, 1927).

[20] *Bulletin de la société internationale des études pratiques d'économie sociale,* 1874, Vol. iv, p. 469.

[21] *Journal des Economistes,* 1872, Vol. xxvii, p. 227; Vol. xxviii, pp. 123, 196, 203, 215; 1874, Vol. xxxiv, pp. 179-180.

[22] *Ibid.,* 1872, Vol. xxviii, pp. 178, 294-295.

[23] P. T. Moon, *The Labor Problem and the Social Catholic Movement in France,* p. 61.

[24] "The family in which the chosen son takes the place as head of the family and proprietor of the family patrimony." Moon, *op. cit.,* p. 60.

[25] Le Play, *Organization of Labor,* p. 314.

[26] *Ibid.,* pp. 155-156.

[27] *Bulletin de la société internationale des études pratiques d'économie sociale,* 1873, Vol. iv, pp. 225 *et seq.*

[28] See list of members in *ibid.,* pp. 883 *et seq.*

[29] Moon, *op. cit.,* p. 356.

[30] *Ibid.,* p. 85.

[31] Weill, *Histoire du mouvement social en France,* pp. 182-183.

[32] Pierre Lafitte, *Le positivisme et l'économie politique,* pp. 36, 41, 70-71.

[33] *Revue occidentale,* 1878, Vols. i-ii, pp. 265, 270; Lafitte, *op. cit.,* pp. 74, 78.

NOTES

[34] Laporte, Magnin et Finance, *Le positivisme au congrès ouvrier,* p. 95.

[35] Fabian Magnin, *Etudes sociales,* pp. 159 *et seq.*

[36] *Cf. infra,* p. 64.

[37] *Revue occidentale,* 1881, Vol. i, p. 140; Laporte, etc., *op. cit.,* p. 58; Lafitte, *op. cit.,* pp. 31 *et seq.*

[38] See Gabriel Mollin, *Les jobards et les roublards du positivisme,* p. 49.

[39] Charles Gide, *Le familistère de Guise et la verrerie ouvrière,* pp. 3-13.

[40] Godin, *Solutions sociales,* pp. 317 *et seq.,* 348, 418 *et seq.,* 460 *et seq.,* 652.

[41] *Bulletin du mouvement social,* January 1, February 1, 1873.

[42] *Ibid.,* December 1, 1873.

[43] Weill, *Histoire du mouvement social,* p. 211.

[44] *Revue des Deux Mondes,* 1870, Vol. xc, p. 118.

[45] Emile Levasseur, *Questions ouvrières et industrielles en France,* pp. 643, 649 n. 3.

[46] *L'Economiste Français,* March 23, 1878, p. 360.

[47] *Bulletin de la Fédération Jurassienne,* May 15, 1872.

[48] *La Liberté,* September 1, 1872.

[49] For statistics on French production after the Commune see Paul Louis, *Histoire de la classe ouvrière en France,* pp. 142 *et seq.*

[50] Dubreuilh, *op. cit.,* p. 489.

[51] *Bulletin de la société internationale des études pratiques d'économie sociale,* 1872, Vol. iv, p. 11.

[52] Quoted in Ducarre, *Rapport sur les conditions du travail en France,* pp. 105-106.

[53] On Thiers' protectionist policy see *Journal des Economistes,* 3rd series, 1872, Vol. xxv, pp. 177-187; *Journal of Economic and Business History,* 1929, Vol. i, pp. 302-324.

[54] Quoted in Ducarre, *op. cit.,* p. 106.

[55] J. Barberet, *Le mouvement ouvrier à Paris de 1870 à 1874,* pp. 23-24 (Paris, 1874); Malon, *"Le mouvement syndical de 1872 à 1878," La Revue Socialiste,* 1886, Vol. iv, pp. 866 *et seq.*

[56] Barberet, *op. cit.,* p. 56.

[57] *Ibid.,* pp. 70 *et seq.,* 83 *et seq.*

[58] *Ibid.,* p. 148.

[59] Barberet, *Les grèves et la loi sur les coalitions,* pp. 146-147 (Paris, 1873).

[60] *Ibid.,* pp. 6, 16.

[61] *Ibid.,* p. 58.

[62] *Ibid.,* pp. 65-66.

[63] *Ibid.,* p. 119.

[64] *Ibid.,* pp. 131 *et seq.*

NOTES

[65] *Ibid.*, p. 136.

[66] Barberet, *Le mouvement ouvrier à Paris de 1870 à 1874*, pp. 92 *et seq.*; *Monographies professionnelles*, Vol. i, pp. 24-25.

[67] Quoted in Weill, *Histoire du mouvement social en France*, p. 189.

[68] Barberet, *Le mouvement ouvrier à Paris de 1870 à 1874*, pp. 110 *et seq.*

[69] Lewis Lorwin, *Syndicalism in France*, p. 46, 2nd edition (New York, 1914).

[70] The *Conseils de Prud'hommes*, or councils of wise and honest men are tribunals set up "to adjudicate differences arising out of relations between employers and employees." The institution has its roots in the medieval guilds. The abolition of the guilds by the Constituent Assembly ended its existence and it became necessary to find a substitute. This was supplied by Napoleon I who created the first *Conseil de Prud'hommes* in Lyons in 1806. The institution spread to other cities during the first half of the nineteenth century. From 1810 to 1907 various laws were passed, increasing the workers' influence in the *Conseils de Prud'hommes* and extending the powers and jurisdiction of the latter. See David J. Saposs, *The Labor Movement in Post-War France* (Social and Economic Studies of Post-War France, Vol. iv, ed. Carlton J. H. Hayes), pp. 292 *et seq.* For a summary of the laws on the *Conseils de Prud'hommes* see Paul Louis, *L'Ouvrier devant l'état*, pp. 443-448.

[71] Hubert Lagardelle, *L'Evolution des syndicats ouvriers en France*, p. 231.

[72] Gaumont, *op. cit.*, Vol. ii, pp. 31 *et seq.*

[73] *Ibid.*, pp. 33-34.

[74] *Ibid.*, p. 31.

[75] For the statutes of the group see *Bulletin du mouvement social*, March 1, 1873.

[76] Gaumont, *op. cit.*, Vol. ii, pp. 36-37.

[77] Lafitte, *op. cit.*, pp. 27 *et seq.*

[78] *Infra*, p. 85.

[79] *Séances du congrès ouvrier de Paris*, 1876, p. 317.

[80] *Ibid.*, p. 327.

[81] *Ibid.*, pp. 334 *et seq.*

[82] *Ibid.*, pp. 340 *et seq.*

[83] *Rapports de la délégation ouvrière française à l'exposition universelle de Vienne*, Vol. i, "Rapport des délégués de Paris sur la marbrerie," p. 8. The reports of the syndical chambers were published during 1874 and 1875. The joint report appeared in 1876.

[84] Weill, *Histoire du mouvement social en France*, p. 193.

[85] *Rapports de la délégation ouvrière française à l'exposition universelle de Vienne*, Vol. ii, "Rapport des délégués de Paris sur la gravure," p. 66.

NOTES

[86] *Ibid.*, Vol. ii, *"Rapport des délégués de Paris, tailleurs d'habits,"* p. 90.

[87] *Ibid.*, Vol. i, *"Rapport du délégué de Paris sur la marqueterie,"* pp. 31 et seq.

[88] *Ibid.*, Vol. ii, *"Rapport des délégués lyonnais sur les tissus,"* p. 66.

[89] *Ibid.*, p. 67.

[90] *Ibid.*

[91] *Ibid.*, *"Rapport des délégués de Paris, tailleurs d'habits,"* p. 84.

[92] *Ibid.*, Vol. i, *"Rapport du délégué de Paris sur la marqueterie,"* p. 26.

[93] Reprinted in *ibid.*, *"Rapport des délégués de Paris, modeleurs-mécaniciens,"* pp. 45-46; Malon, *"Le mouvement syndical de 1872 à 1878,"* La Revue Socialiste, 1886, Vol. iv, p. 875.

[94] Quoted in Malon, *Histoire du socialisme*, pp. 377-378.

[95] Ducarre, *op. cit.*, pp. 185-186.

[96] Lagardelle, *op. cit.*, pp. 240 et seq.

[97] Weill, *Histoire du mouvement social*, p. 202.

[98] Barberet, *Monographies professionnelles*, Vol. i, p. 26.

[99] *Bulletin du mouvement social*, January 1, 1875.

[100] Quoted in Guillaume, *op. cit.*, Vol. iii, p. 91.

[101] Zévaès, *Histoire de la troisième république*, p. 103.

[102] Halévy, *La fin des notables*, p. 247; Zévaès, *op. cit.*, p. 104.

[103] See Ch. Seignobos, *Le déclin de l'empire et l'établissement de la 3ᵉ république*, p. 75.

[104] Joseph Reinach, *Discours et plaidoyers politiques de M. Gambetta*, Vol. ii, p. 261.

[105] *Ibid.*, Vol. iii, p. 101.

[106] *Ibid.*, Vol. ii, pp. 262-263.

[107] Weill, *Histoire du mouvement social*, p. 195.

[108] *Ibid.*, pp. 196-197.

[109] Quoted in G. Hanotaux, *Contemporary France*, Vol. iii, pp. 452-453; Zévaès, *op. cit.*, p. 138.

[110] Zévaès, *op. cit.*, p. 139.

[111] Gaumont, *op. cit.*, Vol. ii, p. 82.

[112] Weill, *Histoire du mouvement social*, pp. 200-201.

[113] *Cf.* p. 50.

[114] *Journal des Economistes*, 3rd series, 1877, Vol. xlv, p. 217.

[115] June 19, 1876, cited in *Séances du congrès ouvrier de France*, 1876, p. 5.

[116] *Ibid.*, p. 3.

[117] *Ibid.*, pp. 6, 9.

[118] *Ibid.*, p. 4.

[119] *Ibid.*, p. 72.

[120] *Ibid.*, pp. 85 et seq.

[121] *Ibid.*, pp. 511-512.

NOTES

[122] *Ibid.*, p. 513.

[123] *Ibid.*, p. 145.

[124] *Ibid.*, p. 117.

[125] *Ibid.*, pp. 114 *et seq.*

[126] *Ibid.*, pp. 131-132.

[127] *Ibid.*, pp. 173 *et seq.*

[128] *Ibid.*, p. 208.

[129] *Ibid.*, p. 294.

[130] *Ibid.*, p. 281.

[131] *Ibid.*, p. 288.

[132] *Ibid.*, pp. 518 *et seq.*

[133] *Ibid.*, pp. 383 *et seq.*

[134] *Ibid.*, pp. 523 *et seq.*

[135] *Cf. supra*, p. 65.

[136] *Séances du congrès ouvrier de Paris*, p. 344.

[137] *Ibid.*, pp. 44, 448 *et seq.*

[138] *Ibid.*, p. 22.

[139] *Ibid.*, p. 518.

[140] *Ibid.*, p. 27.

[141] *Ibid.*, p. 23.

[142] Quoted in A. May, *Les origines du syndicalisme révolutionnaire*, pp. 22-23.

[143] Third series, 1876, Vol. xliv, pp. 187, 191.

[144] *Ibid.*, p. 178.

[145] Guillaume, *op. cit.*, Vol. iv, p. 69.

[146] *Cf. infra*, p. 105.

[147] *La Philosophie de l'Avenir*, 1876-1877, Vol. ii, pp. 146, 189.

[148] This manifesto is reprinted in Mermeix, *La France socialiste*, pp. 278-285 (Paris, 1886). Parts of it appear in Charles da Costa, *Les blanquistes*, pp. 53-54 (Paris, 1912), and in Alexandre Zévaès, *Auguste Blanqui*, p. 237 (Paris, 1920).

[149] Mermeix, *op. cit.*, p. 278.

[150] *Ibid.*, p. 282.

[151] *Ibid.*, p. 284.

[152] These articles are reprinted in his *Ça et Là*, pp. 107-152 (Paris, 1914).

[153] Jules Guesde, *op. cit.*, p. 107.

[154] For the program see *Séances du congrès ouvrier de France*, 1878, p. 8.

[155] *Ibid.*, pp. 335 *et seq.*, 434 *et seq.*, 505.

NOTES TO CHAPTER III

[1] *La critique philosophique*, 1872, Vol. i, p. 208. Dr. Pellarin showed his unabated enthusiasm for Fourier's ideas by issuing a new edition of his life of Fourier. Charles Pellarin, *Fourier, sa vie et sa théorie*, 5th edition (Paris, 1872).

[2] Quoted in Weill, *Histoire du mouvement social*, p. 211. See Renouvier, *"La situation critique de l'école de Fourier,"* *La critique philosophique*, 1872, Vol. ii, pp. 49-52.

[3] *Supra*, p. 55.

[4] *Journal des Economistes*, 1874, Vol. xxxii, p. 355.

[5] *Bulletin du mouvement social*, March 15, 1874.

[6] When a group of reformers published their program in 1876, in which they used the word "socialism," they spent more than a page to explain that the significance they attached to the word was entirely different from that which public opinion attributed to it. They were careful to repudiate any recourse to violence. *Manifeste et programme des socialistes garantistes*, pp. 4-5 (Paris, 1876).

[7] See Engels' letter to Sorge in F. A. Sorge, *Briefe and Auszüge aus Briefen von Joh. Phil. Becker, Jof. Dietzgen, Friedrich Engels, Karl Marx u. A. an F. A. Sorge und Andere*, p. 85 (Stuttgart, 1906). See also *Procès de l'internationale, compte rendu des débats* (Toulouse, 1873), pp. 11 *et seq.*

[8] Guillaume, *op. cit.*, Vol. iii, pp. 62-65; *Procès de l'internationale, compte rendu*, Toulouse, pp. 29 *et seq.*, 38 *et seq.* The counsel for the defense, referring to Dentraygues, said: "He is the prime mover of the accusation, the pivot on which it rests." *Procès de l'internationale*, p. 48.

[9] Sorge, *op. cit.*, pp. 106, 111.

[10] Weill, *Histoire du mouvement social*, pp. 167 *et seq.*; Zévaès, *De la semaine sanglante au congrès de Marseille*, pp. 17-18.

[11] The document is reprinted in Charles da Costa, *Les blanquistes*, pp. 44-51, and in Compère-Morel, *Grand dictionnaire socialiste*, pp. 137-139.

[12] Da Costa, *op. cit.*, pp. 46-47.

[13] Engels, *"Programm der blanquistischen Kommune-Flüchtlinge,"* *Volkstaat*, 1874, no. lxxiii; Sorge, *Briefe und Auszüge aus Briefen*, etc., Engels to Sorge, November 16, 1872, pp. 77 *et seq.*

[14] For a list of his anarchist writings, see Max Nettlau, *Bibliographie de l'anarchie*, pp. 66-67 (Paris, 1897).

[15] Brousse, *L'Etat à Versailles et dans l'association internationale des travailleurs*, pp. 12-13 (1873).

[16] *Ibid.*, p. 18.

NOTES

[17] Brousse, *Le suffrage universel, et le problème de la souveraineté du peuple*, pp. 42 *et seq.* (Geneva, 1874).

[18] Guillaume, *op. cit.*, Vol. iii, p. 90. The word "collectivist" was generally employed by those anarchists who demanded the collective ownership of the land and the means of production, but who wished to maintain the individual ownership of the products. In the Early Eighties, Kropotkin and his followers, who became known as anarchist communists, advanced the theory that in the future society not only the land and the means of production, but also the products should be owned in common. *Cf. infra*, p. 166.

[19] Max Nettlau, *Der Anarchismus von Proudhon zu Kropotkin*, p. 288.

[20] For summaries of certain phases of his life see the memoirs of his childhood days, "*Fragments de mémoire*," *La Revue Socialiste*, 1907, Vol. xlv, pp. 1-10, 97-106, 307-320, 496-507; Vol. xlvi, pp. 16-25; Elie Peyron, "*Benoît Malon*," *La Revue Socialiste*, 1901, Vol. xxxiii, pp. 257-288; Hermann Thurow, "*Benoît Malon*," *Sozialistische Monatshefte*, 1897, Vol. i, pp. 75-82; François Simon, *Une belle figure du peuple, Benoît Malon, sa vie, son oeuvre* (Courbevoie, 1926).

[21] Guillaume, *op. cit.*, Vol. ii, p. 315.

[22] See *Bulletin de la Fédération Jurassienne*, June 15, 1872; *Réponse de quelques internationaux à la circulaire privée du conseil général de Londres*, p. 9 (1872).

[23] The name "alliancist" was used by Marxists to denote members of Bakunin's Alliance of Socialist Democracy.

[24] *Les prétendus scissions dans l'internationale, circulaire privée du conseil général*, p. 14. Malon answered Marx's accusations in the anarchist organ, *Bulletin de la Fédération Jurassienne*. His response and those of others, accused by Marx, were published in a pamphlet, *Réponse de quelques internationaux à la circulaire privée du conseil général de Londres*. Lafarge, a son-in-law of Marx, also participated in the controversy. On one occasion, carried away by his own satire, he advised the members of the Federation of the Jura to read some of Marx's writings because, as he said, "he [Marx] will give you an idea of the application of the materialistic method to social science. I am not referring you to his book, *Capital;* it is too large." Quoted in *Réponse de quelques internationaux*, etc., p. 33.

[25] Guillaume, *op. cit.*, Vol. ii, p. 314.

[26] *Ibid.*, Vol. iv, p. 12 *et seq.*

[27] *Le Socialisme Progressif*, No. i, p. 2; No. iv, p. 63; No. vi, p. 106.

[28] See his letters to Jourde written in 1875, *La Revue Socialiste*, 1896, Vol. xxiv, pp. 286, 287.

[29] A good biography of Jules Guesde is unfortunately lacking. For a sum-

mary of his career and of his ideas see Alexandre Zévaès, *Jules Guesde* (Paris, 1929) ; Georges Bourgin, *"Jules Guesde," Archiv für die Geschichte des Sozialismus und der Arbeiterbewegung,* Jahrg. xiv, 1929, pp. 88-101 ; Bracke, *"Jules Guesde," La Nouvelle Revue Socialiste,* July, 1926, pp. 509-517 ; Compère-Morel, *Grand dictionnaire socialiste,* pp. 356-363.

[30] Guillaume, *op. cit.,* Vol. ii, p. 244.

[31] The statutes of the Federation, stressing the absolute autonomy of the sections, were signed by Guesde. See *La Révolution sociale,* December 14, 1871.

[32] *Ibid.*

[33] *L'Alliance de la démocratie socialiste et l'association internationale des travailleurs,* pp. 50 *et seq.* (London, 1873). This document was written by Marx, Engels and Lafargue. See Engels' letter to Sorge, July 26, 1873, in Sorge, *op. cit.,* p. 116.

[34] Guillaume, *op. cit.,* Vol. iii, p. 63.

[35] Guesde, *Essai de catéchisme socialiste,* p. 37 (Paris, 1912).

[36] *Ibid.,* ch. iv.

[37] *Ibid.,* p. 51.

[38] *Ibid.,* pp. 60 *et seq.*

[39] Malon, *Histoire du socialisme,* pp. 389, 569.

[40] Edited by Brousse, Allerini and Camet, three anarchists.

[41] Guillaume, *op. cit.,* Vol. iii, p. 91.

[42] Other articles in this pamphlet were by such prominent anarchists as Elisée Reclus and Schwitzguebel.

[43] This article was reprinted in an anarchist paper sixteen years later. See *Le Drapeau Noir,* August 8, 1889.

[44] The letter was first published in Italian in the *Plebe* of Milan in 1877, and appeared for the first time in French in 1914 in a volume, *Ça et Là.*

[45] Guesde, *Ça et Là,* pp. 3-30.

[46] *Cf. infra,* p. 108.

[47] For a summary of his ideas, see Gabriel Parent, *Le socialisme de Colins* (Paris, 1912).

[48] *La Philosophie de l'Avenir,* 1876-1877, Vol. ii, pp. 5-6.

[49] *Ibid.,* p. 244.

[50] *Ibid.,* 1877-1878, Vol. iii, p. 358.

[51] *Ibid.,* 1876-1877, Vol. ii, pp. 173 *et seq.*

[52] *Ibid.,* pp. 61-62.

[53] *Ibid.,* p. 52; Vol. iii, pp. 180-181.

[54] *Ibid.,* 1875-1876, Vol. i, pp. 690 *et seq.;* 1879-1880, Vol. v, pp. 290-291.

[55] *Ibid.,* 1878-1879, Vol. iv, pp. 112-113.

[56] *Séances du congrès ouvrier de France,* 1878, pp. 432 *et seq.,* 595.

NOTES

⁵⁷ Proudhon, however, filled Marx's answer to his *Système des contradictions économiques* with numerous marginal notes which were more an expression of Proudhon's emotions while he read the book than a refutation of Marx's assertions. They are, therefore, of greater value to the psychologist than to the social scientist. The notes are reprinted in Proudhon, *Système des contradictions économiques*, Vol. ii, pp. 415-423 (Paris, 1923). To his publisher Proudhon wrote: "I have received *The Poverty of Philosophy*, the lampoon of a Dr. Marx. It is a texture of coarseness, slander, debasement and plagiarism." Proudhon, *Correspondance*, Vol. ii, pp. 267-268.

⁵⁸ Malon, *"Karl Marx et Proudhon,"* *La Revue Socialiste*, 1887, Vol. v, pp. 15-16. The Manifesto had little immediate influence in countries other than France. Concerning this Engels wrote in the preface to the German edition of 1890: "Greeted with enthusiasm at the date of its first appearance by the little handful of those who constituted the advance guard of scientific socialism, . . . it was soon forced into the background by the reaction which followed upon the defeat of the Parisian workers in June, 1848. Later, as the result of the trial of the communists at Cologne in November, 1852, it was banned. The workers' movement which had surged upwards as a consequence of the revolutionary upheaval of the February days passed into the background, and the *Communist Manifesto* followed in its wake." D. Ryazanoff, *The Communist Manifesto of Karl Marx and Friedrich Engels*, p. 266, tr. Eden and Cedar Paul.

⁵⁹ Albert Richard, *"Les propagateurs de l'internationale en France,"* *La Revue Socialiste*, 1896, Vol. xxiii, p. 643.

⁶⁰ A. Richard, *L'Association internationale des travailleurs* (Lyons, 1870).

⁶¹ Malon, *"Karl Marx et Proudhon,"* *La Revue Socialiste*, 1887, Vol. v, p. 16.

⁶² *La Revue Socialiste*, 1887, Vol. v, p. 235. A second French edition of the Manifesto was printed in 1882.

⁶³ *Enquête parlementaire sur l'insurrection du 18 mars*, Vol. i, p. 200. The error was probably borrowed from E. E. Fribourg, *op. cit.*, p. 46.

⁶⁴ *Bulletin de la société internationale des études pratiques d'économie sociale*, 1876, Vol. v, pp. 205-206. Thirty years earlier, a review in a French periodical contained the following misinformation: "Marx is a shoemaker, just as another German communist, Weitling, is a tailor. The first does not hold in high esteem the French communism which he has been fortunate to study on the spot. Nevertheless, Marx also adheres to abstract formulas; he refrains from broaching any really practical question. According to him, the emancipation of the Germans will be the signal of the emancipation of humanity. Philosophy should be the head of this emancipation,

206

the proletariat its heart. When everything is prepared, the Gallican cock will sound the rising of the Germans." *Journal des Economistes,* 1846, Vol. xv, p. 88.

[65] *Journal des Economistes,* 3rd series, 1872, Vol. xxvii, p. 7.

[66] *Revue des Deux Mondes,* 3rd series, 1876, Vol. xvii, p. 143. Marx, having read the article, said in a letter to Pierre Lavrov: "It must be read to conceive of the imbecility of our bourgeois 'thinkers.'" *La Revue Marxiste,* 1929, Vol. i, p. 436.

[67] *Bulletin de la société internationale des études pratiques d'économie sociale,* 1876, Vol. v, pp. 215-216.

[68] Malon, *L'Internationale,* Lyons, 1872.

[69] Malon, *Exposé des écoles socialistes françaises,* pp. 236-237 (Paris, 1872).

[70] *Ibid.,* pp. 286 *et seq.*

[71] *Le Capital* (Paris, 1875), translated by J. Roy from the second German edition, Maurice Lachâtre et Cie. The translation was completed under Marx's supervision, and with the advice of his son-in-law, Charles Longuet. See Engels' letter to Sorge, November 16, 1872, in Sorge, *op. cit.,* p. 80.

[72] Both letters are printed as a preface to the edition of 1875.

[73] See E. Acollas, *Manuel de droit civil,* Vol. i, pp. xiv, 572-573. For a sketch of his ideas see Malon, *"Emile Acollas,"* La Revue Socialiste, 1891, Vol. xiv, pp. 594-598.

[74] Quoted in Guillaume, *op. cit.,* Vol. iv, p. 22.

[75] Quoted in Zévaès, *De la semaine sanglante au congrès de Marseille,* p. 26.

[76] Guesde, *Ça et Là,* p. 108.

[77] These articles were reprinted in Guesde, *Ça et Là,* pp. 83-104.

[78] *Ibid.,* p. 84.

[79] *Ibid.,* p. 96.

[80] *La Philosophie de l'Avenir,* 1877, Vol. ii, p. 259.

[81] Zévaès, *Jules Guesde,* p. 37.

[82] Franz Mehring, *Karl Marx,* p. 524, 4th edition (Leipzig, 1923); O. Zetkin, *Der Sozialismus in Frankreich,* pp. 11-12 (Berlin, 1893).

[83] Gabriel Deville, *Le Capital de Karl Marx,* pp. 7-8 (Paris, 1897).

[84] Stekloff, *History of the First International,* pp. 342 *et seq.*

[85] *La Revue Socialiste,* 1886, Vol. iv, p. 996.

[86] *L'Egalité,* November 18, 1877.

[87] Quoted in Guillaume, *op. cit.,* Vol. iv, pp. 296 *et seq. Cf. supra,* p. 103.

[88] Zévaès, *Jules Guesde,* p. 38.

[89] Edouard Drumont, *La fin d'un monde,* p. 157 (Paris, 1889).

[90] *L'Egalité,* November 18, 1877.

[91] *Ibid.,* November 25, 1877.

[92] *Ibid.,* December 23, 1877.

[93] *Ibid.,* December 30, 1877.

[94] *Ibid.*, November 25, 1877.
[95] *Ibid.*, December 16, 1877.
[96] *Ibid.*, June 2, 1878.
[97] *Ibid.*, July 14, 1878.
[98] *Ibid.*, November 18, 1877.
[99] *Ibid.*
[100] *Ibid.*, June 2, 1878.
[101] *Ibid.*, January 13, 1878.
[102] *Ibid.*, January 13, March 2, 1878.
[103] *Cf.* e.g. *ibid.*, November 18, 1877; March 2, June 2, June 16, 1878.
[104] *Ibid.*, June 9, 1878.
[105] *Ibid.*, December 30, 1877; January 13, 1878.
[106] *Ibid.*, February 10, 1878.
[107] *Ibid.*, January 13, 1878.
[108] *Ibid.*, July 14, 1878.
[109] Gabriel Deville, "*Aperçu sur le socialisme scientifique*," *Le Capital de Karl Marx*, p. 9.
[110] See his report on the Lyons Congress in *La Philosophie de l'Avenir*, 1877-1878, Vol. iii, p. 575.
[111] *Séances du congrès ouvrier de France*, 1878, p. 432.
[112] *Ibid.*, pp. 436-437.
[113] *Ibid.*, pp. 441, 444.
[114] *Ibid.*, p. 595.
[115] Léon de Seilhac, *Les congrès ouvriers en France de 1876 à 1897*, p. 26.
[116] Quoted in Léon Blum, *Les congrès ouvriers et socialistes français*, Vol. i, p. 30 (Paris, 1901).
[117] *Journal des Economistes*, 4th series, 1878, Vol. i, pp. 420-421.
[118] *Le Socialisme Progressif*, February 15, 1878, No. iv, p. 81.
[119] *L'Egalité*, February 17, 1878.
[120] Guesde, *Ça et Là*, pp. 156-158.
[121] Léon de Seilhac, *op. cit.*, p. 28; Malon, *Histoire du socialisme*, p. 379.
[122] Léon de Seilhac, *op. cit.*, p. 28.
[123] His defense is reprinted in Guesde, *Ça et Là*, pp. 155-183.
[124] Zévaès, *Jules Guesde*, p. 44.
[125] The manifesto was later published in the second series of the *Egalité*, February 21, 1880.
[126] *L'Egalité*, February 21, 1880.
[127] It lasted until December, 1878. Its chief contributors were César de Paepe, Arthur Cornette, Louis Bertrand, Jean Lombard and André Léo.
[128] *Le Socialisme Progressif*, February 15, 1878, No. iv, p. 66.
[129] *La Revue Socialiste*, 1886, Vol. iv, p. 1016.

NOTES

[130] *Le Prolétaire,* November 23, 1878.

[131] *Ibid.*

[132] *Ibid.,* January 1, 1879.

[133] *Ibid.,* December 25-28, 1878; January 8, 1879.

[134] *Ibid.,* December 7, 1878.

[135] *Ibid.,* December 21, 1878.

[136] *Ibid.,* January 18, 1879.

[137] *Ibid.,* December 7, 1878.

[138] *Ibid.,* December 18, 1878.

[139] *Ibid.,* February 1, April 26, October 11, December 6, 1879.

[140] *Ibid.,* January 8, 1879.

[141] *Ibid.,* August 2, 1879.

[142] *Ibid.,* January 10, 1880.

[143] *Ibid.,* January 24, 1880.

[144] *Ibid.,* January 1, December 6, 1879.

[145] *La Philosophie de l'Avenir,* 1878-1879, Vol. iv, pp. 422 *et seq.*

[146] G. Renard and A. Dulac, *L'Evolution industrielle et agricole,* p. 187, cite
the following figures concerning the introduction of machinery into France:

	No. of machines	h. p.
1859	13,691	169,000
1869	26,211	320,000
1879	39,556	516,000

[147] Levasseur, *op. cit.,* pp. 644 *et seq.*

[148] *Le Prolétaire,* November 23, 1878. See Zévaès, *De la semaine sanglante
au congrès de Marseille,* pp. 25 *et seq.*

[149] Charles da Costa, *op. cit.,* p. 55; Zévaès, *Auguste Blanqui,* pp. 107
et seq.; Gustave Geffroy, *L'Enfermé,* pp. 421 *et seq.* (Paris, 1897).

[150] *Le Prolétaire,* May 10, June 7, 1879.

[151] *Le Prolétaire,* December 11, 1878, quoted in Weill, *Histoire du mouvement social,* p. 227.

[152] After the disappearance of the paper the group continued to exist.

[153] Mermeix, *La France socialiste,* p. 91 (Paris, 1886).

[154] *Le Socialisme Progressif,* June 16, 1878, No. xii, p. 213.

[155] See e.g. *Le Prolétaire,* December 21, 1878; February 8, 1879.

[156] *L'Egalité,* January 6, 1878; *Le Socialisme Progressif,* January 15, 1878,
No. ii, p. 21.

[157] These three pamphlets are *La république et les grèves* (Paris, 1878);
La loi des salaires et ses conséquences (Paris, 1878); *Collectivisme et
révolution* (Paris, 1879).

[158] Guesde, *La république et les grèves.*

[159] Guesde, *Collectivisme et révolution,* pp. 12 *et seq.*

[160] *Ibid.,* pp. 10 *et seq.*

NOTES

[161] *Ibid.*, p. 16, n. 1.
[162] Guesde, *La loi des salaires et ses conséquences*, p. 24.
[163] Guesde, *Collectivisme et révolution*, p. 22.
[164] *Ibid.*, p. 20, n. 1.
[165] P. Kropotkin, *Memoirs of a Revolutionist*, p. 423 (New York, 1899). See also Jean Grave, *Le mouvement libertaire sous la troisième république*, pp. 42-43.
[166] *Le Révolté*, October 4, 18, November 1, 1879; May 15, 1880.
[167] *La Revue Socialiste*, 1886, Vol. iv, p. 880.
[168] Quoted in Blum, *op. cit.*, Vol. i, pp. 34-35.
[169] *Ibid.*, p. 40.
[170] Léon de Seilhac, *op. cit.*, p. 30.
[171] *Ibid.*, p. 31.
[172] For brief sketches of his career see Robert Bernier, *"Jean Lombard,"* *La Revue Socialiste*, 1891, Vol. xiv, pp. 190-197; Paul Lombard, *"Jean Lombard et le cinquantenaire du socialisme,"* *Revue des Vivants*, 1930, Vol. iv, pp. 383-395.
[173] *Séances du congrès ouvrier de France*, 1878, p. 350.
[174] Quoted in *La Revue Socialiste*, 1886, Vol. iv, pp. 1070-1071.
[175] Léon de Seilhac, *op. cit.*, pp. 32-33.
[176] *Ibid.*, p. 34.
[177] *La Revue Socialiste*, 1886, Vol. iv, p. 1074.
[178] Blum, *op. cit.*, p. 41.
[179] *Séances du congrès ouvrier socialiste de France*, 1879, p. 808
[180] Blum, *op. cit.*, pp. 47-48.
[181] *Séances du congrès ouvrier socialiste de France*, 1879, pp. 811-812.
[182] Blum, *op. cit.*, pp. 48-49; Léon de Seilhac, *op. cit.*, pp. 43-44.
[183] *Séances du congrès ouvrier socialiste de France*, 1879, pp. 604, 611.
[184] *Ibid.*, p. 814.
[185] Gaumont, *op. cit.*, Vol. ii, pp. 29-31, 35, 39.
[186] November 1, 1879, p. 537.
[187] November 7, 1879.
[188] *Ibid.*, November 9, 1879.
[189] *Le Prolétaire*, February 17, 1880.
[190] *Ibid.*, November 8, 1879.
[191] *La Revue Socialiste*, January 20, 1880, p. 19.
[192] *Le Révolté*, November 15, 1879.

NOTES TO CHAPTER IV

[1] *Cf. supra*, p. 4.
[2] *Séances du congrès ouvrier de Paris*, 1876, p. 519.

NOTES

[3] *Séances du congrès ouvrier*, 1878, pp. 283, 286, 287-288, 293, 311, 318, 359.

[4] *Ibid.*, p. 600.

[5] Hirsch was compelled to leave France after the trial of the Thirty-nine.

[6] See Bebel's letter to Vollmar, November 30, 1879, quoted in Bebel, *op. cit.*, Vol. iii, pp. 86-87.

[7] *Séances du congrès ouvrier socialiste de France*, 1879, pp. 816-817.

[8] *La Revue Socialiste*, 1886, Vol. iv, p. 1066.

[9] *Séances du congrès ouvrier socialiste de France*, 1879, pp. 817-818.

[10] *L'Egalité*, March 24, 1880.

[11] *Ibid.*, June 9, 1880.

[12] *Ibid.*, July 28, 1880.

[13] *Ibid.*, March 10, July 14, 21, 1880.

[14] *Ibid.*, April 21, 1880.

[15] *Ibid.*, August 4, 1880.

[16] *Ibid.*, July 7, 1880; *La Revue Socialiste*, 1887, Vol. v, p. 40.

[17] *L'Egalité*, August 18, 1880.

[18] *La Revue Socialiste*, 1887, Vol. v, p. 41.

[19] Engels to Bebel, March 18/28, 1875, quoted in Bebel, *op. cit.*, Vol. ii, p. 323.

[20] *La Revue Socialiste*, March 20, April 20, May 5, 1880.

[21] *Ibid.*, April 20, 1880, pp. 193 *et seq.* See also Marx's letter in Sorge, *Briefe und Auszüge aus Briefen*, etc., p. 170.

[22] *L'Egalité*, February 18, 25, 1880.

[23] Malon, *Histoire du socialisme*, pp. 410-419, 443-451.

[24] E. Bernstein, *My Years of Exile*, p. 64; *La Revue Socialiste*, 1887, Vol. v, p. 45, n.

[25] Sorge, *Briefe und Auszüge aus Briefen*, etc., p. 185.

[26] Bernstein, *Die Briefe von Engels an Bernstein*, p. 35.

[27] *Ibid.*, p. 34.

[28] *Ibid.*

[29] Marx's letter to Sorge, November 5, 1880, in Sorge, *op. cit.*, p. 170. The italics are in Marx's own English version.

[30] *Ibid.*

[31] Letter quoted in *Compte rendu du sixième congrès national*, Saint-Etienne, 1882, p. 79.

[32] *La Revue Socialiste*, 1887, Vol. v, p. 47.

[33] *Ibid.*

[34] For a list of the groups which approved of the program see *La Revue Socialiste*, July 20, 1880, pp. 418-420.

[35] *L'Egalité*, June 30, 1880; *Le Prolétaire*, July 10, 1880; *La Revue Socialiste*, July 20, 1880, pp. 417-418.

[36] *L'Egalité*, June 30, 1880.

NOTES

[37] *Le Prolétaire*, September 11, 1880.

[38] *Ibid.*, June 12, 1880.

[39] *Ibid.*, July 3, 1880.

[40] *La Revue Socialiste*, July 20, 1880, p. 423.

[41] For a summary of these congresses see Stekloff, *op. cit.*, Part ii, chs. ii-iii, v-x; Guillaume, *op. cit.*, Vols. iii-iv, *passim*. Stekloff presents the Marxist side, while Guillaume is partial to the anarchists.

[42] *Cf. supra*, p. 116.

[43] Guillaume, *op. cit.*, Vol. iv, p. 279.

[44] Kropotkin, *Memoirs of a Revolutionist*, p. 406.

[45] Some of these pamphlets were: Colonna, *Aux travailleurs manuels de la France* (Geneva, 1876); A. Perrare, *Aux travailleurs manuels lyonnais* (1876) and *Encore un soufflet* (n.d.); *La question électorale* (Paris, 1880), published by L'Alliance des groupes socialistes révolutionnaires.

[46] *La question électorale*, p. 5.

[47] *Séances du congrès ouvrier de France*, 1878, pp. 601-602.

[48] Kropotkin, *op. cit.*, p. 423.

[49] *Le Révolté*, October 18, November 1, 1879; October 17, 1880. For the beginnings of anarchist communism see Nettlau, *Der Anarchismus von Proudhon zu Kropotkin*, chs. xiv, xix-xx.

[50] M. Nettlau, *Der Anarchismus von Proudhon zu Kropotkin*, p. 299; *Anarchisten und Sozialrevolutionäre*, pp. 65, 67; Grave, *Le mouvement libertaire sous la troisième république*, pp. 5, 7, 13.

[51] Hervé was a member of the French Socialist Party, who was violently antimilitaristic and antipatriotic.

[52] Eugène Fournière, *La crise socialiste*, pp. 41-42 (Paris, 1908); Grave, *op. cit.*, p. 13.

[53] Grave, *op. cit.*, p. 4.

[54] Louis Andrieux, *Souvenirs d'un préfet de police*, Vol. i, pp. 338 *et seq.*; Grave, *op. cit.*, pp. 192-194.

[55] See Elisée Reclus' interpretation of the conditions which produce anarchism. *Correspondance*, Vol. ii, pp. 441-442.

[56] *Qu'est-ce que la propriété?*, p. 339.

[57] Kropotkin, *The Place of Anarchism in Socialistic Evolution*, p. 14 (London, 1887).

[58] *Ibid.*, pp. 9 *et seq.*

[59] J. Grave, *La société au lendemain de la révolution*, pp. 36-37 (Paris, 1893). It was first published in *Le Droit Social*, Lyons, April 9–September 22, 1882.

[60] Roger N. Baldwin, ed., *Kropotkin's Revolutionary Pamphlets*, p. 110 (New York, 1927).

NOTES

[61] Kropotkin, *The Place of Anarchism in Socialistic Evolution*, p. 14.

[62] *Ibid.*

[63] *Le Révolté*, May 29, 1880.

[64] Baldwin, *op. cit.*, p. 238. Anarchist communists did not agree among themselves on the method of effecting the transition to the new society. Elisée Reclus, for example, did not advocate the insurrectionary method. See *Correspondance*, Vol. ii, pp. 279, 325; Vol. iii, pp. 130, 182.

[65] *Le Révolté*, November 1, 1879.

[66] *Ibid.*, June 8, 1884.

[67] Baldwin, *op. cit.*, p. 248; *Le Révolté*, October 14, 1882.

[68] *Le Révolté*, April 13, 1884.

[69] Grave, *La société au lendemain de la révolution*, pp. 14 *et seq.*

[70] *Ibid.*, p. 89.

[71] *Le Révolté*, July 23, 1881. In the same resolution the congress advised anarchists to study and apply the chemical and technical sciences "for the purpose of defense and attack."

[72] *L'Anarchie*, n.d., c. 1880-1881.

[73] Kropotkin, *Paroles d'un révolté*, pp. 311-312; Grave, *op. cit.*, pp. 5-6.

[74] On the instability of the anarchist groups and the smallness of their membership, see Nettlau, *Anarchisten und Sozialrevolutionäre*, p. 62. See also the reports of French anarchists at the congress of August 13, 1882. *Le Révolté*, August 19, 1882.

[75] *La Revue Socialiste*, May 5, 1880, p. 267.

[76] *Ibid.*, July 20, 1880, p. 423.

[77] *L'Emancipation*, November 15, 1880.

[78] *Le Prolétaire*, January 29, August 3, 1881.

[79] *La Revue Socialiste*, April 20, 1880, pp. 66, 223; *L'Emancipation*, November 6, 1880; *L'Egalité*, May 21, 28, 1882.

[80] *L'Egalité*, August 11, 1880.

[81] *Ibid.*, July 21, 1880; Deville, *Aperçu sur le socialisme scientifique*, p. 47, reprinted in his *Le Capital de Karl Marx*.

[82] *Cf. supra*, p. 154.

[83] *Cf. supra*, p. 159.

[84] *La Justice*, July 22, 1880.

[85] *Ibid.*, July 23, 1880.

[86] *Le Citoyen*, August 1, 1880; *L'Egalité*, July 28, 1880.

[87] Léon de Seilhac, *Les congrès ouvriers en France de 1876 à 1897*, pp. 52-53.

[88] *Le Citoyen*, August 1, 1880; *L'Egalité*, July 28, 1880; *La Revue Socialiste*, August 5, 1880, p. 453. These modifications were all in the section dealing with economic demands. They were: (1) a change in the

wording of article four; (2) the addition of an article to the effect that the aged and the disabled should be maintained at the expense of society; (3) the addition to the last article of a section on the abolition of inheritance in order to satisfy the Colinsists. The last addition was opposed by Guesde on the ground that it was unscientific.

[89] See Crié's article on the anarchist movement written for *La Nation*. The article is in page-proof, corrected by the author, and is bound in a volume of articles by Louise Michel. Columbia University Library, B.335.8–M589.

[90] *Cf. supra*, p. 176.

[91] *La Justice*, August 30, 1880.

[92] Gaumont, *op. cit.*, Vol. ii, p. 81.

[93] *La Justice*, November 1, 1880.

[94] Gaumont, *op. cit.*, Vol. ii, p. 70; Charles Gide, *Les coopératives de production et l'état*, p. 15.

[95] Gaumont, *op. cit.*, Vol. ii, p. 84.

[96] *L'Egalité*, April 14, 1880.

[97] *L'Emancipation*, November 1, 14, 1880.

[98] *Le Prolétaire*, November 27, 1880.

[99] *Séances du congrès ouvrier socialiste de France*, 1879, p. 821.

[100] *Le Prolétaire*, September 18, 1880.

[101] November 20, 1880.

[102] August 25, 1880.

[103] *MSS., Congrès ouvrier du Havre*, cercle Franklin, 1880, Musée Social, no. 6794.

[104] *Ibid.*

[105] Léon de Seilhac, *op. cit.*, p. 67.

[106] *Ibid.* The moderates, inspired by Barberet's ideas, held two more congresses: in 1881 in Paris and in 1882 in Bordeaux, both of which passed unnoticed by the public. The proceedings of both of these congresses are in the library of the Musée Social in Paris, no. 6518.

[107] Léon de Seilhac, *op. cit.*, p. 70.

[108] *La Justice*, November 19, 1880.

[109] *MSS., Congrès national socialiste ouvrier*, Havre, salle de l'Union Lyrique, 1880, Musée Social, no. 6974; *L'Emancipation*, November 20, 21, 22, 1880.

[110] Léon de Seilhac, *op. cit.*, p. 73.

[111] *La Revue Socialiste*, 1887, Vol. v, pp. 111-112.

[112] *Cf. supra*, p. 176.

[113] *Ibid.*, p. 58; *La Justice*, November 19-25, 1880.

CONCLUSION

[1] *La crise socialiste*, pp. 44 et seq.

BIBLIOGRAPHY

Bibliographies and Handbooks

Compère-Morel, *Grand dictionnaire socialiste*, Paris, 1924.

Nettlau, Max, *Bibliographie de l'anarchie*, Paris, 1897.

Stammhammer, Josef, *Bibliographie des Socialismus und Communismus*, 3 vols., Jena, 1893-1909.

Stegmann und Hugo, *Handbuch des Sozialismus*, Zürich, 1897.

Vérecque, Charles, *Dictionnaire du socialisme*, Paris, 1911.

Secondary material

A. Books

Augé-Laribé, Berthod, Bouglé, etc., *Proudhon et notre temps*, Paris, 1920.

Bebel, August, *Aus meinem Leben*, 3 vols., Stuttgart, 1910-1914.

Bourgin, Georges, *Histoire de la Commune*, Paris, 1907.

————, *Les premières journées de la Commune*, Paris, 1928.

Bourgin, Hubert, *Proudhon*, Paris, 1901.

————, *Les systèmes socialistes*, Paris, 1923.

Ceinmar, Olivier de, *Les doctrines des congrès ouvriers de France*, Paris, 1880.

Chaboseau, A., *De Babeuf à la Commune (Histoire des partis socialistes en France*, Vol. I, ed. A. Zévaès), Paris, 1911.

Chang, Sherman Hsiao-Ming, *The Marxian Theory of the State*, Philadelphia, 1931.

Clère, Jules, *Les hommes de la Commune*, 4th edition, Paris, 1871.

Delevsky, J., *Les antinomies socialistes et l'évolution du socialisme français*, Paris, 1930.

Desjardins, Arthur, *P. J. Proudhon, sa vie, ses oeuvres, sa doctrine*, 2 vols., Paris, 1896.

Dommanget, Maurice, *Blanqui*, Paris, 1924.

Droz, Edouard, *P. J. Proudhon*, Paris, 1909.

Dubreuilh, Louis, *La Commune* (*Histoire socialiste*, Vol. XI, ed. Jean Jaurès), Paris, 1908.

Fontanille, Henri André Lucien, *L'Oeuvre social d'Albert de Mun*, Paris, 1926.

Fribourg, E. E., *L'Association internationale des travailleurs*, Paris, 1871.

Gaumont, Jean, *Histoire générale de la coopération en France*, 2 vols., Paris, 1924.

Geffroy, Gustave, *L'Enfermé*, Paris, 1897.

Gide and Rist, *A History of Economic Doctrines*, London, 1919.

Guillaume, James, *L'Internationale, documents et souvenirs*, 4 vols., Paris, 1907-1910.

Halévy, Daniel, *Essais sur le mouvement ouvrier*, Paris, 1901.

———, *La fin des notables*, Paris, 1930.

Iswolsky, Hélène, *La vie de Bakounine*, Paris, 1930.

Kritsky, N., *L'Evolution du syndicalisme en France*, Paris, 1908.

Labusquière, John, *La troisième république* (*Histoire socialiste*, Vol. XII, ed. Jean Jaurès), Paris, 1909.

Lagardelle, Hubert, *L'Evolution des syndicats ouvriers en France*, Paris, 1901.

Laronze, Georges, *Histoire de la Commune de 1871: la justice*, Paris, 1928.

Levasseur, E., *Questions ouvrières et industrielles en France sous la troisième république*, Paris, 1907.

Lorwin, Lewis, *Syndicalism in France*, revised edition, New York, 1914.

Louis, Paul, *Histoire du mouvement syndical en France*, Paris, 1907.

———, *Histoire de la classe ouvrière en France de la révolution à nos jours*, Paris, 1927.

Lu, S. Y., *The Political Theories of P. J. Proudhon*, New York, 1922.

Malon, Benoît, *La troisième défaite du prolétariat français*, Neuchâtel, 1871.

———, *L'Internationale, son histoire et ses principes*, 1872.

———, *Exposé des écoles socialistes françaises*, Paris, 1872.

———, *Histoire du socialisme depuis ses origines probables jusqu'à nos jours*, Lugano-Castagnola, 1879.

Mason, Edward S., *The Paris Commune, An Episode in the History of the Socialist Movement*, New York, 1930.

May, André, *Les origines du syndicalisme révolutionnaire*, Paris, 1913.

Mehring, Franz, *Karl Marx*, 4th edition, Leipzig, 1923.

Mermeix (Terrail), *Le syndicalisme contre le socialisme*, 6th edition, Paris, 1907.

Michel, Louise, *La Commune*, 5th edition, Paris, 1921.

Milhaud, Albert, *La lutte des classes à travers l'histoire et la politique*, Paris, 1908.

Moon, Parker Thomas, *The Labor Problem and the Social Catholic Movement in France*, New York, 1921.

Moreau, Georges, *Essai sur les théories et l'histoire du syndicalisme ouvrier en France*, Paris, 1925.

Moriac, Edouard, *Paris sous la Commune*, Paris, 1872.

Muller, Jean, *L'idée de lutte de classes et son évolution depuis le manifeste communiste*, Paris, 1911.

Nettlau, Max, *Der Anarchismus von Proudhon zu Kropotkin; seine historische Entwicklung in den Jahren 1859-1880*, Berlin, 1927.

————, *Anarchisten und Sozialrevolutionäre; die historische Entwicklung des Anarchismus in den Jahren 1880-1886*, Berlin, 1931.

Parent, Gabriel, *Le socialisme de Colins*, Paris, 1912.

Posse, Ernest H., *Der Marxismus in Frankreich, 1871-1905*, Berlin, 1930.

Postgate, R. W., *The Workers' International*, London, 1920.

————, *Out of the Past*, London, 1922.

Prudhommeaux, J., *Les expériences sociales de J.-B. A. Godin*, Nîmes, 1911.

Puech, J. L., *Le proudhonisme dans l'association internationale des travailleurs*, Paris, 1907.

Ralea, Michel, *Proudhon, sa conception du progrès et son attitude sociale*, Paris, 1922.

————, *L'Idée de révolution dans les doctrines socialistes*, Paris, 1923.

Richard, A., *L'Association internationale des travailleurs*, Lyons, 1870.

Sainte-Beuve, C. A., *P. J. Proudhon, sa vie et sa correspondance, 1838-1849*, Paris, 1872.

Sée, Henri, *Esquisse d'une histoire économique et sociale de la France*, Paris, 1929.

Seignobos, Ch., *Le déclin de l'empire et l'établissement de la*

3ᵉ république (*Histoire de France contemporaine*, Vol. VII, ed. Ernest Lavisse), Paris, 1921.

————, *L'Evolution de la 3ᵉ république* (*Histoire de France contemporaine*, Vol. VIII, ed. Ernest Lavisse), Paris, 1921.

Simon, François, *Une belle figure du peuple, Benoît Malon, sa vie, son oeuvre*, Courbevoie, 1926.

Stekloff, G. M., *History of the First International*, London, 1928.

Steklow (Stekloff), G., *Michael Bakunin, ein Lebensbild*, Stuttgart, 1920.

Tchernoff, I., *Le parti républicain au coup d'état et sous le second empire*, Paris, 1906.

Thomas, Albert, *Le second empire* (*Histoire socialiste*, Vol. X, ed. Jean Jaurès), Paris, 1907.

Weill, Georges, *Histoire du parti républicain en France de 1814 à 1870*, Paris, 1900.

————, *Histoire du mouvement social en France*, Paris, 1924.

Yorke, Onslow, *Secret History of The International Workingmen's Association*, London, 1872.

Zetkin, O., *Der Sozialismus in Frankreich*, Berlin, 1893.

Zévaès, Alexandre, *Le socialisme en France depuis 1871*, Paris, 1908.

————, *Le syndicalisme contemporain*, Paris, 1911.

————, *De la semaine sanglante au congrès de Marseille* (*Histoire des partis socialistes en France*, Vol. II, ed. A. Zévaès), Paris, 1911.

————, *Auguste Blanqui*, Paris, 1920.

————, *Jules Guesde*, Paris, 1929.

Zévort, Edgar, *Histoire de la troisième république*, 4 vols., Paris, 1899.

B. Special articles

Bourgin, Georges, *"Jules Guesde,"* *Archiv für die Geschichte des Sozialismus und der Arbeiterbewegung,* 1929, Jahrg. XIV, pp. 88-101.

———, "Commune of Paris," *Encyclopaedia of the Social Sciences,* Vol. IV, pp. 63-66.

Bourguin, M., *"Des rapports entre Proudhon et Karl Marx,"* *Revue d'Economie Politique,* 1893, Vol. VII, pp. 177-207.

Bracke, *"Jules Guesde,"* *La Nouvelle Revue Socialiste,* July 15-August 15, 1926, pp. 509-517.

Engels, F., *"Programm der blanquistischen Kommune-Flüchtlinge,"* *Volkstaat,* 1874, No. LXXIII.

Laveleye, Emile de, *"Le socialisme contemporain en Allemagne,"* *Revue des Deux Mondes,* September 1, 1876, 3rd series, Vol. XVII, pp. 120-149.

Kritschewsky, B., *"Aus Auguste Blanqui's Leben,"* *Sozialistische Monatshefte,* 1897, Vol. I, pp. 10-17; 109-115.

Lombard, Paul, *"Jean Lombard et le cinquantenaire du socialisme,"* *Revue des Vivants,* March, 1930, Vol. IV, pp. 383-395.

Mason, Edward S., "Blanqui and Communism," *Political Science Quarterly,* Vol. XLIV, No. IV, pp. 498-527.

Mathiez, A., *"Notes inédits de Blanqui sur Robespierre,"* *Annales historiques de la Révolution française,* new series, 1928, Vol. V, pp. 305-321.

Pilon, F., *"Le socialisme d'Auguste Blanqui,"* *La critique philosophique,* new series, 1888, Vol. VIII, pp. 61-75, 126-137.

Thurow, Hermann, *"Benoît Malon,"* *Sozialistische Monatshefte,* 1897, Vol. I, pp. 75-82.

Zévaès, Alexandre, *"Les candidatures ouvrières et révolutionnaires sous le second empire,"* La Révolution de *1848*, 1932, Vol. XXIX, no. CXLII, pp. 132-154.

Source material

A. Books

Acollas, Emile, *Manuel de droit civil*, 3 vols., Paris, 1874-1877.

Bakounine, Michel, *Oeuvres*, 6 vols., Paris, 1895-1913.

Baldwin, Roger N., ed., *Kropotkin's Revolutionary Pamphlets*, New York, 1927.

Barberet, J., *Les grèves et la loi sur les coalitions*, Paris, 1873.

———, *Le mouvement ouvrier à Paris de 1870 à 1874*, Paris, 1874.

———, *Monographies professionnelles*, 7 vols., Paris, 1886-1890.

Bebel u. Bernstein, *Briefwechsel zwischen Friedrich Engels u. Karl Marx*, 4 vols., Stuttgart, 1913.

Bernstein, Edouard, *Die Briefe von Friedrich Engels an Edouard Bernstein*, Berlin, 1925.

Blanqui, Auguste, *La patrie en danger*, Paris, 1871.

———, *Critique sociale*, 2 vols., Paris, 1885.

Deville, Gabriel, *Le capital de Karl Marx*, Paris, 1897.

Godin, André, *Solutions sociales*, Paris, 1871.

———, *La richesse au service du peuple*, Paris, 1874.

———, *Le gouvernement*, Paris, 1883.

Grave, Jean, *La société au lendemain de la révolution*, Paris, 1893.

————, *Le mouvement libertaire sous la troisième république* (*Souvenirs d'un révolté*), Paris, 1930.

Guesde, Jules, *Ça et là*, Paris, 1914.

Kropotkine, Pierre, *Paroles d'un révolté*, Paris, 1885.

————, *La conquête du pain*, Paris, 1921.

Magnin, Fabien, *Etudes sociales*, Paris, 1913.

Marx, Karl, *Le capital*, Paris, 1875.

————, *The Poverty of Philosophy*, tr. H. Quelch, Chicago, n.d.

Le Play, F., *Organization of Labor*, Philadelphia, 1872.

Proudhon, P. J., *Du principe fédératif*, Paris, 1921.

————, *Idée générale de la révolution au XIXᵉ siècle*, Paris, 1923.

————, *Système des contradictions économiques ou Philosophie de la misère*, 2 vols., Paris, 1923.

————, *De la capacité politique des classes ouvrières*, Paris, 1924.

————, *Qu'est-ce que la propriété?* Paris, 1926.

————, *Les confessions d'un révolutionnaire*, Paris, 1929.

————, *De la justice dans la révolution et dans l'église*, 3 vols., Paris, 1930-1932.

Reclus, Elisée, *L'Evolution, la révolution, et l'idéal anarchique*, Paris, 1921.

————, *Correspondance*, 3 vols., Paris, 1911-1925.

Ryazanoff, D., ed., *The Communist Manifesto of Karl Marx and Friedrich Engels*, tr. Eden and Cedar Paul, New York, 1930.

Sorge, F. A., *Briefe und Auszüge aus Briefen von Joh. Phil. Becker, Jof. Dietzgen, Friedrich Engels, Karl Marx u. A. an F. A. Sorge und Andere*, Stuttgart, 1906.

Schwitzguébel, Adhémar, *Quelques écrits*, Paris, 1908.

Tridon, G., *Les hébertistes*, 2nd edition, 1871.

B. Pamphlets

L'Alliance de la démocratie socialiste et l'association internationale des travailleurs, London, 1873.

Brousse, Paul, *L'Etat à Versailles et dans l'association internationale des travailleurs*, 1873.

——, *Le suffrage universel et le problème de la souveraineté du peuple*, Geneva, 1874.

Colonna, T., *Aux travailleurs manuels de la France*, Geneva, 1876.

Deville, Gabriel, *L'Anarchisme*, Paris, 1887.

Gide, Charles, *Le Familistère de Guise et la verrerie ouvrière*, Paris, 1923.

——, *Historique des associations coopératives de production*, Paris, 1923.

——, *Les divers types d'association coopératives de production*, Paris, 1923.

Guesde, Jules, *Le collectivisme devant la Xe chambre*, Paris, 1878.

——, *La république et les grèves*, Paris, 1878.

——, *Collectivisme et révolution*, Lille, 1906.

——, *La loi des salaires et ses conséquences*, Lille, 1906.

——, *Essai de catéchisme socialiste*, Paris, 1912.

Junius, *Le citoyen Proudhon devant l'assemblée nationale*, Paris, 1848.

Kropotkin, P., *The Place of Anarchism in Socialistic Evolution*, London, 1887.

——, *An Appeal to the Young*, London, 189

Kropotkine, P., *Le salariat*, Paris, 1892.

Lafitte, Pierre, *Le positivisme et l'économie politique*, 3rd edition, Paris, 1876.

Laporte, Magnin et Finance, *Le positivisme au congrès ouvrier*, Paris, 1877.

Léo, Bakounine, Lefrançais, Schwitzguébel, *Simples questions sociales*, Saint-Imier, c. 1872.

Marx, Karl, *The Civil War in France*, Chicago, n.d., tr. E. Belfort Bax.

Mollin, Gabriel, *Les jobards et les roublards du positivisme*, Paris, 1879.

Perrare, A., *Aux travailleurs manuels lyonnais*, Geneva, 1876.

Les prétendus scissions dans l'internationale, circulaire privée du conseil général de l'association internationale des travailleurs, Geneva, 1872.

Proudhon, P. J., *Résumé de la question sociale, banque d'échange*, Paris, 1849.

———, *Banque du peuple*, Paris, 1849.

Reclus, Elisée, *A mon frère le paysan*, Geneva, 1893.

Réponse de quelques internationaux, membres de la fédération jurassienne à la circulaire privée du conseil général de Londres, 1872.

Rienzi (Van Kol), *L'Anarchisme*, Brussels, 1893.

Shaw, G. B., *Anarchism v. State Socialism*, London, 1896.

C. Reports, Proceedings, etc.

Blum, Léon, *Les congrès ouvriers et socialistes français*, Paris, 1901.

Bulletin de la société internationale des études pratiques d'économie sociale, 9 vols., Paris, 1865-1884.

Chambre de Commerce de Paris, *Enquête sur les conditions du travail en France pendant l'année 1872*, Paris, 1875.

Congrès national socialiste ouvrier, salle de l'Union Lyrique, Havre, 1880, MSS., Musée Social, no. 6794.

Congrès ouvrier, cercle Franklin, Havre, 1880, MSS., Musée Social, no. 6794.

Ducarre, M., *Rapport fait au nom de la commission d'enquête parlementaire sur les conditions du travail en France,* Versailles, 1875.

Enquête parlementaire sur l'insurrection du 18 mars, 3 vols., Versailles, 1872.

Procès de l'internationale, compte rendu des débats devant la chambre de police correctionnelle de Toulouse, Paris, 1873.

Procès-verbaux des séances officielles de l'internationale pendant le siège et pendant la Commune, Paris, 1872.

Rapports de la délégation ouvrière française à l'exposition universelle de Vienne, 3 vols., Paris, 1874-1876.

Séances du congrès ouvrier de France, tenu à Paris du 2 au 10 octobre, 1876, Paris, 1877.

Séances du congrès ouvrier de France, tenu à Lyon du 28 janvier au 8 février, 1878, Lyons, 1878.

Séances du congrès ouvrier socialiste de France, tenu à Marseille du 20 au 31 octobre, Paris, 1879.

Seilhac, Léon de, *Les congrès ouvriers en France, 1876-1897,* Paris, 1899.

Les 31 séances officielles de la Commune de Paris, Paris, 1871.

"*Troisième congrès de l'association internationale des travailleurs, compte rendu officiel,*" *Le Peuple Belge,* Brussels, September, 1868.

D. *Newspapers and Periodicals*

L'Autonomie individuelle, anarchist, monthly, Paris, May, 1887-March, 1888.

L'Avant-Garde cosmopolite, anarchist, weekly, Paris, May 28-August 5, 1887.

Bulletin de la Fédération Jurassienne de l'Association Internationale des Travailleurs, anarchist, fortnightly, Sonvillier, February 15, 1872-March 25, 1878.

Bulletin du mouvement social, Fourierist, monthly and semi-monthly, Paris, December 1, 1872-December 1, 1875.

Le Défi, anarchist, weekly, Lyons, February 3-17, 1884.

Le Drapeau Noir, anarchist, weekly, Lyons, August 12-December 2, 1883.

Le Droit anarchique, anarchist, weekly, Lyons, June 8-22, 1884.

L'Economiste Français, weekly, Paris, April 19, 1873——.

L'Egalité, Marxist, weekly, Meaux, November 18, 1877-July 14, 1878; January 21-August 25, 1880; December 11, 1881-November 5, 1882.

L'Emancipation, socialist, daily, Lyons, October 31-November 23, 1880.

L'Emeute, anarchist, weekly, Lyons, December 9, 1883-January 20, 1884.

L'Etendard révolutionnaire, anarchist, weekly, Lyons, July 30-October 15, 1882.

La Guerre sociale, anarchist, fortnightly, Brussels, November 23, 1885-March 15, 1886.

L'Insurgé, anarchist, weekly, Brussels, March 15-May 17, 1885.

L'International, anarchist, fortnightly, London, May, 1890-January 11, 1891.

Journal des Economistes, monthly, Paris, January, 1870—.

Journal officiel de la Commune, daily, March 20-May 24, 1871.

BIBLIOGRAPHY

La Justice, radical republican, daily, Paris, January, 1880-
December, 1885.
La Lutte sociale, anarchist, weekly, Lyons, August 28-October 2, 1886.
Ni Dieu ni Maître, Blanquist, daily and weekly, Paris November 20, 1880-November 6, 1881.
La Philosophie de l'Avenir, Colinsist, monthly, August, 1875-June, 1889.
Le Prolétaire, labor, later possibilist, weekly, Paris, November 23, 1878-March 29, 1884.
Le Révolté, anarchist, fortnightly, Geneva and Paris, February 22, 1879-September 10, 1887.
Revue occidentale, positivist, bi-monthly, Paris, 1878-1889.
La Révolution sociale, anarchist, weekly, Geneva, October 26, 1871-January 4, 1872.
La Revue Socialiste, socialist, fortnightly and monthly, Paris, January 20-September 5, 1880.
Le Socialisme Progressif, socialist, semi-monthly and monthly, Lugano, January 1-November 30,'1878.

INDEX

228

INDEX

229